I0415434

CONTENTS

What is Freedom and Other Essays

PREFACE

My political views are based firmly on advocating individual freedom or authoritarian government and concept such as "group rights" and group entitlements. In the last 70 years our governments, both state and local, have become larger, much more expensive, and far more intrusive in our daily lives. The problems that more government and higher taxes are supposed to solve only get worse, or at best persist, as we pay higher taxes for more big government. The only solution is to reduce the size of government and re-emphasize individual rights and individual responsibility.

I agree entirely what former Senator Barry Goldwater said and wrote about politics. Seeking the presidency in 1964, Goldwater said:

I have little interest in streamlining government or in making it more efficient, for I mean to reduce its size. I do not undertake to promote welfare, for I propose to extend freedom. My aim is not to pass laws, but to repeal them. It is not to inaugurate new programs, but to cancel old ones that do violence to the Constitution, or that have failed in their purpose, or that impose on the people an unwarranted financial burden. I will not attempt to discover whether legislation is 'needed' before I have first determined whether it is constitutionally permissible. And if I should later be attacked for neglecting my constituents' 'interests,' I shall reply that I was informed their main interest is liberty and that in that case I am doing the very best I can.

That statement was the basis of Barry Goldwater's campaign for the presidency in 1964. Like many, I was first exposed to Barry Goldwater through the biased and sleazy misrepresentations of Senator Goldwater that have lived on since the sleazy mudslinging he withstood from the dirty campaign run against him by Lyndon Johnson. That misrepresentation of Goldwater's views is much like that which demonizes conservative views in general. As a matter of fact, it was upon reading Goldwater's The Conscience of a Conservative that I discovered a home for my own views in what is commonly called conservative.

I hope that offering my articles on a variety of issues from this consistently individual-rights point of view will lead others to this same realization. As others realize how and why collectivist and socialist politics are delusions that do not lead to more freedom, many more will realize how important it is that we embrace individual rights. If we demand that the government simply return to living within the Constitution and The Bill of Rights, we'll enjoy much more freedom than we do now. Benjamin Franklin commented about the Constitutional Convention in Philadelphia. He said it created a "Republic, if you can keep it." Before we have lost it entirely, we need to return to living within this Constitution and its amendments, and completely upholding The Bill of Rights. Not just some of the rights recognized by Constitution's first ten amendments, but ALL of those rights.

What is Freedom?

"There is no reason that all human existence should be constructed on some one or some small number of patterns. If a person possesses any tolerable amount of common sense and experience, his own mode of laying out his existence is the best, not because it is the best in itself, but because it is his own mode."

- John Stuart Mill

Freedom is just that, as described by John Stuart Mill. Freedom is the ability of the individual to live ones life as one chooses, without violating the rights of others as well as the ability to make one's own decisions on exactly how to pursue such life choices. But freedom, like many other words, has been twisted, distorted, and contorted by the twin influences of political correctness and corporate marketing.

The politically correct left has defined freedom in all manners of material goods that constitute freedom (housing, education, health care, a "living wage," etc.) that can only be guaranteed as "fundamental rights" when the state takes money from Peter in order to furnish these "rights" to Paul. But politicians have found quite effective ways to have more Peters than Pauls, and make sure that most Pauls show up at the polls to collectively vote in their self interest over those of the Pauls who advocate, in many instances, individual freedom over such collective welfarism.

I am one of the Pauls who seeks to show that life under individual freedom would be a better life of freedom and individual responsibility, not only for those of us who can see this, but for the Peters as well. I don't advocate forcing this choice on the Peters, but I certainly would like to convince them of this and have them later make this choice as well. After all, we quickly find out on April 15 that the other choice, that which is in favor of taking out money to re-distribute to the Peters, is a choice that is forced on us. Individual freedom is about not having that choice forced on any of us, regardless of which choices we make.

What is Freedom and How Much of it do We Enjoy?

April 11, 2000

First, think of freedom as measured on a continuum. At one end is absolutely zero freedom, essentially living your life on a day to day basis where ALL your decisions at all times are made by someone else. The other extreme is anarchy, a condition where you can do anything you want at any time, including even violating the rights of others. Naturally, you can see that maximum practical levels of freedom are to be found somewhere between the two.

But where is that point? For me personally that point is easy to find. Personal freedom should be respected in all areas except where it can be demonstrated an action or decision directly violates someone else's freedom. My point here isn't to debate on the label for this philosophy other than to simply say I agree with the late Senator Barry Goldwater, who called it conservative. That point on the continuum I mention is what I call maximum practical achievable freedom. Another term I use is Q-Star, which means quality of life raised to highest exponential value.

But the question I do want to pose here in this essay is how much of this freedom do we really enjoy? How close are we, as a society, from realizing the maximum level of personal freedom that I call Q Star. Again, Q Star is that point between fascism and anarchy that is maximum freedom. So in short, let's give the status quo a Freedom Report Card, so to speak. And this will be only a partial grading, as a full grading would perhaps take the length of a full volume. In no particular order, here are some issues of freedom.

Earnings/Wages/Fruits of One's Labor:

Freedom here is limited, between 25-50% (depending on income level) of our money is taken in state and federal taxes, most of which funds programs and policies the Constitution does not authorize. Most Americans work 3-4 months of each year to pay taxes, the remainder to pay their own bills.

Religious Freedom/Education Related:

Two areas here we'll consider. While your church can file paperwork to IRS bureaucrats to be tax free (that requirement itself is an obligation to "petition" for something the First Amendment recognizes as a Right) you can not choose to send your children to the schools of your choice without also paying separately for public schools through taxes as well. In many areas of the country vouchers to send your children to religious based schools are disallowed under a distorted interpretation of the First Amendment.

Rights to Keep and Bear Arms and Religious Freedom, Freedom of Association:

All of these rights were clearly violated when Attorney General Janet STERNO sent the BATF agent to gas and fry the Branch Davidians in Waco, Texas in 1993. The standoff had begun with a completely fraudulent warrant being served on the group's leader, David Koresh. Based on false allegations of gun law violations and child abuse, Clinton and his attorney general authorized the government to murder 82 law abiding, innocent citizens including 22 children. I could also mention the Randy Weaver affair here, he was framed in a bogus weapons violations case and later missed a court date he was never duly informed of which lead the FBI siege of his home. It ended when several family members who shot at by FBI agents, including the murder of his pregnant wife and the family dog. The murderer I mean sniper who shot Randy Weaver's pregnant wife, killing both her and the unborn child, was later promoted to a higher rank under Bill Clinton's FBI director.

Eating/Smoking/Drinking/etc.:

The proliferation of policies to "regulate/promote" so-called "public health" should alarm anyone who cares deeply about individual freedom. The anti-tobacco suits are nothing more than judicially created taxes on those who choose to smoke cigarettes. Likewise, there are some that want to add extra taxes to foods high in fat and/or cholesterol. These are ideas from those who wish to use the tax code or the regulatory ability of the government to force you choices on personal lifestyle issues. Those who choose to drink alcoholic beverages already pay high levels of tax on their drink of choice. Freedom here is definitely under attack.

There are numerous other areas of freedom that I urge you to look at. Ask yourself what areas of personal choices one can make that violate no one's rights that are also subject to laws or regulations either proposed or already on the books. Consider your own day to day life, examine not only the areas of freedom you do enjoy, but also the ones that are either limited or restricted. What can you do that isn't either taxed, regulated or that you don't need a license, permit, or other government authorization in some way to do it?

I don't doubt that we in fact enjoy freedom in many areas and many contexts. I'm writing this article right now and don't expect to be put in jail once it's published. I have absolutely no fear of that whatsoever. In many areas of my day to day life, I like most will enjoy basic freedoms. But we shouldn't be content to sit back and think this is good enough. No freedom is ever secure in the long run if the freedoms of some of our fellow citizens, or some of our own freedoms, are under attack. We will have to stand up for individual freedom until we've reached that point on the continuum if we hope to enjoy freedom in the future. And we will need to do this all the more if we hope our children and their children will enjoy freedom.

If You're not interested in politics, this is for You

June 7, 2000

I talk to so many good people who say, "I'm not interested in politics." This is no doubt the negative connotation of the word politics that is being used in this statement. In an ideal world, politics (defined as such) would not exist. But, as we all know, we don't now and probably never will live in an ideal world. In the world, or namely the country, we do live, politics is extremely important.

We as people are more busy then ever, have more sources of information and entertainment then ever, especially those of us who frequently find information and entertainment on the internet. Many Americans work longer hours to make enough money to pay the bills. Many are married, have children, careers, hobbies, etc. I fully understand there's often little time left to follow and keep up with politics, even if one is interested. And I know many find it difficult to become interested. I'll start making my case in favor of being interested in politics by mentioned one date below.

APRIL 15.

As you know, that is the infamous date on which state (most states) and Federal income taxes are due. The amount of money you are legally obligated to send in on April 15 is determined by politics. The very existence of April 15 as tax day was created by politics. What and where, and on whom, your tax dollars are spent is a process that is decided by politics. At all levels, including federal and down to your local city or town government, laws and policies and ordinances are determined by politics. Much of what you do on a daily basis, especially every time you leave your own property (whether owned or rented) is affected by politics. Even much of what you do on your own property is affected by politics. Try adding an additional room on to your own house, your local government regulates this process and you likely need a permit from them to do this. This is because of politics.

I'm not defending the ubiquitous involvement of politics in every crack and crevice of our lives, including our personal lives and personal decisions. Not only am I not defending this, I'm against it. I'm against our personal decisions and our own business constantly being decided, regulated, and affected by politicians, bureaucrats, and government agents.

I think if you own your home you have a right to build a deck or an addition without getting permission (same route as word permit) from the town or city government. I think you should decide what food you eat and whether or not you smoke in your own home. I think paying 35-50% of your earnings and income into taxes is far too high. Do you not agree with me? I suspect you probably agree with most, if not all, of those statements? So how do you and I get these things changed? By now you know the answer, politics. We must first make the effort to be informed. And then we must vote for the candidates most likely to make these needed changes, when we vote on Election Day. You don't vote, you say. Start doing so. When we the people lead, the politicians will follow.

You might be saying voting affects little change, so why bother. Or you might be saying voting makes no difference because we don't have real choices on Election

Day. I disagree with both statements. Cynicism about the value of voting is easy when you see a story like today's primary election in New Jersey. Democrat Jon Corzine wins his party's nomination for U.S. Senate with 58%, defeating former governor Jim Florio. Corzine spent $33 million of his own money, mostly on negative advertisement against Florio. But guess what, all the money didn't put votes into the ballot box. I admit money makes it easy to get votes, but that alone doesn't do it. If the voters of New Jersey, or at least the 58% of the Democrats who voted today, didn't vote for this guy, he would not have won. Simply put, if you don't want your vote "bought" by someone willing to spend $33 million of his own money to be a Senator, don't vote for the character who does this. It's that simple.

Those who think we don't have choices on Election Day, consider this. Those choices are put on the ballot in primaries, in most cases, like the ones today in New Jersey and New Mexico. Most voters don't participate in primary elections. We all should, these are the key chances we have to decide who is on the ballot in November. If enough of us, as voters, demand candidates who will lower taxes and do a number of other things we want done, the politicians will follow. If we make those preferences heard loudly, the politicians will follow and we'll have those choices on Election Day. But making this happen requires that we follow politics. Spend at least a little while every day making the effort to be informed. We need to participate. That includes voting and a lot more. Sending in letters to your local newspaper helps.

Politicians, and their advisors, read those letters. Editors do publish them, and many others citizens read them. You influence both your fellow citizens and the politicians when you have a letter printed in your local newspaper. And most newspapers have web sites and accept letters via e-mail. So it couldn't get much easier and convenient than that. If you have time, and you think there's a good candidate running for office in your area, get involved in that campaign and help increase the odds that person gets elected.

I wish that few decisions would be made by politicians and bureaucrats and government agencies in the future, but right now that is not the case. A lot of us would like to change a lot of things related to government. The only way to do that is getting involved in politics. It may not always be the most fun thing to do, or the thing we want to do at any given time. But if enough of us get involved and make a difference, we'll notice the difference and appreciate the positive outcome that our involvement will effect.

If you don't get involved in politics, you're letting others do it for you. If you don't vote, you're letting others choose the politicians who will choose how much you pay in taxes, and where that money is spent. If you want to leave that choice to others, you can remain not interested in politics. But if you want that choice being made with your involvement, that will take getting involved.

Are you still not interested in politics?

What is Freedom? Part Two

April 27, 2000

"There is no reason that all human existence should be
constructed on some one or some small number of
patterns. If a person possesses any tolerable amount of
common sense and experience, his own mode of laying
out his existence is the best, not because it is the best in
itself, but because it is his own mode."
-    John Stuart Mill

    Freedom has been defined many times by many
individuals. Some say freedom is simply the ability one to
do whatever one chooses, regardless of the consequences,
or regardless of anyone else's freedom. This is the view
William Donahue, in his book of the same title, called
The New Freedom. I don't think many serious advocates
of individual freedom support that kind of freedom.
    While out in New Mexico I was working on a
television program with a friend at the local cable access
channel. We spoke briefly with the host of a previous
show that was primarily about exposing the "New World
Order" and various related conspiracy theories. My friend
asked him how he defined freedom. His response,
"freedom is the ability to do what's right." While I asked
who defines what's right, my friend asked him what he
defines as being right. Neither of us were convinced by
that definition of freedom. You and I don't agree 100% on
what's right, so how can we both agree to live in freedom
by that definition?
    Still others believe freedom comes in the form of
following and abiding by the preaching of new age
religions. Living in accordance with the various Eastern

religions will solve all ones problem and allow one to find true freedom, so we are told. What does this do for those of us who don't believe in new age religions? Are we not doing to enjoy freedom? Well not their kind of freedom I suppose. I don't challenge one's right to believe in the religion of one's choice. However, when that belief translates into organizing a political party around that vision of freedom and having a desire to use the levers of government to lead people to that freedom, by choice or by force if needed, then I have a problem with that. When I'm told I need to comply with conformity, then my freedom is violated. Freedom is not a "everyone does the same thing" kind of concept. But when new age religion is combined with politics, this is often the result. My writings about the Natural Law Party will focus on this.

We are left still with the nagging question, what is freedom? I say freedom includes the right of the individual to live life as one chooses so long as the rights of others are not violated in the process. Choose your own preferences for lifestyle, views on issues, music, or movies, etc. and not impose those choices on others.

For instance, if you think drinking is so bad it should be stopped, then simply say so and attempt to convince people of that point. Many will disagree, of course. Both of those are within a reasonable definition of freedom. Try writing a law to say that drinking alcohol should be illegal, thereby making that choice to everyone who is subject to the law, if passed, and that action obviously violates freedom. One has a right to have a few drinks and it only violates the rights of others if one causes harm to others (drinking and driving) or if one attempts to force a drink on someone who chooses to abstain from alcohol. I use this as an example. Remove the reference to booze, replace with any other personal freedom choice and the concept remains the same.

The issues of freedom that get more complicated are those involved in the "don't violate the rights of others" part. That is central to discussion of freedom, and will also be the focus of much writing in this column. That is the main issue at hand when we attempt to define freedom, and then put this into action in seeking to maximize the level of freedom we all enjoy as individuals.

The Politics of Negative Incrementalism

February 1999

Negative Incrementalism is the backward cousin of compromise. It's also the product of the other side taking a long term approach to achieving their agenda, knowing they'll eventually get the entire loaf even if only part of it today. Since the administration of one Abraham Lincoln in the 1860s our country has been traveling down a road that leads surely to socialism and statism. The statists and socialists have known all along that their agenda was too radical to be achieved all at once, but that they could continually push new incremental measures, "steps in the right direction," until socialism is achieved. They successfully practiced a strategy of positive incrementalism, means they incrementally move in a positive direction toward their agenda. That's not to say that their agenda is anything we consider positive.

For decades our two party system has been great at giving us worthless, false dilemma choices. Moderate Republicans, who dominate their party, have a 70-year long very consistent history of negative incrementalism. At every point of ratcheting up the socialist agenda, their response has been "can't we have just a little less socialism than the Democrats want" rather than debating the merits of socialism and saying NO to more socialism and statism. Moderate Republicans never disputed the basic principles behind socialism. They only demanded a little bit less, little more gradual transition to socialism then the Democrats wanted. Sensing this mush, the Democrats have charged on, and over the last 70 years have achieved most of the major goals of socialism. Karl Marx called for, and we now have: state run schools, largely state controlled health care, more money taxed or controlled by the government than by private hands, minimum wage laws, in many places rent control laws, gun control laws, welfare and other income re-distribution programs, social security, etc. If Hillary's womb-to-the-tomb "health security" were implemented all at once (rather than through the incremental plans receiving bi-partisan support from both wings of our two-party monopoly) it would just about complete the socialist agenda's successful implementation.

Currently we can see negative incrementalism at work in the gun control debate. There's no doubt that gun control advocates won't stop until the entire U. S. population is completely disarmed and the right to keep and bear arms is repealed. Whether stated or not, that is in fact their goal. The gun control movement is made up of the leaders of the movement who desire that goals, as well as some duped into thinking they support a more moderate course on gun control without realizing they back a movement that will seek to achieve the most extreme gun control agenda.

The gun controllers propose waiting periods, and the Moderate Republicans and their friends and allies, the National Rifle Association (NRA), propose instead more limited violation of the 2nd Amendment: electronic background checks instead of both waiting period and background checks. We have 20,000 gun laws already on the books; they are the products of years of Republican/NRA compromise, in a negative direction, with the gun control movement. With friends like these to sell us out, gun owners don't need enemies.

We this trend with taxes. The record tax increases of 1990 and 1993 dramatically increased taxes paid by the middle class taxpayers. Now the Moderate Republicans propose a "ten percent tax cut." This will only be followed, if passed, but future bi-partisan tax increases. Make no mistake about it, the moderate Republicans are no friends of the taxpayers, any more than Frank Perdue is the friends of the chickens. Voting Republican and expecting lower taxes and more freedom is as smart as the chicken voting for Frank Perdue. You and the chicken are both headed in the same direction.

Negative incrementalism is both short-term and long-term defeat. Freedom fighters will never achieve freedom practicing the politics of negative incrementalism. Never fall for the allusion that we just cooperate and compromise, accepting partial socialism today that the other side will somehow magically go along with incremental moves toward freedom tomorrow. It will never happen, they'll come back to the table tomorrow asking we compromise in their direction yet again. And again and again and again, until their agenda I achieved. Until they've established the socialist workers paradise.

We have to vigorously debate and win the debate against socialism, and oppose it in all it forms, and in all it's sub-agendas, including gun control, state-run education, etc. We need to turn change the direction of public policy, by winning that debate, and make the statists compromise by accepting parts of the pro-freedom agenda. We never compromise on principle and should only compromise when freedom is increased by the passage of any proposal with our support. Like Goldwater said, we should only agree to the proposal when it involves wiping out regulations not passing new regulations over old ones, repealing laws that violate freedom not passing new laws to try to fix old failed laws, and eliminating programs that are unconstitutional, not creating new bureaucracies to solve problems created by old failed programs.

If you support moderate Republicans and/or the NRA and expect a different outcome, you're not only wasting your time and effort, you're contributing to the problem. You're aiding those who steal our money, violate our 2nd Amendment rights, and ultimately sell out to the socialists and statists that won't stop until they've stolen all our money and have full control over our lives.

Libertarians Right on a Lot of Issues

April 27, 2000

As a strong supporter of individual liberty I've often been critical of the Libertarian Party on strategic matters. But I applaud their stands on a number of public policy issues and it is this reason I wish they were more strategically successful in selling their views to the voters.

Below are the just some of the numerous public policy areas where Libertarians are and have been right:

Affirmative Action. I call it Affirmative Discrimination, because that is exactly what it is. Regardless of which euphemisms one used, quotas, set-asides, goals and time tables, etc. any system of policies which takes race or sex into consideration for hiring, promotion, financial decisions, housing or other such decisions is simply put, racist or sexist. Period. Dr. Martin Luther King called to people to be judged by "the content of their character, not the color of their skin." Libertarians, any myself, are in agreement on this.

Bosnia and Kosovo. We had no national interest in participating in the military intervention in the wars of the former Yugoslavia. Opposing that policy of the Clinton Administration and the U.N. is isolationism, it's common sense.

Capital Gains Taxes. Eliminate them, don't lower them, get rid of them altogether. Nuking the capital gains tax is not a "tax cut for the wealthy" it's a tax cut for everyone who believes we'll be better off with more economic prosperity. If you think capital gains taxes are in your interest, try unemployment too.

Farm subsidies. Like all corporate subsidies, they are neither good for economic prosperity nor good for the industries they tend to corrupt. Farming like any other industry would be better served to earn it's place in the economy via the free market. When will more Republicans join this point of view and pledge to REFORM government by getting rid of corporate subsidies. Why don't you adopt this issue Senator McCain?

Internet Regulation. Libertarians have come out entirely against the regulation and taxation of the Internet. I agree, and believe that not only should the Internet be recognized as a sphere of freedom (freedom here means tax-free and regulation free) but it should teach us that we should expand this kind of freedom to other sectors of our economic life. While fraud and crime remain illegal in such a sphere of freedom, government corruption and fraud are not tolerated.

War on Drugs. Conservatives in good standing like William F. Buckley and New Mexico Governor Gary Johnson have declared the drug war a failure and called for its end. I agree when Libertarian point out we could far more effectively remedy the true violent crime problem by putting the real violent criminals in the prisons instead of filling up our cells with non-violent drug offenders. Drug addicts belong in treatment, murderers and rapists belong in "the joint." This is not only wise criminal justice policy, it's common sense as well.

Zoning. Libertarians, principled conservatives, and other supporters of property rights worked together to repeal zoning regulations in Houston a few years ago. A friend of mine is fond of the slogan "the only permit you need is your deed." He's right, zoning regulations are a violation of private property rights. Does this mean one can violate the property of others, such as engaging in pollution that effects the entire neighborhood? Of course not, but it means you can paint your house whatever color you choose, and if someone down the street doesn't like it he doesn't have look at it.

There are several others areas of public policy I could cover here. We've had our public policy pulled in the direction of the socialist left for the past 70 years. We've had weak-kneed moderate Republicans often posing at the alternative to status-quo liberal Democrats; both of which have combined to preserve the current system of big government over the years. Barry Goldwater said in 1964 the Republicans should represent "a choice not an echo." This is true now more than ever.

Libertarian Integrity fades under scrutiny of Abortion Discussion

March 17, 2000

Like most groups of Americans, Libertarians are divided on the abortion issue. But unlike most groups of Americans, Libertarians claim their views are strictly based on the principles they adopt and that is what sets them aside from other parties. The Libertarian Party has both its pro-life faction and a "pro choice" faction. And you guessed it, both sides say their abortion position is consistent with party principle and the other one is not. And a few of the more intellectually opportunistic Libertarians, who don't like to debate the issue, simply say "both sides are right" and leave it at that. But of course both sides can't be right on an issue like Life.

The main principle involved is what Libertarians call the "non-aggression" axiom, which is the pledge they take as guiding their philosophy on the issues. That pledge is, "I do not believe in or advocate the initiation of force as a means of achieving political or social goals." While force is reasonably easy to define the initiation part is not always so easy. Defining initiation can get like the old school yard fight, when the teacher comes out both students point the other way and say he started it. This becomes true about the abortion issue for Libertarians too, both sides say the other is advocating the initiation of force.

The summary of the arguments is as follows: pro-life libertarians believe the act of abortion is initiation of force against the unborn human fetus. They obviously recognize the unborn human fetus as human life that is worthy of protection its right to life. The pro-choice

Libertarian side argues the unborn human fetus is simply property of the mother and she can expel it at any time. While I disagree with this premise, at least they admit something liberal abortion supporters will not, simply that they do not recognize the unborn human fetus as human life. They call it property, which is not the first time a group of people has declared human lives to be property.

What's important with this issue is how most Libertarians don't want to talk about abortion. And that's against their general nature, Libertarians otherwise love to talk and debate most issues until they turn blue in the face. But why do they not want to debate this issue at such length? Answer is simple: Libertarian political philosophy (and Libertarian's confidence in it) is so heavily dependent on the non-aggression axiom that any issue that calls to question the effectiveness of that axiom as a guide to politics calls the whole Libertarian dogma into question. You see, an issue, which shows that the non-aggression axiom can't answer all political questions, is one that shows the limitations of accepted Libertarian philosophy. In doing so, the inadequacy of that philosophy is what Libertarians don't want to consider, and therefore they don't want to debate abortion. Otherwise, a good vigorous discussion of abortion might cause some to question the Libertarian Orthodoxy handed down on high from libertarian scholars like Murray Rothbard and Ayn Rand.

But the true test of a party that wants to hold the highest offices in the land is how they tackle the most controversial and challenging issues of the day. Can they debate that issue and have their principles withstand the challenge that issue might offer. I suspect that Pro-Life Libertarians would answer that question yes. But their status as the minor in the Libertarian Party calls that into question, or at least shows they have yet to win over enough members of their own party to get their party's officially pro-choice platform stance reversed. The wide majority of Libertarians who either want to tell you they're pro-choice and not back up the position, or the others who say "there's disagreement in our party and let's leave it at that" are both in agreement with not wanting to debate the abortion issue. In that way they show that most Libertarians really want to run and hide when this issue comes up.

A political party that wants to run and hide on the most controversial issues of the day is one that is not yet prepared to play politics in prime time. It's one party that is not yet ready to lead us.

Big Government is a Huge Racket
March 17, 2000

The federal government is buying, with money confiscated from taxpayers, advertisement telling you filling out the census paperwork is important in the distribution of government money. Except when government runs the printing presses and inflates the currency, it can only get money by borrowing or collecting taxes. The notion is, the more your local community has its members "stand up and be counted" the more your community will get in money from various government programs that dole out the bucks based on local demographics.

The occasion of the census is also a great opportunity to question the wisdom of this establishment political scientists call "the Modern Administrative State," in plain English, Big Government. Supporters of this way of governing have created the perception that government does a lot of functions that would not be done otherwise. Additionally, that perception includes the notion that most people get more benefit out of Big Government than they pay in taxes to support this system. But is that really true?

Let's start at the individual level. Ask yourself, do you really get more benefit from the government than you pay into it? Now I realize you might be thinking, "I paid X amount into state and federal taxes" but add to that all the hidden taxes and costs of Big Government. Add to that state sales taxes if your state has them, any excise taxes you might pay, and on top of all that the costs of taxes and regulations on business. Corporations pay those so I don't, you say. Not so, corporations raise the price of their products and services which means you and I pay those taxes at the cash register. So adding in all those hidden taxes and indirect but also hidden taxes, it's estimated most of us end up sending half the money we earn to the government. Now add up how much you personally get from various government programs in one form or another. Does that equal half of what you earn from income? For most I doubt it will.

Let's consider your local and state governments. They get some money from the Federal government, who collected that money from us to then send SOME of it back to the state and local levels. But the government in Washington D.C. has erected great bureaucracies to re-distribute all this tax money. Those great bureaucracies are themselves funded by this money. So for every dollar paid in taxes toward these functions, such as taxes on gasoline, a fraction of that money actually comes back to pay for those functions, such as repairing of roads and highways. If the road and highway repair money was never cycled through the great bureaucracies of Washington D.C. we'd either have more roads and highways better repaired and maintained, or we could do the same for roads and highways for a whole lot less money. But the bureaucrats and politicians of the Washington D.C. inside-the-beltway culture will have it no other way.

Every once in a while the statistics are published on which states get back more or fewer dollars for what their citizens pay into Washington D.C. If ALL the money was going to Washington and coming back to the states, you would either see all states getting the same back. Or you might see one state that gets more back for every state that gets less back. But what you do see are a few states that get a little bit more back, maybe one state (usually New Mexico) that gets quite a bit back, and then about

30-something to nearly 40 states that get a LOT less back. For most state, sending money to Washington D.C. to get SOME of it back is a raw deal.

And at the Federal level itself much of the money is eaten up in fraud, waste, and abuse. The Federal government can't do anything with creating massive bureaucracies. Medicare and Medicaid costs nine times as much as was estimated when those programs were created. The more government gets involved and spends in the health care industry the more those products and service rise in cost. Government has put millions into student loans for college students and the cost of going to college has risen three times faster than the rate of inflation over the past 30 years since the inception of student loan programs. Anyone see a pattern here?

Most of us simply don't get much back for all the taxes we pay. Some will say we get relative freedom and a reasonable level of security from government. But let me tell you, those "public goods" if you consider them that are paid for by a SMALL FRACTION of current government spending. We could have all the freedom and security (and probably a lot more freedom) with a lot less government and many fewer and lower levels of taxes. Many people are afraid to go this route, thinking they will lose a lot of the benefits of Big Government. We've been sold the Big Government snow job for decades now. But many of us don't realize how little we really get from Big Government. If Charles Ponzi could have only sold his schemes as well as Uncle Sam has, he would been named the world's most brilliant businessman of all time.

Big Government is a huge racket that benefits primarily those in the government. Under minimal government we all do much better to provide support for charities and private efforts to help those who truly need it. And with the rest of the money we'd not being paying taxes or giving to charity we'd live a better standard of life and work many fewer hours for better money. Let's give up our addiction to big government and try more freedom. It works.

Green Party Road to Serfdom: This Policy Stinks

May 18, 2000

Like many third parties, the Green Party focuses a great deal of their effort in trying to win local offices. And in some cases they succeed. The Green Party advocates a hard leftwing platform that is a mixture of new age values, socialist economics, and extreme anti-industrialist, anti-capitalist environmental politics. Rush Limbaugh has observed that the extreme environmental movement is the new home of socialism since the fall of communism. He's right, but I add it's the home of authoritarian socialism.

The latest showcase of Green Party governance from the extreme left comes from New Mexico. One of the looniest left-wing cities in the nation, Santa Fe has elected a Green Party member, Fran Gallegos, to the position of municipal judge. But don't look for this judge to be tough on crime, at least real crime. This judge has previously attracted media attention for being the most lenient judge in the state for giving light sentences to repeat drunk driving offenders. But you don't want to be in Judge Gallegos' court because your dog has pooped in the public park in Santa Fe, that's a serious crime in Fran's kangaroo court.

Today's Albuquerque (NM) Journal reports that Judge Gallegos has issued 70 warrants for the arrest of pet owners who failed to appear in court over alleged dog pooping in the public park incidents. I'm not making this up, this is true as reported. By serving these bench warrants, these individuals can be arrested, booked, and spend the night in the local jail. This is all over doggy poop, imagine it. There are rapists, murderers, and lots of politicians (it's the state capital) driving drunk in Santa Fe in need of being arrested and prosecuted. But Judge Gallegos illustrates the wacky Green philosophy of her party by placing more priority on jailing owners of dogs to leave their droppings in the park.

Some did show up at the court. Gallegos sentenced them to wear brown hats and be part of crews that will clean up doggy droppings at city parks. And they had to pay fines as well, but the article didn't say what amount the fines were.

But dogs aren't the only animals out there leaving behind their droppings. What about birds? They certainly leave their droppings in undesired places as well. What will Judge Gallegos do about them? Perhaps it's not easy since birds don't have specific owners the way dogs do. Greens claim to understand nature, but apparently they don't. The droppings of the birds, dogs and other animals are washed away by nature itself. None of this stuff is a real problem. But extreme environmentalists wishing to control people and their pets will invent "problems" like this to solve with authoritarian government policy. Commit such "crimes" and you're doing jail time. Commit real crime, and instead of doing the time, Judge Gallegos and other Greens will "understand" your behavior and give you a free pass.

This is proof that radicals like the Greens have no place being elected or appointed judges. Throwing the book after non-crimes and minor offences and giving away free passes to real criminals is simply ineffective criminal justice policy. It also sends the wrong message to criminals. This kind of criminal justice approach is itself criminal. Santa Fe dog owners need to start collecting signatures to have Judge Gallegos re-called or impeached from office.

Criminals LOVE Gun Control

March 16, 2000

Gun control laws are the criminals' favorite laws. The more you take firearms out of the hands of law abiding citizens you made them easier targets for robbers and other criminals. I know the knee-jerk response to this from some is "that's so simplistic" and the like. But it's simple because it's simply TRUE.

Remember the rash of highway killings and robberies that happened a few years ago in Florida and in all the publicized cases it was tourists driving rented cars being car-jacked, robbed and murdered? This was because the criminals KNEW these people were not carrying firearms and would be easy targets. This is why criminal also love laws prohibiting concealed carry of firearms. Those who openly carry are to be avoided, and anyone not carrying is therefore an easier target.

Let's remember the simple fact about how criminals obtain their firearms. They don't go to a gun shop and fill out the Brady Waiting Period paperwork and register for them and such. They buy their guns from the underground market, often getting inexpensive firearms with serial numbers ground off, or imported firearms, etc. Criminals don't obey laws, why does anyone think they'll obey gun control laws? Politicians know this. But the real intent is to eventually pass restrictions on law-abiding citizens to keep and bear arms. This from the same set of politicians who use the bogus argument "its to protect children" when passing legislation to restrict the freedoms of adults. They also use this argument for gun control as well. If just one of those teachers at Columbine High School was carrying a concealed firearm, perhaps numerous children would have been spared from death if Harris and Klebold were to have been gunned down sooner in defense of the rest of the students. In other such school shooting incidents, teachers have prevented further student deaths by having a firearm available.

Politicians, especially those that are calling for more laws in addition to the 20,000 gun laws already on the books, are most hypocritical about gun control. Armed Secret Service agents guard the president as well as members of Congress. Yet most members of Congress, and the current President, advocate laws that limit or restrict your ability to carry firearms for self-defense.

If you want a great way to effectively show the hypocrisy of politicians who support gun control try this: ask any member of Congress or state legislator who supports gun control legislation to put a sign a up on their homes saying "this residence is a gun free zone." See how many will take you up on the offer, even if you offer to make the signs for them. Politicians that vote for gun control should live as they vote, and take this suggestion. But I wouldn't hold my breath waiting for any honest gun control supporting politician to do this.

And for those politicians and demagogues who trot out that "gun control makes communities safer" tripe, remind them of these facts. Washington, D.C. is the murder capital of the world. It almost always leads in most categories of violent crimes. Washington, D.C. also has the nation's strictest gun control laws. Most of our big cities are crime capitals and have very strict gun control laws. Yet the inner cities of most of those cities are war zones. What does that tell you about gun control?

Latest Supreme Court Ruling Again Endangers the Bill of Rights

May 16, 2000

The current membership of the Supreme Court of the United States has been quite good at ruling in major cases by seeming to make up as they go along. On many occasions the court hands down legal sophistry that should get a failing grade from any legitimate college of Constitutional Law.

The latest exercise in legal sophistry is the Court's recent ruling regarding adult entertainment establishments, or more specifically topless nightclubs. Keep in mind, regardless of whether you personally condone or patronize such establishments, no one is dragged kicking and screaming into these places. The issue was a local ordinance in Erie, Pennsylvania regulating these businesses.

Justices O'Connor, Rehnquist, Kennedy and Breyer concurred that local communities could ban nude dancing at such establishments because such constitutes a manner of expression and it not in itself expression. Therefore, according to the ruling majority, such an ordinance of that type doesn't ban the expression itself and does not violate the First Amendment. The justices also cited precedent from a case on the burning of draft cards by anti-Vietnam war protesters. That ruling upheld restrictions on the burning of draft cards on the reasoning that the law didn't ban protesting of the war, but banned only that method of protest. Additionally, the Court ruled that the First Amendment didn't repeal previously existing "police powers" of the state to regular or ban such behavior. Antonin Scalia and Clarence Thomas concurred separately, upholding a "right of the government" to enact ordinances regulating adult entertainment. The justices argued that the First Amendment is not violated because expression itself is not banned but only a single manner of that expression is banned.

This ruling is legal sophistry, plain and simple. A right to free expression is meaningless if the individual is legally prohibited from choosing his own method of expression providing he does not violate the rights of others in doing so. If I choose to speak out against this court ruling, it is my right under the First Amendment to choose the method. It might including writing an article like this one, appearing on a radio talk show, writing a letter to the editor, or taking out advertisement in the local newspaper.

Apply the Court's logic to other amendments in The Bill of Rights. Could a law banning handguns be said not to ban our right to keep and bears arms because it only bans one type of firearms and not all types? Consider the ludicrous "good faith exception to conduct search and seizure without a warrant" that was debated in Congress in 1995. Sponsored argued it was consistent with the Fourth Amendment since it only addressed one type of search and seizure but don't entirely repeal the Fourth Amendment? Using this bogus reasoning, would a law allowing coerced confessions be allowed under the Fifth Amendment using this bogus reasoning? Perhaps it is this reasoning that has rendered the Ninth and Tenth Amendments virtually impotent as protections against intrusive government.

Consider the other premise of the ruling: that the First Amendment didn't repeal allegedly pre-existing state authority to regulate adult entertainment establishments. Anyone who has studied history knows that the Bill of

Rights was drafted and enacted for precisely the VERY REASON of repealing a great deal of pre-existing and commonly exercised uses of government authority. Pre-Constitutional violations of Free Speech, gun ownership, property rights, and other rights were the very reason that Jefferson and his colleagues insisted on enacting The Bill of Rights.

What's next? What other earlier state authority to regulate freedom will the Supreme Court now resurrect with this reasoning to uphold further encroachments of individual freedom, and do further violence to The Bill of Rights?

The World is Ruled by Force, but Who Will Control It?

May 22, 2000

In stating the world is controlled by force, I'm not condoning. Instead I'm pointing out reality. Ultimately, the military force the nations around the world build up control world politics, directly or indirectly. While this may not be the best world we could live in, it is in fact the world we do live in. And remember the purpose of a military is to kill people and break things. It's not for international meals-on-wheels missions or any of this "humanitarian" nonsense you see the Clinton administration preaching about in press conferences.

Left wing liberals love to talk about their idealist principles of self-determination and democracy, about international law, and protecting human rights around the world, etc. Liberals tell you they want to make the world such a nice place to live. Remember Wilson's "making the world safe for democracy." This is all poppycock and gobbledegook. The real issues in world politics are who holds the power and just what policies are pursued when they exercise that power. Liberals, while serving up all their idealist spin, know this too.

Liberals love to promote the United Nations and so-called International Law as the solutions to problems around the world. The South Korean side of the Korean conflict was backed by the U.N. but it was primarily the force of the U.S. military that beat back the North Korean and Chinese forces. The Gulf War was backed officially by U.N. resolutions but it was primarily the U.S. military forces that beat back Saddam Hussein's armies. U.N support made little or no difference in those conflicts.

Likewise, the lack of U.N. support has not prevented the use of force around the world either. Saddam Hussein took over Kuwait without U.N. approval. The U.S. invaded Grenada without U.N. approval. The Reagan Administration, despite U.N. disapproval, sent arms to the democratic resistance in Nicaragua. The communist Sandinista government of Nicaragua was ultimately toppled from power despite having U.N. support.

But the left wing liberals know that gaining power will be needed in order to impose their agenda on the world. That is exactly why liberals want to see the United Nations take on more power and resources, and it is why they would like to see it take on authority to enforce "International Law." Right now International Law comes from treaties negotiated and signed by the nations of the world. But liberal supporters of one-world government ultimately want to see the established of an international parliament that would have the authority to pass legislation that would be binding on all nations and peoples of the earth. Most of us oppose that idea, and for good reason. The government of a large country is already too disconnected with the concerns of the people it represents.

Most treaties signed do not in fact deal with relations between nations anymore, which is what they are supposed to be used for. Most treaties now deal with issues of domestic policy within the various nations. Look at the recent treaties that have been promoted and signed by many countries. They deal with rights of children, pollution and global warming, economic development, education and civil right, etc. Since when are these issues between nations rather than issues that are actually between individual nations' government and THEIR OWN citizens?

These are the areas of policy that liberal supporters of world government seek to take from your elected leaders and place them in the hands of un-elected U.N. bureaucrats. There's already numerous precedents showing how the one-world supporters would use the United Nations, if given the power, to impose their socialist agenda on the world. The so-called World Court was the where they attempted to enforce the liberal foreign policy agenda on the United States in regard to the Nicaragua policy in the 1980s.

Little imagination is needed to see how the United States could be declared in violation of several recent treaties for not stopping global warming, for failing to enact national health care legislation, for failing to equally offer free education to all children, for failing to reduce emissions of greenhouse gases, etc. We are not very far away at all from the time when one-world government supporting liberals will start using the international bureaucracies to try to compel the U.S. government into legislating socialism here. And they have their willing allies in the form of Congressional Democrats, the NEA preaching socialism in the public schools, and the nightly propaganda of the three major network news programs and PBS's news programs.

But there's one way to stop all this nonsense. Insist on full enforcement of the Constitution and the Bill of Rights. The Constitution explicitly prohibits the United States from signing treaties that would over-ride the authority of the elected institutions of our federal and state governments as well as the rights of the people contained in The Bill of Rights. This is exactly why liberals constantly fight for court decisions that interpret the amendments of The Bill of Rights as saying we really don't have these rights.

To win the battle for individual freedom around the world, or to simply defend our own freedom, we must maintain and protect individual freedom by enforcing the Bill of Rights. Exposing and opposing the move toward one-world government imposed socialism is a good step in the right direction as well.

Prosecution of Medical Marijuana User Steve Kubby is neither Compassionate nor Conservative

May 18, 2000

The nanny-state has gotten so far out of control it will let you die to protect you. If you're unfortunate enough to suffer from an illness that can only be effectively treated by a drug not yet approved by the FDA you might die sooner than necessary. This may sound like a human rights case from some third world state. It's not.

The 1998 Libertarian candidate for Governor of California, Steve Kubby, and his wife are on trial for possessing and producing the only drugs Kubby's physicians have found treats his illness: marijuana. The voters in California legalized its medicinal use in 1996, but prosecutors are acting under federal marijuana prohibition laws.

Steve Kubby has a rare and fatal form of cancer of the adrenal system. You can read more information at their web site, http://www.Kubby.com. Using medical marijuana keeps the cancer in check and allows him to lead a normal and healthy life. His doctors don't understand how it works and or why, and they have been studying his progress under marijuana treatment. Kubby is one of the few alive with this rare form of cancer and his physicians tell him the marijuana is precisely what is keeping him alive.

Numerous other cancer and AIDS patients have found smoking marijuana to help in their treatment as well. As a political activist, Kubby was instrumental in leading the campaign to pass Proposition 215 on the 1996 California ballot, legalizing the use of medically prescribed marijuana. Under the advice and supervision of their physicians, Steve and Michelle Kubby had been growing and producing marijuana for medicinal use. The statewide vote enacting Prop. 215 legalized this practice. So they thought.

Proposition 215 was essentially declared null and void by the Drug Enforcement Agency. The DEA advised prosecution of anyone attempting to produce their own marijuana, despite the fact the new law legalized it for those having a prescription from their physician. In early January 1999, (comma) the Feds barged into the Kubby's home in an early morning raid. Thus, the Kubbys are currently on trial for possession and production of marijuana.

Dr. Vincent DeQuattro, of the University of Southern California's School of Medicine, supervises Kubby's treatment via medical marijuana. Several physicians and scientists have concluded his life has been spared from death because of the use of medical marijuana. If he were to stop using it, they say he would surely die shortly after that. And it would appear that is precisely what the Placer County Prosecutor wants. A guilty verdict and a jail sentence would effectively deny Kubby access to the politically incorrect medicine that keeps him alive. A jail sentence would be his death sentence.

Furthermore, such actions are anathema to principles of fiscal conservatism. The state is spending the scarce resources of the prosecutor's offices, the law enforcement agencies, to prosecute, and try, and attempt to put someone in jail for treating his rare illness with medical marijuana? Isn't this a massive waste of money? There are too many rapists and murderers and scam artists to prosecute rather than spend the resources going after someone for using medical marijuana. But this is more than someone; the individual is the political activist who lead the campaign to secure voter approved legalization of medical marijuana.

If convicted, the Kubbys will go to jail and their children will become wards of the state. A healthy and happy family will be broken up, and two productive law abiding adults (yes Prop. 215 is part of that law) will be put in jail. Is this compassionate?

Do we value and respect the patient-physician relationship? Politicians, the same ones who preach about the "war on drugs," claim to value this relationship. But they are ones advocating prosecution when physicians prescribe medical marijuana. Why is it the government's business what form of medication physicians prescribe to their patients? It's not being forced on anyone, and the patients who use medical marijuana aren't engaging in behaviors that are violating the rights of others.

So why can't the Kubbys be left alone to grow their own marijuana to treat this illness under the supervision of Dr. DeQuattro? Why can't the rest of us mind our own business? This really isn't a problem, is it?

For most of us who value individual freedom it's not a problem. But to the politicians who prop up the nanny-state it is. Those who seek to control your life to protect you from yourself are willing to protect you from anything they disapprove of. Including the very remedy that might even save your life.

I Would Vote for this Presidential Candidate Part I

April 25, 2000

I would easily vote for a presidential candidate who announced his or her campaign like this:

My fellow Americans, I believe we can and should pursue a better America where we enjoy Freedom, Quality of Life, and Economic Prosperity. We can enjoy freedom to live as we choose so long as we respect the rights of others, have a quality of life that will mean our freedom is meaningful, and economic prosperity for everyone is an attainable goal.

Individual freedom is the principle on which our nation is built. I want to live in an America where the right of the individual to live his life as he choose while respecting the rights of others will not be infringed. A vision of family values in a free society means parents, not government bureaucrats, choose which schools their children will attend. It means families can raise their children free of the meddling bureaucrats of state agencies. It means that marriage is an agreement between the married couple and not a contract with the state. Freedom means your house, your automobile, the food you eat, and other necessities of life are free from taxes and regulations that drive up the cost of living. Freedom means you choose your health and medical care rather than being subject to government-created one-size-fits-all plan.

I believe we can build an America where we can enjoy a better quality of life. Enjoying a quality of life is more than simple economic prosperity. We need to ask

ourselves as individuals if we are well off not just
financially but in overall quality of life. Many families are
better off financially than in the past must sacrifice their
quality of life for that financial improvement. Many
Americans work longer hours for the same or little more
income than ten years ago. Decreased family or leisure
time, and therefore quality of life, is the price of our
recent prosperity. And the tax burden on families is partly
to blame. In many cases both parents work full time and
one works to pay the taxes while the other works to
support the family. Eliminating income taxes on working
families improves both quality of life and economic
prosperity. This is yet another reason we must reduce the
size of government so that we will enhance prosperity and
quality of life.

And economic prosperity must reach all our citizens
rather than benefit the few. To create economic prosperity
that will reach all individuals and families we must reduce
and eliminate needless taxes and government regulations
that prevent you from getting better work, higher pay, and
more opportunity to advance. Creating an economy that
offers opportunity for all is only possible if we eliminate
the impediments to economic growth emplaced by
endless red tape, bureaucracy, and the dozens of
unconstitutional government agencies that get in the way
of progress. We must recognize that in most instances
freedom and economic growth is The Solution and that
government programs, regulations, and needless failed
policies are The Problem. We will promote more freedom
and prosperity by having fewer laws, many fewer
government agencies, and by eliminating economically
destructive taxes and regulations.

The vision of my candidacy is that we can have
Freedom, Quality of Life, and Economic Prosperity for

All through less government, lower taxes and ending needless regulations. In the coming months I will outline this vision in more detail.

Presidential Candidate Part II: Statement on the Elian Gonzalez Raid in Miami

April 22, 2000

In a speech to an audience of Cuban Americans the candidate would offer the following remarks at a community center near the Little Havana neighborhood in Miami:

What happened in the dark of early morning last Saturday in your community last Saturday an outrage and a disgrace that the entire world witnessed. The AP photo showing the INS agent aiming a machine gun at Elian Gonzalez and his rescuer shows the true nature of this administration of corrupt thugs and low-rent fascists we currently have in the White House. Jackbooted Janet Reno and Waco Willie Clinton have really shown their true colors with this action.

American values do not include justification for midnight raids to kidnap a six year old child to turn over to the Cuban dictator where he and his psychiatrists will be ready to subject him to brainwashing that will be essentially a detoxification from freedom. American values don't include over-riding the wishes of Elian Gonzalez's late mother and his family here in this community, to hand him over to Fidel Castro. Elian's Dad is a victim of the Castro dictatorship. The fact that all his actions and moves here in the United States are scripted and controlled by the Cuban Interest Section is proof of this. American values do not include our own government siding with the Castro dictatorship and against freedom, against Elian Gonzalez, against your community, and against the values symbolized by the Statue of Liberty.

What we need here is a new immigration policy that stands for the values symbolize by the Statue of Liberty. We must once again open our borders and open our country to the people of oppressed lands seeking to become productive, freedom-loving members of our society and who risk their own lives to come here. You folks and/or your parents risked everything to come here to enjoy a better standard of life. My ancestors and those of most Americans did the same thing. It is both hypocritical and wrong if our immigration policy is based on the idea that the very same ladder of opportunity to this society that welcomed us is something we pull up behind us.

If I'm elected we'll change policy on Cuban Americans from day one. Any future Elian Gonzalez will be welcomed with open arms and immediately granted to his family here if he has family here. We'll have INS officials who believe in America's value and not Fidel Castro's values. We'll uphold the Rule of Law and the civility of our communities. And we certainly will immediately stop the practice of midnight raids to snatch children. And I can assure you that every single political appointee of the Janet Reno Injustice Department will be unemployed on January 21, 2000.

Let us hope that Lazaro Gonzalez will ultimately win custody of Elian so he might have a future of freedom here in this community. We can only hope the community will be healed and that never again will the Federal Government send in Gestapo agents to tear up a community and steal one of its children again. We can hope to have a president in the White House who values human life, the children of our communities, and stands for American values on Cuban immigration rather than Fidel Castro's values.

Presidential Candidate Part III: Putting Justice Back into the Justice Department
April 23, 2000

In a speech to a law enforcement convention the candidate would offer the following remarks about the Janet Reno Department of Justice under Bill Clinton:

We've witnessed the most corrupt and politicized Justice Department under Bill Clinton's Attorney General, Janet Reno that we've ever had. Early in the Clinton Administration the American Spectator predicted that Bill Clinton would radicalize the justice department. I'm not sure they realized how true that prediction would become.

This justice department has turned its back to blatant large-scale internal political corruption while pursuing the most authoritarian justice mentality of any recent justice department. Senator Ted Kennedy argued against the confirmation of Supreme Court nominee Robert Bork, claiming he advocated rogue police agencies making midnight raids on the homes of citizens. The Clinton-Reno Justice Department ordered a midnight raid in Miami to seize Elian Gonzalez. Senator Kennedy's silence on that raid has been deafening.

Under eight years of Bill Clinton virtually every government agency has created a paramilitary branch staffed with the most psychologically unstable jackbooted thugs who were released from the military as a result of downsizing our national defenses. Our government has invented missions and created agencies to employ these forces. The same people who called conservatives fascists, and said Barry Goldwater was nuts, have turned out to build the most authoritarian police state we've ever seen. Why does our government even have a Bureau of Alcohol Tobacco and Firearms when all three are legal, and the right to own them is recognized by The Bill of Rights? The Federal Bureau of Investigation should be just that, a bureau of investigation aiding the effort to expose criminals and help secure the safety of the community and the nation. But this administration abused by the FBI by sending its agents and forces in to Waco in order to gas and fry 86 human beings to death, including 24 children. And then the political appointees of Waco Willie Clinton and Jackboot Janet Reno engaged in lies, misinformation, and blatant cover up to hide the real truth about the Waco tragedy.

This Injustice Department has put The Bill of Rights into a shredder. Remember it was Bill Clinton who signed the so-called Communications Indecency Act into law that would have regulated content published on the Internet. Sorry Bill, but the First Amendment applies to the Internet as well. Bill Clinton has been the biggest enemy of the Right of law-abiding citizens to keep and bear arms we've ever had in the White House. The best friend of law enforcement officers is the law-abiding citizens who defends himself, prevents crime, and has no need to call on the police. You folks know this, and if I'm elected we'll have an Attorney General that knows this.

Under this administration of Bill Clinton, the Fourth Amendment has become a casualty of the Janet Reno Injustice Department. The right to be secure on one's person, papers, and effects is just that, and is recognized by The Bill of Rights. There are reasons why searches and seizures must be allowed only after properly obtaining a correctly certified warrant. Insuring the peace of the community and the enforcement of the laws means we effectively find and convict the guilty and make sure we leave alone the innocent. We must respect the Fourth Amendment to make this vision of Justice a Reality. Anyone who doesn't fully believe in and value the Fourth Amendment has no place in a Department of Justice in my administration.

This administration has presided over a so-called "war on drugs" where the theft of property, automobiles and real estate to be re-sold for government revenues is justified in the name of law enforcement and stopping drugs. These actions do nothing to help those afflicted by drug abuse and are entirely in violation of the Fifth Amendment. Civil asset forfeiture is wrong and unconstitutional and must immediately be stopped.

We'll also appoint judges and justices who rule in favor of The Bill of Rights, and who will interpret the Constitution for what is says and not what they think is says or should say. The First Amendment says Congress Shall Make No Law regulating free speech. It means exactly what it says, and I'll appoint judges and justices who know that. If Congress violated The Bill of Rights by enacting laws that restrict those rights, I'll veto those acts of legislation. Should my veto be over-ridden in Congress we'll make sure the laws are challenged in the courts. And judges appointed by my administration will strike down such laws because they'll know that "No Law" means exactly that.

If nominated, by my party, I'll be the candidate of Bill of Rights Enforcement and if elected President, freedom will be my flight plan. Our earliest freedom fighters drafted and enacted The Bill of Rights so we can insure our freedom today. The next president needs to have a Department of Justice based on sound law enforcement principles, the highest of which is Bill of Rights Enforcement. If elected, I'll appoint an Attorney General who will lead the Department of Justice toward the defense and enforcement of The Bill of Rights.

Disposable Pets and Disposable Humans
March 18, 2000

Last night I read an article here on Themestream about someone who was willing to have their dog put to sleep before going away for a few months if they didn't find a dog-sitter and then obtain another dog after returning. The article showed how this makes one think that perhaps some have added pets to the list of "commodities" that are disposable.

We have become increasingly a disposable society, and I think it's time we seriously question the wisdom of this. I don't question this on the grounds of suggesting we do more "re-cycling" of resources but I question this on conservative grounds. Disposal products being used needlessly are wasteful. But aside from devaluing material goods have we devalued that which is far more important to life?

I agree that considering pets a disposable commodity is outrageous. As the author said, dogs and cats should be considered to be like members of the family. I can't understand how one can become attached to a dog (if this kind of individual does) but then later on have the dog put to sleep only to soon after get another one. I can't understand this. But outrageous as this is, I suspect many of us don't realize how disposals something other than the lives of pets have become.

In our current society, human beings are disposable. That's right, I said human beings are disposable. This is deplorable but very true. Just think of the many ways we condone and excuse the sacrificing of human lives for various reasons. Wars are an ultimate sacrifice of human life. And this is unjustified in many cases, especially the deaths that have occurred in many of the most needless wars our government has authorized lately that were not consistent with the constitutional mandate for national defense. Wars have killed millions in needless wars. But millions of human lives have been disposed outside of wars as well.

Abortions. That's right, abortions are the disposal of human beings. Those who aren't in denial of the relevant facts know that an unborn HUMAN fetus is in fact scientifically a human being. And most abortions are in fact done for the same reason that article said the neighbor wanted to put the dog to sleep if he didn't find a dog-sitter: Convenience. Let me say that again, because this is important. Most abortions are committed for pure convenience. Self-centered crass convenience of the individual who seeks to get out of the responsibility one has taken on by engaging in the actions which produce that result.

And this disposal is the most tragic and colossal waste of our most valuable "commodity" which is of course human life. Since the legalization of abortion in 1973 more than 35 million unborn human beings have been aborted. Many of those people might have grown up to become productive citizens and leaders in the community and the country. But they were aborted instead. One of them might have gone on to become a great scientist and find the cure for cancer or AIDS. One of them might well have developed technology we can't even imagine right now. But they were aborted instead. This has been the ultimate waste of human life and human potential.

I know many are outraged at my comments here. But what you are outraged not at me, I'm simply the messenger. What you are outraged at, if you are, is the inner realized that I'm right and difficulty reconciling that with opinions on the issue, the current reality of the situation, and other factors. Most of you, regardless of your views on making abortion legal or illegal, believe that abortion itself is wrong. There is a really simple reason most people believe this. Those of us who refuse to have out thinking clouded by wishful thinking can see the reasons this destructive practice is wrong in a society that claims to value human life.

The disposal society, at its most wasteful, is ultimately self-defeating. Devaluing the products of our time and effort has given way to devaluing our pets and this logically extends to the ultimate devaluation of human life itself. All of this has happened far too often in our increasingly disposable society. And if we don't place highest value on human life, we else will we place any value in? How can we call ourselves a civilized society if the sanctity of human life is not worthy of our highest level of protection?

On Libertarians and the Right to Life

April 23, 2000

A member of the Libertarian Party posted a note about abortion on an e-mail list to which I subscribe. The individual argued that opposition to abortion is not promoting a position of advocating liberty. I disagreed and posted the comments below.

If one accepts the premise that the unborn human being deserves the Right to Life, then opposing abortion is defending liberty for all, child and mother, included.

But...let's play with words a second time so we can examine the logic involved or the lack of it. Here's the argument from the e-mail to which I responded.

"Opposing abortion is NOT necessarily promoting liberty for the mother. There is nothing liberating about being force to bring a pregnancy to term against your will."

In mathematics the negative of a negative is a positive, but that's not always true in logic.

For me the full span of human life goes from conception to natural death. When a couple decides to have a child they CHOOSE (that is choice, not after the fact) to bear the RESPONSIBILITY to raise that child to adulthood. Making that choice and then deciding later to change the decision is evading personal responsibility. But since adoption shows that decision to in essence be changed without violating the Right to Life of the Child, I'm in favor of the "pro-choice" option on ADOPTION. But since the "pro-choice" option on abortion violates the Right to Life of the child by ending it's life, I don't believe that should be an option until medical technology allows for the unborn child to be removed from the womb and still allowed to be brought to life in a healthy manner. Given that, let's replace abortion with childhood and see how the sentence sounds.

Opposing release from child rearing responsibility is NOT necessarily promoting liberty for the mother. There is nothing liberating about being force to raise a child to adulthood against your will.

See how absurd the argument is? Don't want children, your choice is to not create them. The "pro-choice" position where children before birth have no legal rights and those after birth do have the right to life is simply put, discriminatory. I'm against this discrimination and in favor of upholding the right to life of human beings, including the unborn ones.

And for those who call themselves "libertarians" and say discussing abortion is a waste of time, I feel sorry for you. If we can't defend the Right to Life, we are worthy of defending any rights. If the Libertarian Party lacks the courage to stand up for Human Life, I don't view them as having any value to stand up for any other rights. Without the Right to Life we have no other rights. If my mother hadn't chosen Life I would have no Rights at all. Think about that.

Abortion, Slavery, and Civil Liberties

April 26, 2000

In the 1800's, U.S. citizens used to own slaves, as most of us have learned in our junior high school history classes. And one slave broke free, and resisted being returned to his "owner," and the Supreme Court, in the then landmark Dred Scott decision, ruled against the ex-slave's claim to being human, and ruled that he be returned to his master.

In doing so, the court determined that the black skinned human being was not human, but was property to be owned by white skinned humans. And this would not be the first mistaken precedent from the Supreme Court that would divide American society.

In 1973, in another similar Constitutional blunder, the Supreme Court once again ruled that a certain class of human life is not human, and is, in effect, someone's property. The court ruled, in effect, that the human fetus is not human life, that it is property owned by the pregnant woman, and privacy allows the woman to dispose of this "property" at her own will. This was the second time in our history that an entire class of human life was pronounced to be lifeless property by the Supreme Court.

As for the human fetus being human life, it is life, scientifically speaking, by the fact that it has 46 chromosomes. And scientifically, a living being, with 46 chromosomes that is, or will become at the end of gestation, a living human is in fact human life. And the U.S. Constitution states that no human may deprived of "life, limb, or liberty" without the benefit of due process. The Roe vs. Wade pro-abortion decision is not only lacking Constitutional justification, it is blatantly against the Constitution. This citation is from the Bill of Rights, the Fifth Amendment, and it (as the first ten amendments do) is for the purpose of protecting civil liberties, the most fundamental of which is the RIGHT TO LIFE.

But the ideologues of the leftist and feminist variety chant slogans like "anti-choice is Anti-women." First, to put this in plain English, the backwards term "anti-choice" describes those who favor something being illegal that should be illegal. For example, I am quite sure that most readers of this article are "anti-choice" on rape, robbery, murder, child pornography, etc. Many of us are also "anti-choice" on allowing the murder of the unborn human being.

With all the various effective form of contraception, there is nearly no excuse for "unwanted pregnancies." And less than one percent, according to all measures of this, of all abortions annually are due to rape and incest. The remaining 99% of abortions were instances of two adults consenting to sexual behavior and causing pregnancy. If two adults create human life, they are responsible for it's protection for at least the nine months of pregnancy. The "choice" was made prior to having sex and creating the pregnancy.

In the many polls taken, the wide majority of U.S. citizens agree with the contention that the act of aborting an unborn human being is an act of murder, and that they recognize that the human fetus is human life. And many practices of American society are congruent with this fact of life no pun intended. Surgeons perform delicate surgery on unborn fetuses, and surely they don't do this if the human fetus is not human life. In many states, and rightly so in my view, mothers are charged with crime if there babies are born addicted to illegal drugs. This would still be a crime even if drugs such as cocaine and crack were made legal, because in this case the drug is being forced on another human being with that human being's consent. And when a woman gets pregnant, Doctors advise the mother (and the pregnant woman is called the mother, even while pregnant with her first child) to quit smoking (tobacco, crack, or otherwise), quit drinking, and to eat enough nutrition to feed both the mother and the fetus/baby. And surely this is not done merely for an "unviable tissue mass" that resides in the woman's womb.

In light of this, we might see what, and why, organizations like Operation Rescue, are up to. One can reasonably debate their tactics, but one cannot reasonably deny that they are following in the tradition of non-violent civil disobedience. But in our current politically correct atmosphere, those who engage in civil disobedience on this issue are somehow less justified in doing so than those who picket large corporations who are allegedly destroying the environment, for example. The hard left can be very selective in who they think should be able to engage in civil disobedience and on what issues.

The anti-civil libertarian bent of the abortion industry, and its political supporters, becomes obvious. But then again, why would a group of people opposed to protecting the most fundamental of civil liberties, that of the right of life, be so concerned with other civil liberties such as free speech and freedom of association?

What is Freedom? The McMartin Preschool Case Reconsidered

May 7, 2000

An innocent family had their livelihood taken away, their lives and reputations destroyed, and the preschool they opened up was ultimately closed and leveled. The McMartin family had been recognized as pillars of the community in Manhattan Beach, Cal. and received numerous civic awards on behalf of their preschool. It all came crashing down when one child abuse allegation came out. Child abuse, real and unfortunate as it is, can often be one of the charges which one is charged and assumed guilty before a single item of evidence is ever presented in a court of law. Having a chance to watch the HBO documentary, Indictment - The McMartin Trial, has given me a chance to reflect back on this story that I had followed very little of when it hit the news.

At the vortex of this case was sensationalistic media, a children's advocacy group needing to boost fundraising, a single initial child abuse allegation against the child's father, an activist social worker seeking to build a career as a child abuse counselor, and career prosecutors working for two District Attorneys in the heat of election and re-election campaigns. All these factors worked to put the McMartin family on trial, and despite ringing acquittal in the court of law, the family was convicted in the court of public opinion via the press.

One child, who attended the preschool, complained of being abused and the rush to judgement set in and lead to allegations against the McMartin preschool. This lead to the local police sending a letter to the parents off all the preschool's children. Soon these children were being referred to interviews at the Los Angeles-based Children's Institute International with a social worker named Kee MacFarlane.

As demonstrated in the two trials, MacFarlane used heavily suggestive questions and behavior modification techniques to get the children to answer questions as she desired and get them to claim they were abused. This was so skillfully done it had children making believable claims (that they themselves believed) of events happening that did not and could not happen. While parents were shown just parts of these videotaped interviews, and therefore believed the allegations, the jury saw these tapes in their entirety and ruled in favor of the defendants and not-guilty verdicts. MacFarlane, who was not licensed as a therapist for children, was attempting to build a career as an expert on child abuse. MacFarlane at times suggested the entire preschool and day care industry was over-run by a conspiracy to engage in systematic and ritualistic abuse of children across the nation. Such a conspiracy would aid greatly in the careers and fundraising of those in her profession. The prosecution was later shown to have concealed evidence, most notably about the first child abuse charge that started the case, and engaged in blatant prosecutorial misconduct.

As with many high-profile cases, the press bought the prosecution's story and aided and abetted in the conviction-in-the media of the defendants. The charges were brought by an appointed district attorney seeking re-election and then continued by the district attorney that defeated him. The second district attorney, Ira Reiner, later sought the Democratic nomination for Attorney General of California. Political considerations, and public pressure from those convinced of the guilt of the McMartin family by the press, constantly threatened to disrupt the process of finding truth and justice in a court of law.

In the end no convictions were obtained. The family lost their livelihood and their business, namely the school and the property they had worked all their lives to build up. They were impoverished and had their reputation and names destroyed in the process. When politics and government authority can do this to that family, it can happen to any other family. In fact, this case spawned several copycat aggressive prosecutions of very questions, in some cases bogus, cases of child abuse allegations. The cases seriously diminished public confidence in the entire preschool and child care industry. Its no coincidence that the politically partisan activist groups, such as the Children's Institute International are the very same people who would like to see all preschool and child care provision nationalized by the Federal government. Cases like this are cited as reasons for regulations, and ultimately government control, of this industry.

These cases and the politics behind them are part of a systematic campaign to destroy public confidence in the institutions, especially the private ones, which have made this country prosperous and free. The McMartin family exemplified the American Dream and represented the ideals our Republic was founded on. When people like that are not free from this kind of destruction via the legal system, we ultimately are not free from it either. When one citizen is not free, you are not free either.

What is Freedom: Gay Marriage Controversy in Vermont

May 29, 2000

You may know Vermont as place where one can find great ski resorts like Stowe, Killington, and Mount Snow. You might also remember that Ben and Jerry's Ice Cream and Cabot cheese are made in Vermont. If you're a fan of alternative rock music you know the band Phish hails from Burlington, Vermont. Fans of alternative politics (and those not fans of such) also know that Vermont's only Congressmen is the self-proclaimed socialist and former mayor of Burlington, Bernie Sanders.

The state of Vermont might also become known for something else, especially among members of one "community." The state has become the first to legislatively grant full benefits and rights, including full entitlements to all the welfare a state has to offer, to gay "married" couples.

That's right, under recently signed state law in Vermont, joining a partner in a "gay marriage" will get one enhanced access to welfare benefits and other entitlements. And citizens of the state, who still believe individual rights are more important then collecting checks from the state, are outraged. But the debate isn't about homosexuality versus so-called "homophobia," it's about the state's governor signing a law that will transfer yet more money from those who work for a living to those who can now use "gay marriage" as a way to get more money from the state.

Governor Howard Dean, currently serving his fourth 2-year term, signed H 847, an act granting full legal rights of married, heterosexual couples to homosexuals in "civil

unions." The term civil union is a convenient euphemism
for gay marriage. The legislation instantly opens the
"spouses" in such "civil unions" to eligibility to all state
and federal benefits afforded otherwise to married
couples. Those who crusade for gay rights don't want the
voters to know that the real agenda of the homosexual
lobby is entitlements that will have to be funded at
taxpayer expense.

One of the great rallying cries of the homosexual lobby
is to require health insurance coverage for the partners in
such "civil unions." They say it's unfair that married
couples get something that is granted to those in so-called
gay marriages. But polls have shown the public is against
extending this class of entitlements to homosexual
couples. Non-binding votes in Vermont town meetings
this past spring were almost all overwhelmingly against
legally recognizing gay marriages, or "civil unions."

Thousands of citizens in the state have plastered their
cars with bumper stickers that feature the slogan "Howard
the Coward sign H847 Homo Sex Law." One resident in
Southern Vermont displays a sign in his yard saying, "I'm
not gay, our state government is." A sign displayed along
route 9, which crosses from East to West in Southern
Vermont, says "Howard the Coward, governor of
Vermont, signed H847 Homo Sex law" with the words
Howard, Coward, and Homo Sex painted in bright pink.
Next to the sign is a life-size wooden cutout of Dean
wearing shoes and women's underwear briefs both painted
bright pink. Yet another sign at that same location reads,
"Howie Dean, Vermont's 1st queen."

Along with the grassroots opposition, the legislation is
spurring oppositions from conservatives and Republicans,
who vow to defeat the liberal Democrats who passed the

legislation and repeal H 847 in the next legislative session.

The outrage is perfectly understandable. This is what happens when one group, in this case the homosexual lobby, defines their "rights" in a way that requires someone else to pay for it. In this case the someone else is the public and the price to be paid is tax dollars for entitlements to gays in "civil unions" and the continued moral decadence as displayed by the demand for public acceptance of a lifestyle that is fast proving to be a death style.

The next battle over these issues will take place over the use of public school programs to "educate" school children about homosexuality. This is already taking place in many states, including Vermont. Taxpayer money is being mis-appropriated for "awareness" programs designed by rabid homosexual "rights" activists and included in school curriculums as "civility training" designed to reduce "homophobia."

Those who don't think we are in the midst of a culture war, where individual freedom values are on trial against the values of the 1960s, should just simply talk to the citizens of Vermont who are personally facing the prospect of paying the price for this agenda. You probably don't realize it yet, but odds are very good you are paying taxes for programs and entitlements of the like in your state.

What is Slavery and Who Advocates It
June 20, 2000

Advocates of individual freedom will tell you that politics is the process by which we decide whether we'll live in a society of freedom or one of slavery. The word slavery is loaded with so much distracting baggage that I'm hesitant to use it but I used it because it is the most accurate word to describe that which is the opposite of freedom. If one believes that freedom is possible, one must logically accept that slavery is possible as well. ? I define freedom as the individual living life as one chooses so long as the rights of others are not violated in the process. I define slavery as any law, policy, or regulation handed down from any level of government that violates this freedom.

We think of slavery by the historic definition of it, namely slaves working on plantations and being owned by the plantation owners. That practice was called slavery because the human beings enslaved were denied their basic freedoms. No one admits to being in support of slavery. They will deny they support slavery in one of two ways. One either denies the "slaves" are in fact human beings, or otherwise must deny that the condition violates the freedom of the human beings involved. Slaves owners denied the humanity of their victims while today's advocates of slavery deny that the political views they espouse would lead to policies that violate individual freedom. But this denial doesn't change reality. One must remember that members of the Flat Earth Society are in similar denial despite the evidence that the earth is round.

I have illustrated in previous essays how the rights of free expression, property ownership, Life, etc. important elements of individual freedom. Without them there is no human freedom. Those who advocate policies that result in slavery necessarily advocate the limiting or elimination of these fundamental rights. Remember, as Franklin says, freedom of the press cannot be limited without being lost. That is also true of our other individual rights.

There are several "movements" that make up the opposition to freedom. The fact that many in these movements use the language of freedom masks the reality of their real opposition to individual freedom. In no particular order, the pro-abortion movement, the extreme environmental movement, the extreme animal rights/vegetarian movement, the so-called welfare rights movement, the homosexual political movement, the extreme feminist movement, and the broader leftist "political correctness" movement are all spokes in the wheel of the larger leftist, authoritarian, socialist movement against individual freedom. The common thread in all of these movements is advocacy of policies and laws that will limit individual choice over legitimate personal decisions and impose statist and socialist policies on all of us.

One can talk to devoted activists in these movements and quickly realize they support all elements of this movement. You will see they take a "holistic" approach to supporting the importance in all of these movements. The reason is always anything but freedom. They will cite "saving the earth" or "realizing fairness in society" or some one excuse. While there are exceptions, most active members of one or more of these radical movements support all the others. Those who support them are essentially the same kind of people. Again, experience will bear this out. All of these movements are designed to destroy the value and institutions of individual freedom.

Effectively opposing those who seek to limit our freedom starts first with recognizing these movements and activists. By being more aware of them we can be more effective in standing up for freedom.

The coming essays in this series will address these movements, and demonstrate exactly how they are in opposition to individual freedom.

What is Freedom: Congressman Ron Paul's Freedom Principles

June 2, 2000

The best example of a citizen politician entering the halls of Congress and consistently standing up for Freedom is that of Congressman Ron Paul from the 14th Congressional District of Texas. Paul, a physician, served in Congress during the 1980s and was nominated for president by the Libertarian Party in 1988. He was re-elected in 1996 and 1998 by the voters of his district. Congressman Ron Paul has consistently stood solidly in favor of the Pro-Life view and individual freedom.

On his Congressional web site, Paul has listed what his Freedom Principles. I will quote them below, with my own comments about them.

Rights belong to individuals, not groups.

This is extremely important. Virtually all other agendas, other then the individual freedom, view rights as being held by groups rather then individuals. Group rights are the negation of rights, since if the group holds them, it follows they are exercised by the group, and therefore the individual who is in the minority in the group is deprived of those rights. But when individual decisions, that don't violate the rights of others, are made by the individual, the rights of all individual are upheld.

Property should be owned by people, not government.

Property rights mean the right of the individual to own himself, the fruits of his own labor, and then any property that he chooses to purchase with that. Taxing an individual's earnings and income is essentially making him a slave for the state for that period of time he must work to earn that money which must be paid in taxes. Property taxes are really, in effect, income taxes because they are paid from one's income.

All voluntary associations should be permissionable -- economic and social.

This is real simple, individuals can freely associate with other individuals in any groups or activities that don't violate the rights of others. Now, it's important to understand this right doesn't confer any claims to receive monetary entitlements that must be paid for by others. See my comments below on redistribution of wealth and special privileges.

The government's monetary role is to maintain the integrity of the monetary unit, not participate in fraud.

Currently, our money is coined and regulated by the Federal Government through the semi-private Federal Reserve System, which manipulates and alters the value of the currency at will, often to suit the interests of those in government. Congressman Paul advocates replacing our phony paper money with real currency backed by gold, taking the money supply out of the hands of political appointees and putting it back under the domain of the free market.

Government exists to protect liberty, not to redistribute wealth or to grant special privileges.

Socialists and leftist-liberals believe the government is here to establish financial equality and assure a minimum standard of living to all citizens, regardless of what they do to earn their living. You hear these concepts when leftists and other collectivists speak of a "right" to education, affordable housing, health care coverage, etc. These are not rights. There's a fairly reliable way to tell the difference between rights and those that are not rights but entitlements or privileges. Simply ask yourself, if X is established to be a right, do anyone else have to pay or be taxed to insure this "right." If the answer is no, it is likely a legitimate rights claim. Otherwise, it is not.

The lives and actions of people are their own responsibility, not the government's.

Responsibility over individual decisions rests with the individual. The competing perspective on this is the view of "social responsibility" where individuals are not responsible but the group is. The typical 1960s leftist liberal advocated individual freedom but social responsibility. This meant the individual could do as he pleases and not be personally held responsible. William Donahue calls this view the "New Freedom." As the children of the 1960s grew up, many of them switched on those and have adopted individual responsibility along with advocacy of group rights. This view influences much leftist and liberal thinking today. But the only consistent and workable view on rights and responsibilities is centering both at the level of the individual. True rights and real responsibility can only be held if they are held by individuals. If the group is responsible, it ultimately means no one is responsible. If we have group rights, no one has rights.

You can read more at Congressman Ron Paul's web site:

http://www.house.gov/paul/freedomprinciples.htm

What is Slavery: Big Brother wants to decide your Diet for You

June 3, 2000

What foods you choose to eat are distinctly a matter of personal freedom. But politically correct do-gooder liberals think otherwise. Regulation of your personal diet decisions has become the latest so-called "public health" issue taken up by those who would like to run our lives and make all our day-to-day personal decisions for us, if they could get away with it.

Just recently, the U.S. Department of Agriculture and the Department of Health & Human Services organized, at taxpayer expense, a "Nutrition Summit" on health and nutrition involving more 1,800 advocates of government regulations of personal diet choices. Just the mere fact that government now likes to convene major high-level meetings to discuss what most of us regard as a matter of personal choice should make people aware of just how much politicians and bureaucrats are bent on running our lives.

The Libertarian Party national director Steve Dasbach issued a statement about the summit, saying "It's official: The War on Fat has begun -- and the first victim of this war could be our right to choose the foods we want to eat." Dasbach also referred to the "war on tobacco" as an example of the end result of this assault on personal health choices.

An Associated Press story on the same summit quoted government statistics claiming that 52 percent of the U. S. population is more than 20 pounds above what is considered ideal healthy body weight. The government intends to do something about this trend, the story reported. Eileen Kennedy, deputy undersecretary of agriculture said, "There are a lot of strategies being planned..." Since diet decisions are personal choices, just what strategies do government bureaucrats have planned to impose on us?

One professor with the Harvard University of Public Health has advocated imposing higher taxes on foods considering fattening. A so-called fat-tax would attempt to use the tax code, as Canada does already with excessively high cigarettes taxes, to coerce individuals into not consuming as much of the targeted foods. This obvious disregard for personal choice is be further compounded by spending this ill-gotten money on more programs to tell people the food they choose to eat is not healthy. Revenues from cigarette taxes, in many states, are used to fund anti-smoking advertising campaigns.

The Colorado legislature has already gotten into this game. They've passed legislation directing the appropriate state agency in Colorado to commission a study to measure the percentage of that state's population that is overweight and propose "public health" solutions designed to lower that percentage. The legislation was passed with scant opposition.

However well intentioned these efforts may be, they will always end in collectivist "solutions" to what are strictly individual choices. What each of us chooses to eat is our own decision, and is not the business of politicians, bureaucrats, or so-called experts in "public health." So just how will "public health" expert recommend the government gets around our own personal choices to get us eating less "fattening" diets?

One possibility is the fat taxes I mentioned above. Another is to begin collecting data from our purchasing decisions (I can see it now, personal diet questions on the

2010 Census forms) as a first step to figuring out how to influence us to change such decisions. In addition to taxes and regulations of food providers, perhaps diet supervision will become the next condition which health insurance will be based on. Government control of the health care industry was, of course, an attempt to control this issue from that side of the situation. If the state decides what medical coverage you have, then the state will next make an effort to tell you which health risks you can and cannot incur in your eating and other lifestyle choices.

While I believe individuals should be responsible for their own choices, I have serious problems with the government defining both the responsibility and consequences of those choices. And government will define them by dictating for the individual those choices and the consequences associated with them.

In previous essay I asked if you've invited Big Brother to join you for dinner. No doubt you haven't, but Big Brother is still trying desperately to decide for you what you'll have for dinner tonight. Are you prepared to tolerate this, or will you stand up and say no to the lifestyles and health regulators who wish to decide your diet and personal health decisions for you?

Freedom v. Slavery: a Conflict of Visions

June 14, 2000

There are two major visions on structuring both our lives and society, both competing for support among individuals and political interests. One is individual freedom, while the other is that which supporters of individual freedom call statism, socialism, authoritarianism, or, as it should be called, slavery. When you allow the government, the bureaucracies, and the bought and paid for corporate system dictate your lifestyle and personal decisions, you've bought into slavery to some extent. That remains true regardless of whether or not you realize it.

The conflict of visions is quite easy to spot in debates on many of the day's political issues. Ultimately all of these debates will help determine whether we continue down what F. A. Hayek called "the Road to Serfdom" or we will re-establish our nation's tradition of individual freedom and liberty. If those of us who believe in freedom sit back and do nothing, the Brave New World will be assured of becoming reality.

I've long maintained that income taxes are slavery. If you must work a certain number of hours per day to make money to pay taxes, then it logically follows you're working for the state for those hours for free. Does that not constitute slavery? Ultimately, those who advocate the Marxist-socialist slavery vision are seeking the day when we will pay 100% of our earnings into income taxes.

We're headed in that direction already. No one can dispute the fact that income taxes began at a rate lower than five percent and are heading closer to 50 percent each year. Countries in Europe operating on basically socialist economies have tax rates in excess of 70% with the state providing most necessities of life from that money. In other words, the government in such societies has nationalized most major "vital" industries. Private industry is gradually replaced by state run industry.

In the United States the vision slavery is being promoted through welfarism and corporatism, respectively through the establishment of the welfare state and corporate welfare. The welfare state will provide a safety net for those not able to make in the heavily corporate "New Economy." The New Economy is all about people working in "service industries" doing the equivalent of flipping burgers while working longer hours for few dollars per hours. Most of the new jobs created by the New Corporate Economy of the last decade have been temporary, part-time jobs paying lower rates of compensation and fewer or no benefits. Today one-third of college graduates will take dead-end jobs that do not require any college degree at all. This is the New Economy.

A great deal of corporate welfare has built up this New Economy. The corporate trend has been toward concentration of power and market share. The news every day reports major corporations merging with others to form yet larger ones. The connections between those who run these mega-corporations and those in power in government are more inter-connected than the strings in a piece of weaved cloth. Few people realize what a corporation is. It's a government-sanction organization that is granted government-recognized legal rights that shield it from being held accountable, legally, from most of the consequences of most of its actions. In essence, a corporation is an agent of the government.

Some incorrectly label corporations, and their excesses, as being the consequences of "capitalism." Corporations are the building blocks of capitalism but they are really the building blocks of statism, or state corporatism. Most of what's traded, and speculated upon, on Wall Street every day is not privately owned or managed. Most of that is stock in corporations that are no more privately managed or freely run than the United State Postal Service. Corporations that are nominally in private hands, regulated and controlled by government agencies, owned by numerous stockholders owning that stock under government regulations are essentially government run operations.

Government run operations of this type depend on the ignorance of the people. That is why there is so much debate over education. Advocates of freedom have long support privately-run schools and home schooling as the best ways to educate our young people to be free-thinking, independent-minded citizens of a free society. But those who advocate slavery would prefer children grow up to be good little citizens that don't question the authority of the corporate welfare state regime to run our lives. That is why the politicians who support the statist, authoritarian vision are so dead-set on saving the state run public education system and quashing the home schooling movement. Ultimately the debate over education is a one about freedom.

Free thinking citizens are more likely to question the pabulum served every day in the mainstream media as well as seek out alternative sources of news such as talk radio and the internet. It is no coincidence that talk radio and the internet have been targets of recent attempts at content regulation. Those who don't want the people to know the truth seek to regulate the ability of the people to know the truth through other sources.

Every day more citizens become aware of these issues. As more people become aware of this reality, more are facing the need to oppose the latest attempts to limit freedom by those in government, as well as their willing accomplices in the media and major corporations. Freedom will only prevail if enough people stand up and defend it against this movement toward authoritarianism. Otherwise, slavery will prevail and the Brave New World will become reality.

I Have Found the Bogey Man

June 14, 2000

Just about all of us have a sense, at some level, that we are headed in the wrong direction as a society, in a big way. When we look at certain facts and realize what's going on, we can see this. In one of his essays, former Congressman John LeBoutillier discussed what he called the "salami effect." Gradually over time, changes taking place in society are like occasionally taking another slice from the salami that goes unnoticed. Eventually we notice the salami is gone.

I have chronicled a number of issues in these articles and essays. Most of us agree that we pay far more in taxes then we should. Poll after poll shows that most Americans believe the government wastes most of our money. One scandal after another making the daily headlines reinforces this view. Most us don't trust politicians or those that run most major corporations. Most of us like our member of Congress but think Congress is corrupt. Most of us like our physician and lawyer, if we have one. But most of us think doctors and lawyers are too concerned with making money, regardless of how true that may be.

We know that our education system could be much better and see reports in the press about how test scores are getting lower and lower. Yet as a society we spend more on education than we ever have. I've shown in my articles here how the government engages in blatant lies about economics to tell us the economy is better than it really is. Yet most of us know we make less money than we think we should, and have less opportunity for promotion or better employment than we think we should.

Most of us know that we are not as frugal with our money, as individuals, families, and as a country compared to a hundred years ago or more. We live in a so-called economic boom that has been financed by plastic. That includes the plastic we spend as individuals that is called Visa, MasterCard, etc. and the plastic our politicians spend, that is called bond issues, taxes, and deficit spending. Both at the individual level and the government level, in the past 100 years, we've gone from a society that spends money we have to one that spends money we haven't yet earned. In the past decade personal debt has set new records as personal bankruptcies have also set new records. Most of those were individuals and families who couldn't pay the medical bills and/or the credit card bills.

Government at all levels has done the same thing, especially at the federal level. This current talk about a "surplus" is a fraud perpetrated on us by politicians of both major parties. The federal government is liable for more than $6 trillion and all the politicians can do is argue how to spend the so-called surplus. But there's no surplus, it's an accounting trick. The government is still in debt, and still engages in deficit spending.

Who is to blame for all of this? We realize the problem, most of us. I realize some of us are in denial, and hope that number declines as people read this. So who is to blame for this? All of the decisions, that lead to the problems that most of us realize and recognize, were made either through the political process or through the market process. That's right, those who cast votes at the ballot box and those who made consumer choices when buying products and services decided these issues, at one time or another.

I think most would agree we need to find who is responsible for this, and find some solutions to these problems. I can assure you the solutions won't be quick, nor will they be easy. Many of us want quick and easy solutions, but those aren't always possible. But I found who the bogey man is, and I'll let you in on this secret. We can all find, quite quickly and easily, who the bogey man is. Or at least, who ONE of them is. We can all simply look in a mirror. Then we can ask that individual to make a commitment to also be part of the solution.

Freedom Vote in Massachusetts Senate Race Means Supporting Lawler

June 21, 2000

The Massachusetts race for United States Senator is a three-ring circus outside of the one candidate that is qualified to receive our votes and support. Little known Republican Jack E. Robinson and Libertarian candidate Carla Howell oppose incumbent Senator Ted Kennedy (D-Chappaquiddick).

Massachusetts politics are known for sleazy deals. This year the politicians are working together to see to it that voters only have two choices in this race. Democrats know that EVERY SINGLE race between a Democrat and a Libertarian produces a Democrat winner. Kennedy's campaign was all too fast to file a challenge to Jack Robinson's ballot access signatures. The State's Governor Paul Celluci and the party chairman Brian Cresta have officially disavowed Robinson's candidacy. The scandals of the administration of Celluci, and his chosen Lt. Governor Jane Swift, have demoralized the Massachusetts GOP to the point that Libertarians are taking themselves way too seriously.

The Massachusetts Republicans have had a long history of self-destruction. The latest chapter is the implosion of their campaign in this race. The previous GOP candidate, a county district attorney, dropped out because he failed to raise enough money to campaign for the office. Then state GOP leaders quickly endorsed Jack Robinson, then un-endorsed, after negative press reports about past allegations. Now the press reports that Robinson turned in several allegedly forged ballot signatures, including the state chairman of the Republican

Party who claims to have not signed Robinson's petition. It is now looking more likely that Robinson will not appear on the ballot for this race.

Taking advantage of the pathetic circumstances of the Republicans, like children rushing to the cookie jar after their parents leave the house, the Libertarians have joined the Democrats in trying to knock Robinson off the ballot. Libertarians think getting rid of Robinson's candidacy will help their cause. They're running Carla Howell, they 1998 candidate for State Auditor, who is campaigning on an empty campaign platform devoid of substance. Howell is calling herself the candidate with "small government" without offering any specifics on exactly what that means. Basically, she's hoping enough voters will vote for her because she's not Ted Kennedy, and her campaign seems more suited to boosting her chances of getting the 2004 Libertarian nomination for president rather than defeating Ted Kennedy. So to further her own narrow political interests, Howell has joined with Celluci and Kennedy in opposing the Robinson campaign.

So you have the leading politicians from the Democrat, Republican, and Libertarian parties of Massachusetts all conspiring together to deny the Republicans and Independents a conservative choice on Election Day. They're all elitist liberals. Kennedy is the ultimate liberal Democrat. Celluci is a liberal Republican, known for spending taxpayer money on promoting homosexuality in the public schools. Howell appears to be a left-leaning libertarian, but her vapid "small government is beautiful" campaign might be fooling a lot of people. There's only one true conservative limited government, uphold the Constitution and The Bill of Rights candidate in this race.

His name is Phil Lawler, the nominee of The Constitution Party. Like the Libertarian Party, the

Constitution Party (formerly the U.S. Taxpayers Party) was founded by conservative Republicans who bolted the GOP when it adopted more statist economic policies. But unlike the Libertarian Party, the Constitution Party hasn't politically married the leftist and anarchist factions that are attracted to the Libertarian Party. Basically, The Constitution Party is made up of formerly Republican supporters of the principles that Barry Goldwater espoused.

So while Celluci, Kennedy, and Howell work together to deny the voters another choice in this race, conservative pro-Life, limited government voters have a choice. The last eight years of the Clinton administration have shown us the big government fiscally irresponsible policies of the liberal Democrats combined with the moral and ethical abyss of the far left of the 1960s that has taken power under this administration. Many voters are looking for a clean sweep from this political and ethical corruption by voting for candidates that are the absolute antithesis to the Clinton era's values. The politicians of the Celluci-Kennedy-Howell establishment here in Massachusetts are quite fitting heirs of the Clinton legacy of sleazy, backroom, under-the-table dealing. But there is an alternative.

I urge all voters who want to cast their vote for the candidate of integrity and character, a candidate who stands for The Constitution and The Bill of Rights. That candidate is Phil Lawler. Send a message that this dealing is unacceptable. Tell the politicians, Paul Celluci, Ted Kennedy, and Carla Howell, that they can advance their political careers and self interests on their own time and money. In the meantime, the Commonwealth of Massachusetts needs someone qualified, politically and ethically, to serve as U.S. Senator. Phil Lawler offers his candidacy, and is worthy of your support.

The   Lawler   2000   web   site: www.lawler2000.org/

Political Correctness

There is no mistaking what political correctness is all about, and there could be no more perfect term to describe this agenda than the one adopted originally by its advocates: politically correct. In short, advocates of political correctness are a very specific group of left-wing liberals that believe they know better than us how we should live our lives. The ideology of political correctness is entirely opposite, in its results (regardless of stated intentions, good or otherwise) because it seeks to have other individuals make the decisions, collectively, that should be make by the individual, individually.

Supporters of political correctness believe that politics drives everything. I once had a politically correct liberal tell me that everything in inherently political. To these people there are no uniquely individual decisions that should be made by the individual, free of the constraints of politics. All decisions affect politics, therefore all such decisions should be decided on the basis of politics, in the minds of the politically correct. And not just any politics, but THEIR politics. The politics of the politically correct leftist liberals who seek to control the lives of others.

I personally first heard the term while on the college campus at which I was exposed to my first major dose of political correctness. Upon first attending the University of Massachusetts at Amherst in the Fall of 1987 I quickly realized how the politically correct agenda seeks to undermine the values of Western culture. When I arrived on campus and for the first time saw the kind of "in your face" homosexual propaganda that has become far more common now. Several months later I was seeking office as the most conservative candidate for the elected student representative on the University's Board of Trustees. While waiting to attend a meeting of a student government committee, I overheard discussion between a couple leftists, about their inviting to one of my opponents for Student Trustee, to a meeting to select a candidate their faction would support. Worrying that I might be interested, he informed me that I would not be invited because, as he said, "only politically correct candidates are being invited."

Just more than two years after that experience, the word politically correct became part of pop culture after the mainstream press featured stories about political correctness. But this exposure leads many to conclude that political correctness is dead. Quite the opposite is true; it's more alive and well than it has ever been. Advocates of political correctness alternate between denying they are politically correct to then billing the whole concept and its exposure as a "right wing conspiracy" to going back to denial again. But the fact is, leftwing liberals devised the term politically correct to describe themselves, and it has only been after the term's exposure that its advocates run away from it. That is why, on way to winning the culture battles, conservatives much continue to expose the ideas of political correctness as well as those who advocate it.

Latest Extremism in the War on Sanity
Known as Political Correctness
March 17, 2000

As many of you know, political correctness seeks to eventually control thinking through attempting to change the language. It started with such foolishness as replacing "chairman" with "chairperson" and has gone to the most bizarre extremes to try to stamp out of the English language any word that offends the politically correct. Here are two of the latest examples of this nitwittery.

An Associated Press story in my local newspaper reports that the Maine House of Representatives recently voted 129-17 to ban state use of the word "squaw" on various monuments, etc. Lobbyists representing American Indians (or "Native Americans to be politically correct, an inaccurate term since being born in America makes me a native American as well) demanded the legislation, claiming the word "squaw" was imposed on them by the "white man." Opponents of the legislation questioned whether the word really is offensive.

I'm not really concerned who's offended by the word. What I'm more concerned with is the attempts to control thought by declaring certain words in effect "illegal" so to speak Additionally, the use of government resources to pursue this revision of the language. If the state legislature in Maine has time to debate and ultimately pass something like this, apparently they don't have more pressing and important business to attend to. They should have voted to adjourn, and the members gone back to their districts to spend time with constituents as well as do real work.

The other example comes from an e-mail newsletter I received, reporting that a state legislator in Rhode Island is challenging, and trying to change, the official name of the state. You see, the state was incorporated and admitted into the union as Rhode Island and Providence Plantations. The legislator says the word plantation has a racist connotation and should not be used in the state's name. Of course the argument is almost too frivolous to warrant an argument, let alone a hearing in the halls of Rhode Island's state legislature.

We all know how wrong slavery was, but does that mean any word or practice used by slaveholders is wrong and additionally racist? Just how far do we take this extreme political correctness? Do we stop using the word spade because the politically correct say that word is racist, or the cliche "call a spade a spade?" Just how far will ideological cleansing of the English language go before the politically correct are happy?

Political correctness never ends unless enough of us defend the language and defend the culture and stand up against this campaign of intolerance masking itself as tolerance. Advocates of this ideological cleansing of the language will not give up until the goal of thought control is achieved. The only answer is say no, defeating these attempts to revise the language, and putting this extremism back in its place.

Did You Vote for This? Taxpayer-funded Homosex Propaganda in Public Schools

May 18, 2000

The Commonwealth of Massachusetts spends $1.5 million to teach high school children about "fisting" and other aspects of the homosexual lifestyle. The Massachusetts News reported recently how the Governor's Commission for Gay and Lesbian Youth spends the money to organize so-called "Gay/Straight Alliance" clubs in which students discuss homosexual practices and view X-rated films depicting homosexual pornography. The story reported how this issue came to light when parents complained about this gross misuse of their tax dollars after hearing about it from their children. You know something is wrong when Johnny comes home and tells Mom and Dad about all the "kewl" stuff he learned about at the Gay/Straight Alliance Club meeting in school today.

The Massachusetts News story quoted a Mass. Education Department bureaucrat, speaking before high school students, as saying, "Fisting [forcing one's entire hand into another person's rectum or vagina] often gets a bad rap...[It's] an experience of letting somebody into your body that you want to be that close and intimate with...[and] to put you into an exploratory mode."

The story also reported how the Mass. Department of Education, the Governor's Commission and a national homosexual organization called the Gay and Lesbian and Straight Education Network proposed homosexual education of this kind for students of lower grades. The fact is, the homosexual movement would like to expose your children to this propaganda at younger and younger ages. The earlier children are reached with this stuff, the more like they are to convince young impressionable children to adopt the homosexual lifestyle. There is one simple fact of nature about homosexuality, the simple unnatural nature of it is that homosexuals can not naturally reproduce. Human reproduction takes place ONLY from heterosexual sex. Therefore, the only way the homosexual movement survives is by recruiting naturally heterosexual children to become homosexuals. That is why the homosexual movement, which includes among its various organizations the North American Man-Boy Love Association, must engage in such recruitment efforts in the public schools.

The fact is, homosexuality is an unnatural lifestyle. Biology did not intend the human body to engage in these kinds of acts. The human hand was not designed to be placed in those body cavities as described above, and the human sex organs were are not for the purposes as used by homosexuals. Additionally, adults should make decisions on sexual lifestyle questions not children who are not yet mature enough to decide such matters. That is why promoting such "alternative lifestyles" should not be done in public schools children who are protected under age-of-consent laws.

The Massachusetts News article include far more information and detail on what is being taught under the guise of these programs. I strongly urge all readers of this article to click the link above and read the story.

This might seem shocking to many that this kind of stuff would be taught in the public schools. Perhaps more surprising is the involvement of the Governor's office, and maybe more surprising considering that Massachusetts Governor Paul Celluci is a Republican. One might assume that most Republicans are conservatives, and therefore would oppose such blatant misuse of taxpayer money. Don't be quick to make such assumptions.

The root of this blatant pandering to the homosexual movement, at taxpayer expense, goes back as far as 1990 and the election of Governor William Weld, a liberal Republican with whom Celluci ran as Republican nominee for Lieutenant Governor. 1990 was the crazy election season, the first following the failed presidential bid of Michael S. Dukakis, in which the Massachusetts economy turned sharply toward recession and voters looked for politicians to hold accountable. Even the weakest Republican candidates, where they ran, were elected in what is generally a strongly Democratic state. And the race for governor was shaped by Democrat and Republican primaries where voters defeated the candidates endorsed by the party conventions. Weld defeated a conservative state legislator for his nomination, and Dukakis's Lt. Governor and a former State Attorney General were defeated by conservative Democrat John Silber, then the president of Boston University.

The Weld-Silber race produced strange alliances among various groups of voters and special interest groups. Many conservatives favored Silber over the liberal Republican William Weld. The growing homosexual movement in Massachusetts faced a tough choice, given that they usually support liberal Democrats. They found it tough to support a Republican but knew that Silber was far more conservative on the issues, including their issues. So many prominent leaders in the homosexual movement publicly and enthusiastically endorsed the Weld-Celluci ticket, after obtaining certain public policy commitments from them. Weld offered such commitments, in exchange for their support, because he knew the election would be close and he was desperate to become governor. Desperate enough to buy homosexual votes at taxpayer expense if that's what it took to get elected. And it did, Weld won by the slimmest of margins over Silber.

The Governor's Commission for Gay and Lesbian Youth was set up under Weld and continued under Paul Celluci, who took over as governor after Weld resigned in 1995. This shows what happens when politicians make deals with special interest groups. You can be sure these deals will always come at taxpayer expense. I oppose Weld in 1990 and voted for Silber because I knew he would sell out to special interest groups, and I knew he had already done so when I saw leading members of the homosexual movement endorse Weld during the Fall 1990 campaign. I knew at the time, that these people don't endorse a nominal Republican without getting something in return. Now we see what they got in return. This disgraceful use of tax dollars would never have happened under John Silber, or the conservative Republican Weld defeated   in   the   Republican   primary.

Did You Invite "Big Brother" to Dinner?

September 1991

The Cable News Network has been reporting a small controversy over the alleged failures and problems of a nutritional survey each decade conducted by one of the several dozen various agencies controlled by the U.S. Department of Agriculture. The report claimed that the survey was not representative because only one third of those contacted responded to the survey.

The report also stated that this study (as they all are) is of immense importance, because the results, it's measure of what foods and how often the American people eat them, will effect Federal welfare programs, Federally funded school lunch programs, and other various programs providing food for the poor. I don't doubt that some of the less fortunate need help, but what I do take issue with is Uncle Sam's paternalism, or maternalism, that is evident in Federal policies.

The Federal Government, in giving aid to those who cannot afford to feed and house themselves, puts forth this aid in a specific form, such as food stamps that can only be used for edible (and certain edible items) foods, grants and certificates earmarked for rent payments, the Women, Infants, and Children (WIC) programs which provides certificates for low income women to purchase milk, baby food, etc. for babies and older children, and other such programs. The framers of these programs do not trust the integrity of the people receiving the aid, do not trust the poor recipients to look out for their own interests and efficiently spent the aid they receive. Advocates of this paternalism will tell you that if a welfare recipient were to receive a check, that the person may use the money, rather than for basic living expenses, for drugs, liquor, cigarettes, gambling, lottery tickets, etc.

Now I won't deny that some recipients do this, but they use their benefits to misspend them by selling the food stamps on the "black market," by using the stamps to purchase a low price item in the store and get cash back as change. But the "cheating" with the welfare benefits goes on in the current system, despite the best efforts of the paternalists who place this less dignified restriction on the individuals unfortunate enough to be on the dole.

This is a perfect example of the liberal anti-libertarian philosophy, that they'll help you with taxpayer dollars as long as you live by a code of ethics, and live by their views of how you should live your life.

The nutrition survey also effects those of us who are not on the dole, at least not directly on the dole. An official briefly (brief enough for me to miss the name) stated that the government would have been able to make much progress in the drive to improve people's eating habits (in their view, of course) if the survey had been properly done. In other words, the USDA was planning on engaging in a campaign to convince all of us that should be following a diet as dictated by the Federal Leviathan, that is, Big Brother, or Uncle Sam, as they used to call it.

So the next time, in this "free country" where the unelected and uncontrollable bureaucracy is spending your tax dollars to dream up ways to change your consciously chosen behavior, you sit down to eat a scrumptious pizza with extra cheese, pepperoni, sausage, etc. which is loaded with large quantities of the much maligned fat, cholesterol and a liberal amount of carbohydrates and protein, you can wonder how

Washington is figuring out how to get you to not enjoy that pizza that you've decided to eat knowing the risks that allegedly are a result of its consumption.

Will you be inviting Big Brother to watch you eat dinner, and to record what it is that you'll be eating for tonight?

Freedom of the Press for Liberals Only?
March 21, 2000

Last time I read the First Amendment it included no ideological qualification on who has freedom of the press rights. But some liberals on the Left Coast in the San Luis Obispo County area think otherwise. Members of several local gay rights organizations and their allies are protesting what they say is the "anti-gay" editorial policies of the Gazette community newspapers in that area owned by publisher David Weyrich. Protesters label the newspapers "anti-gay, anti-lesbian, and anti-abortion." It's an easy rhetorical trick to say those who disagree with you are anti everything you espouse. I can therefore imply that Weyrich's editorial stance is in favor of traditional values, the natural heterosexual lifestyle, and the Pro-Life stance on abortion.

Supporters of the protest claim that journalism differs from other businesses, and Weyrich's publications have a "social responsibility" to the community to report the news as they see fit. That's nonsense. Weyrich's Gazettes have a responsibility to not engage in libel on their pages and otherwise serve their customers, the people who pay to subscribe to the newspapers. Period. If the supporters of the gay rights movement don't like his editorial views, they can publish their own newspapers. Weyrich has no obligation to them, their point of view, their movement, or any responsibility to give in to their mob tactics and change his editorial stance.

The homosexual political movement has a long record of getting what it wants through sheer force and in many cases bullying. Based on sound science, the American Psychiatric Association used to pronounce that homosexuality is a mental illness. Many practitioners in field of psychiatry stand behind that. But after disrupting several APA conventions, the organization backed down to their politics and removed homosexuality form the Diagnostic and Statistical Manual of Mental Disorders. The latest versions of that manual, however, still include many other aberrant "sexual orientations" as mental disorders. That is just a single example. The entire history of the homosexual movement is not one of reason but one of politics by mob tactics.

The goal of these people is not to win arguments, it is to stamp out with brute force anyone and all who disagrees with their agenda. They are a cornerstone movement in the larger push for political correctness. The politically correct liberal left seeks to tear down the institutions our society is built on, and replace the values espoused by most Americans with the libertine and entirely permissive values of the 1960s. As one would expect, many Americans do not wish to see our culture re-defined and re-created by those who espouse this leftist, politically correct ethos.

While I'm all for individual freedom, including the right for the INDIVIDUAL to choose one's own lifestyle, I don't want what I believe to be unnatural and unhealthy lifestyle choices to be imposed on others. We are in fact in a culture war in America and it's between the politically correct left that wants to impose its values on all of us and the pro traditional values conservatives who above all value individual freedom. The homosexual movement's leaders are not content to live peacefully in their own community and let the rest of us do the same. They are only content to come out of the closet with all their sex toys and in-your-face rhetoric and do the best they can to offend those who disagree with them.

Weyrich and his newspapers are just one of the latest battles in this culture war. Freedom of the press, and American values are at stake. Standing up for the First Amendment rights of the Gazettes is standing up for both. And it's also right.

In Defense of Intolerance

October 25, 1998

"Extremism in the defense of liberty is no vice. Moderation of the pursuit of justice is no virtue."
-    Senator Barry Goldwater

Those of the politically correct "left" among us often label advocates of freedom intolerant. Recently a fellow advocate of freedom, during a heated argument with a Green Party member, was labeled the usual political correct cliches. He was called intolerant and opposed to "diversity."

Leaving aside the fact that "diversity" to the politically correct almost always means nearly the opposite, conformity and ideological uniformity, I'll address the charge of intolerance. Simply put, we advocates of freedom are intolerant. We're intolerant of that which is inconsistent with basic freedom.

I am intolerant of the violation of individual freedom by the actions and policies of local, state, and federal governments that steal money and property from citizens. Most politicians support mandatory income taxes to achieve their political agendas (usually the process of buying votes with tax dollars.) If objecting to this theft makes me intolerant then I willingly stand guilty as charged.

I am very much intolerant of the government regulating private property in various ways (local zoning, federal wetlands legislation, etc.) that devalues or otherwise changes the value or use of that property by its owners. This form of trespass is clearly in violation of basic property rights. It makes no difference whether the trespass is done by one person or by the bureaucrats backed up by a law passed at the state, local, or federal level. If this stand makes me intolerant, I accept the label and in this context I'll embrace it.

I am intolerant of the so-called "war on drugs." There's no plausible doubt that drug prohibition has been as large if not more so failure as the alcohol prohibition. It has killed tens of thousands of citizens, many of them civilian casualties of this "war." We have filled hundreds of new prisons built during the "war on drugs" over the last two decades with hundreds of thousands of drug users. These people were committing no harm to others but themselves and would be better served in drug treatment rather in jail. One cocaine user (not a dealer) who purchased an amount of his drug of choice comparable to a cigarette smoking buying a carton of cigarettes now sits in a Michigan prison serving a life sentence for simple cocaine possession. The war on drugs is insane policy, and any civilized society should be intolerant of this.

Many on the politically incorrect side have become such fanatics for "tolerance," defined as tolerating just about anything, including the intolerable in the name of being open-minded. If we strive for a just society based on the simple concept that violation of individual freedom is wrong, then we likewise will find much in our current society that we don't tolerate and won't tolerate.

For disagreeing with the many intolerable policy positions of the Green Party, including regulation of private property and limitations on basic personal freedoms, advocates of individual freedom are labeled "intolerant." When it comes to being intolerant of those would sacrifice individual freedom for political agendas, be they false appeals to security or fallacious claims of saving the planet, I stand guilty as charged. Intolerant.

In Defense of Intolerance Part II

April 18, 2000

Libertarians are very intolerant of dissent and disagreement. But to the surprise of many, I'll defend their right to that intolerance. Many Libertarians are fond of saying the individual has a right to be stupid, and make bad choices. I agree. Likewise, I defend their right to be intolerant.

Many weeks ago I joined a few e-mail listservs related to Libertarian discussion and began participating. I offered my views on what the party can do in order to improve itself as well as advice to those serious about achieving freedom in our life times. To the latter I advise doing what I've done, quitting the capital L Libertarian Party and joining the Republican Party in support of freedom-oriented candidates and policies there. In chorus with many other party members, I've pointed out the evidence of the problems with the current LP leadership, their ethics, and their poorly designed and failed political strategies. The Great Libertarian Jacob G. Hornberger as well as founding member L. Neil Smith has been quite eloquent in exposing those issues.

Card-carrying LP members react to comments by others and myself with sheer intolerance. Even worse was their revulsion that I had the audacity to participate in their debate forum once exposed as a small L Libertarian. I will no longer belong to a party and pay its dues where the leadership is more corrupt than any found in the other two parties at this time. My interest is in achieving liberty, not helping Harry Browne and David Bergland sell their books.

After I mildly disagreed with one member, and he announced on the listserv he would put my e-mail address in his software's e-mail filtering system so it would delete any messages I post. He has a right to do that. I defend and support that right. A few others called for me to be banned from the listserv for disagreeing. A few members, acting like libertarians in this case, advised use of the e-mail filtering for those wishing to avoid my messages. And then one member alleged I am part of a large right wing Republican conspiracy to sow dissent in the LP. I'll defend the right to this misguided opinion as well. But it sure makes one look nutty to make statements like that.

I don't care how many decide to filter out my messages via their e-mail programs. I defend their right to do that. But they do so at their own peril. If what I say is so bad, they should want to read it and be the quickest members to respond and refute my supposedly fallacious arguments. After all, in arguing and politics, an argument left unanswered and unchallenged is often viewed as being correct. An allegation left unanswered often stands.

But I'm thrilled with their response. It once again makes me realize the fact that you know you've hit the truth when those who can't face up it choose to attack. The more intolerance I get from closed-minded Libertarians, the more I'll have to say. Hornberger says he likes this kind of confrontation because is allows the true character of those on the other side to show. He's right. These people are really showing how intolerant they are, and proving why they receive so little support on Election Day.

They have a right to be intolerant, ignorant, in denial of political reality, act like space cadets, etc. I'll defend their right to be and act like all of those things. I'll also assert my right to not vote for them in November.

In Defense of Intolerance Part III: I'm Labeled a "Reactionary Conservative" and an "Anarchist" in One Day

April 18, 2000

In addition to other reasons, I defend this intolerance because it displays people showing their true colors. Discussing issues with those who call themselves Libertarians can be a lot of fun, even with the intolerance that one gets from some of them. Officially, the Libertarian Party calls itself the "Party of Principle." But many who call themselves Libertarians can quickly and easily trip and fall over their so-called principles and show themselves to be entirely lacking in any coherent set of principles most of us would recognize.

But to make this understandable I need to provide some background about the discussion. Someone posted a note that many freedom supporting and other libertarian groups would be organizing protest against extreme environmental groups in Washington D.C. on "Earth Day." Those who are aware of what a propaganda fest that day is need little background on why and how freedom is not consistent with the heavy-handed, destructive economic polities advocated by extreme environmentalists.

Someone noted that the hard line environmentalist group Earth First! is among the participants in the Earth Day events in Washington D.C. Earth First! is an group organized in the 1980s in several states who primarily engaged in acts of brutal eco-terrorism against the logging industry. They would drive spikes in trees that would cause chainsaws to literally blow up, causing injury and in some cases death to loggers. This behavior is violent crime plain and simple.

One self-labeled Libertarian claimed to be a member of Earth First! and said he would have a hard time deciding which side of the protest to side with. I ridiculed this. Claiming to be a member of a pro-freedom organization and a eco-terrorist group is like claiming to be a member of both the Anti Defamation League and the Klu Klux Klan.

Another Libertarian, who yesterday called himself a "fan of Clinton" urged the support of "land conservancy" groups instead of groups like Earth First! Libertarians claim to be against anyone who initiates force or any form of fraud. Land conservancy groups fraudulently raise money for land purchases they say will be used for privately owned conservation purposes, and then, in many cases, sells this land to the government. This is outright fraud. Additionally, when government buys this land it purchases such land with money collected from tax dollars. Libertarians oppose all mandatory taxes as government initiation of force. This particular Libertarian admitted the land conservancies sell some land to the government, but saw no problem with that. So he condones violations of the principles his party opposes by excusing both the fraud and the force involved in these transactions. For opposing this position, this self-proclaimed Libertarian and "fan of Clinton" called me an anarchist. Yet he's the one that signed the Libertarian Party anarchist pledge that swears opposition to all taxes and all government actions.

Then another member posts a note basically suggesting driving spikes in publicly owned land is a defendable action. The reasoning is that if logging is done on publicly owned land, a member of the public is owner of that land

and can engage in these acts of eco-terrorism. Go ahead and try applications of this reasoning on public property and see how fast you find yourself in court on criminal charges. I further explained my point about spiking of trees by eco-terrorists, and reinforced my point that such behavior should be prosecuted whether it happens on public or private land because it is nothing more than an act of violent crime with the design intent to injure and main human beings. I think most, who wish to live in a civilized society, agree with me that violent criminals should be prosecuted to the full extent of the law. For this stand, I was labeled a reactionary conservative. My answer to this sophistry is simple. Failure to prosecute violent crime will lead to anarchy. But for opposing the government taking money from the taxpayers to buy land (purchases fraudulently by land conservancies before that) for government use, I'm called an anarchist. Which is it, I can not be both an anarchist and a reactionary conservative? Actually I'm something in between, the individualist pro-freedom Conservative in the Barry Goldwater vein.

Those who call themselves Libertarians are philosophically all over the place, from those who are nearly anarchist to those who are bordering on being Ted Kennedy style liberal Democrats. So much for being so full of principle. And these people call themselves advocates of tolerance too. But the problem is, they're intolerant of anyone who disagrees with them, including other Libertarians who aren't exactly 100% in agreement with them. Their intolerance is quite revealing, and still worthy of my defense.

Politically Correct Brainwashing in the Public Schools

May 18, 2000

There is no doubt in my mind one of the main objectives of many public school administrators is the successful indoctrination of the children. The values they seek to inculcate are the New Age, moral relativist, politically correct, leftist, "diversity" mindset of the educational establishment, namely the large teachers unions. One only needs to look at the hard left agenda that is advocated, in both educational and other policy, by the National Education Association (NEA) and the American Federation of Teachers (ATF) to see this pattern.

Today's new includes a story about a young boy in a recreation center who allegedly, according to the disputed claims of Congressman James Moran (Democrat – Virginia), shaped his hand as gun and threatened to shoot. The parents of the boy dispute the story and claim Moran was bullying their son. But the main issue I highlight here is the allegation the boy was acting out use of a firearm via a "finger gun" and that this proves he needs to be re-educated. I remember doing such things many times as a kid, but I clearly understood the difference between pointing my finger and saying "pow" versus doing the real thing. Moran has demanded the boy be sent to anti-gun re-education, in effect, or has threatened to file charges against the eight year old child to get the court system to order this if the parents will not do so. Congressman Moran, a liberal Democrat and supporters of the agenda of the teachers unions, has a past reputation for violence. He has been accused of engaging in barroom fights in his past.

Children in a New Jersey school plays "cops and robbers" during recess (including the use of "finger guns") and found themselves suspended by school administrators.

A Maryland school recently suspended a child for drawing a picture of a gun on paper in art class. They claimed his artwork violated the schools policy against possession of weapons. It's crazy when a picture of a gun is a "weapon." But then again if the child can be sent home for using a "finger gun" on the playground I suppose it's equally foolish to call his parents in when Johnny draws a gun in art class.

Political correctness found a young violator in a Kansas school. A child drew a confederate flag, and for this was deemed to have violated the school's policy against espousing racism. Do these politically correct types really think a young child is espousing racism by drawing such a thing?

A student in a Michigan school dared to utter some common sense in school and point out that school shootings can be prevented if teachers were allowed to carry firearms. Clearly one teacher with firearm and ability to competently use it would have wiped out Klebold and Harris before too many of their classmates were murdered at Columbine High School just about a year ago. For this "crime" the student received referral to the school's "Hazard and Risk Assessment Team." Can you say re-education?

A Minnesota school rounds out this anti-guns trend. A student there submitted a picture, depicting a World War II howitzer from the local Veterans of Foreign Wars, to his school yearbook. The yearbook declined to publish the picture, saying violated the school's policy against weapons.

But weapons are not the only targets of the PC approach in schools. The aim is to prohibit that which is not politically correct and promote values and thoughts that are believed to be politically correct.

I'm young enough to have seen the first storm clouds of political correctness in the public schools. One of the most important goals of political correctness, remember, is the redefining of traditional clear "gender" roles to vague and fuzzy definitions. One of the most stark examples of this I remember was being shown a film in class during elementary school (I think it was third grade) about a boy who played with dolls. As a kid at the time I thought it was silly fiction and a stupid film. But most kids just appreciated a little entertainment in between the more dull schoolwork. But we didn't realize as kids at the time that this fits into the attempts by the politically correct to redefine sex/gender role ideas.

Despite the best efforts in this direction for decades now, young boys still like to play cops and robbers and pretend to shoot each other, and young girls still like playing with dolls and such. Those are natural tendencies that politically correct brainwashing won't change.

Liberalism Equals Hypocrisy

May 5, 2000

Liberals were the most prominent opponents of government authority and its use. In the 1960s they protested any hint of heavy hard government seeking to quell demonstrations on college and universities campuses. Liberals loathed the military, as Bill Clinton said in his 1969 letter to his draft board, and despised any authority or law enforcement agencies. They called the police "pigs" on a regular basis, the coined and popularized that term in the 1960s as a slur against law enforcement officers.

Despite their excesses, liberals of the 1960s variety are to be commended for fighting for free speech rights, procedural and due process rights, and exposing the excessive uses of government authority at some times. But what has happened to liberals who have betrayed these principles while evolving into such hypocritical schmucks?

Behold the administration of Bill Clinton: lead by the same liberal Democrat who in 1969 said he loathed the military, protested the War in Vietnam on foreign soil, whose current administration has on numerous international meals-on-wheels missions has nothing to do with our miltary's mission of defense, and has increased arms and budgets of virtually every federal agency with SWAT teams, automatic weapons, and other resources as they enhance their paramilitary functions.

The same liberals in this administration, as well as the press, were outraged at the arrest and prosecution of the Black Panthers in the 1960s. They were outraged by the suppression of campus demonstrations by law enforcement officers and the National Guard. Yet these same "liberals" defend and condone the midnight raid of the Lazaro Gonzalez home in Miami to confiscate, against court order, Elian Gonzalez.

The same people who were outraged (justifiably so) at the shootings at Kent State University presided over the execution of 86 human beings at Waco, Texas. And many of the same people in the press who helped stir righteous outrage over the shooting at Kent State willingly aided and abetted in the media snow job and misinformation about what happened at Mount Carmel in Waco. The government served up what are now objectively documented (see Waco -- Rules of Engagement) as blatant lies and propaganda about the Waco tragedy, and virtually all major media outlets supported and assisted as accomplices this campaign to dis-inform the public about Waco.

The same liberals who run in the Clinton administration and support state control enforced by gun point opposed authority in the 1960s and love authority in the 1990s and beyond. These very same people support and defend an administration that abuses authority, and the blatant public display of it, to attempt to goad the public into compliance and fearing the government. In 1993 negotiators were very close to reaching a peaceful agreement with David Koresh, and knowing that, Jackboot-Janet Reno ordered the immediate raid and murder and burning down of Mount Carmel on the morning of April 19, 1993. Similarly, round-the-clock negotiations with Lazaro Gonzalez were very near reaching a settlement regarding Elian. Realizing that was the case, Jackboot Janet Reno ordered the raid on the morning of April 22, 2000. In both cases they wanted maximum show of force. The message is that no one is to defy the Clintons' authority.

This administration of Bill Clinton, made up of liberals who fought for free speech in the 1960s, had a Department of Housing and Urban Development (HUD) that sought to send people to jail for speaking out in opposition to placement of government housing projects in their neighborhood. In some communities, city council members who refused to authorize the building of HUD housing projects were threatened with fines and criminal prosecution until they backed down to the government's demands. Free speech doesn't count anymore if you are speaking out against the policies of liberal government.

Today liberals are hypocrites. They have become the very worst of the kind of authoritarians they claimed to have protested against in the 1960s. This administration and its willing accomplices in the media have proved themselves to be hypocrites of the worst order.

Liberalism Now Means Hypocrisy and Hate

June 3, 2000

Try to talk about issues with most left-wing liberals today and you quickly realize their ideology falls apart into a mess of hypocrisy. And their argument runs out of substance in a few exchanges when the exchange descends into ad hominem attacks and blatant fallacies. Soon after defeating the cliched leftwing liberal arguments on issues, conservatives, sensible libertarians, and other advocates of individual freedom are quickly branded "racist, sexist, homophobic, xenophobic, insensitive, fascist, etc." Politically correct liberals are quick to banter these terms, in many cases without fully understanding many of them.

The liberal argument has proven to be hypocritical. Just look at liberalism as exemplified by the Clintons. Clearly they believe all of us should live under one set of rules, and they will follow any rules they choose to follow. Should any one of us dare to think we could try and get away with just a fraction of what they've done it would be jail time. But the Clintons have evaded responsibility of their actions through cover-up, spin, assistance from their willing accomplices in the mainstream media, and a great deal of ignorance and apathy among the public.

Extreme feminist liberals are great for obvious hypocrisy. They were quick to believe the lying charges of Anita Hill, politically motivated as they obviously were, against Judge Clarence Thomas. Liberals tried to destroy his career and "Bork" his nomination to the Supreme Court. Thomas was brilliant in his own defense, and even sledge hammered the liberal civil rights plantation when he called the hearings a "high tech lynching of an uppity black man." But, where are these same liberals when Jaunita Broaddrick comes forward with credible rape allegations against Bill Clinton, or when Paula Jones described her alleged sexual assault at the hands of Bill Clinton? The extreme feminist movement crumbled in the weight of its silence on these allegations.

Remember author Toni Morrison, anointed a great cultural leader and author by Bill Clinton? Several months ago she got media notoriety for calling Clinton our first "black president." The claim was based on Clinton liking fast junk food, playing the saxophone, cheating on his wife, and being sexually promiscuous. These characteristics are evidence, according to Morrison, to explain his high support levels among black voters. Morrison, black and a liberal herself, can get away with engaging in blatant stereotypical and bigotry. But if a conservative of any skin color had suggested anything half as racist as this, there would be immediate calls for an apology. Remember the Rutgers University official that was called on to resign because he used the term "niggardly" in a graduation speech. The word has nothing to do with race.

Liberals seemed to have the ultimate trump card when they began to promote the politically correct agenda of "diversity" and "compassion" and such. I remember in college in the mid 1980s, the same liberals who demanded "tolerance" and "respect" for the homosexual lifestyle, and anything else they labeled as "diversity" where the quickest to send anyone who disagreed off to the Dean of students office to face unspecified "harassment" charges.

I remember two students senators I knew at the University of Massachusetts got into a hallway argument with one liberal feminist, advocate of gay rights, over whether or not student money should fund a group advancing that political agenda. Without any real evidence, she filed "harassment" charges with the Dean of Students office, that caused them be spending the last weeks of the semester defending themselves in a kangaroo court hearing rather than studying for final exams. They successfully defended themselves, but could have been thrown out of school for disagreeing with a liberal and arguing. On many campuses, students are dismissed for daring to disagree with "compassionate" liberal supporters of "diversity." Obviously, diversity of points of view is not included in the liberal definition of "diversity."

When conservatives exposed the fraud of the politically correct agenda, I suspect many liberals knew their movement had been defeated intellectually. That left them one option in spewing their intellectual impotence: showing their hatred for conservatives. When first exposed as one of the stalwarts of the political correctness movement, Duke University Professor Stanley Fish took to denouncing his critics as "racist, sexist, homophobic, and fascist." He would reel off that epithet each time he commented on critics of his views. Yet it is Fish who authored a book titled, "There's No Such Thing as Free Speech: And It's a Good Thing, Too." Since then liberals have responded much the same way against conservatives.

The goal of left-wing liberals, that which they won't tell you, is real simple. They seek to demonize and destroy that intellectual concepts and institutions that are the basis of individual freedom. But they've lost the argument and have become louder, more shrill, and desperate in their attempts to defeat our values. But never under-estimate leftist liberals, they are still extremely influential in a number of organization and institutions in society including political groups and the entertainment industry, etc.

The politically correct ideology will still fool many people. That is why advocates of individual freedom must continue to refute the leftist, politically correct arguments. Putting up with the hypocrisy and hatred of leftwing liberals is a small price to pay while showing how vapid their arguments truly are.

Liberals Ethically and Morally Homeless Throwing Stones at Glass Windows

June 4, 2000

Liberals are quick to accuse conservatives of hypocrisy, especially when liberal hypocrisy is so vividly demonstrated. But this point-counterpoint isn't simply an exchange of accusations of hypocrisy; it is an important difference that is being confused by blurred by baseless (but typical) liberal distractions from the real issue at hand. That issue, of course, is the moral and ethical bankruptcy of the liberal position. It can not be papered over, regardless of how much effort liberals put forth, by distracting the issue with ad hominem and other non sequitur arguments.

Conservatives, not liberals, are the folks who advocate and advance the idea that we as human beings should consistently live and operate by a higher set of principles. That is not to say that all who call themselves conservative are perfect in living by these, but it is to say the standard is recognized and supported. Liberals take the exact opposite, 180 degrees to the other direction, point of view on this issue of standards. Leftwing liberals deny the very existence of the truths form which these values stem, and espouse the idea that there are no truths, there are no better values, and that all such matters are simply personal opinions and choices by which no individual should ever have to account for the consequences of them. This is the typical liberal view of moral relativism and values-free thinking, so-called that allows for the typical leftwing liberal to condone anything they wish to condone.

The Clinton administration has been scandal central for the last seven years. Exposure of the most sordid scandals the Republic has even seen leads to liberals trying desperately to find scandal on conservatives. Liberals love to play the fallacious partners-in-guilt game by making it look like all are as corrupt, morally and ethically, as their favorite politicians. This cynical strategy is designed to cause the public to conclude all politicians and activists are equally corrupt, and then fail to hold accountable those who engage in the worst acts of brutality and thievery. Unfortunately, it works. This has clearly been the standard operating procedure of the Clinton White House. Anyone exposing or demanding investigation of scandals in this administration must have his or her character smeared on any mud that could be found.

The White House ran an office whose only purpose was to dig mud up on anyone criticizing or exposing the scandals of this administration. While they publicly denied or ignored the allegations, they cynically leveled scurrilous and baseless allegations against conservative critics. Any remember the infamous Filegate scandal? Why else would Hillary Clinton's "security office" Craig Livingstone have FBI file folders on thousands of leading conservative Republican activists? One the most morally ethically corrupt of liberals can condone, deny, or otherwise not be entirely outraged by this behavior.

Liberals, therefore, who do not believe in such values, are in no position, morally and ethically, to criticize those who may not always succeed in living up the standards they advocate. For example, I as a conservative believe it's wrong to steal office supplies from the office. Let's sake, for example, that I go ahead and steal office supplies at the office. I have not only done something that most of us accept as being wrong; I have done something that is clearly wrong according to my own standards. One can definitely say I have engaged in actions inconsistent with my own values, and if I criticize others from stealing from the office, I am also a hypocrite. Conservatives who also agree that stealing from the office is wrong have standing to criticize my actions and accuse me of hypocrisy. That is clear, I think most would agree with the truth of that statement. Now let's say we have a colleague in my office who, for whatever reason he uses to justify it, believe he's justified in stealing stuff from the office. Regardless of whether he acts on that belief, he is in no position to criticize my act of stealing from the office. He simply lacks the moral and ethical standing to criticize my ethical failing, or to call me a hypocrite, because he doesn't believe what I did was wrong. This is true of liberals who are so quick to scream out "hypocrisy" about those who fail to uphold the very values and standards that liberals do not at all espouse.

Leftwing liberals, who are quick to cynically condemn those who espouse family values, love to complain about conservatives preaching about them. We can't have conservative politicians in public office shoving family values down our throat, they say. Yet these are the very same compassionate liberals that use the Force of the State to regulate personal behavior by levying excessive taxes on alcohol, tobacco, and fattening foods if they get their way. It's alright to use government force to tax people out of eating, drinking, or smoking what they choose to, but liberals see nothing wrong with conservatives using the bully pulpit of public office to try to convince people to voluntarily respect and uphold better values. This is liberal hypocrisy of the highest order.

But at the end of this argument, liberals are still wrong because they espouse a "situational ethics" entirely devoid of any substantial moral and ethical standards. Liberals today are profoundly impacted by the corrupt values of the 1960s. They very much believe the "if it feels good it's right" way of thinking, and believe one is not responsible for the consequences of one actions. This brand of thinking, so dominant among today's liberals, is what a friend of mine calls "rancid existentialism."

Conservatives who fail to live by their own standards are wrong. Liberals who cynically jeer them, and find joy and happiness in their failings, are not only wrong and profoundly hypocritical, they are part of the moral and ethical abyss their very morally and ethically relative philosophy has created. In other words, liberals have no basis for criticizing conservatives who've caught the disease when it is liberals who have been agents of the disease all along. To criticize the failure to live by these values requires that one first accepts those values and espouses them. Liberals have no standing to shout "hypocrisy" at others. When they do, they prove themselves to be supremely hypocritical.

Liberalism Stoned Again -- Yet More Evidence that Liberalism Equals Hypocrisy

June 5, 2000

Forgive me to taking the metaphor further. Seeing liberalism from the brick-solid fortress of truth called conservatives makes it quite easy to see the transparently hypocritical nature of today's liberalism and throw literary rocks at it. Liberalism is just so rich in hypocrisy I'll refresh your memory with yet more examples.

Liberals have a skewed view of justice that is even inconsistent among liberals. The standard liberal thinks defendants and prisoners should have more rights in the legal system. I'll admit that at least the old style liberals of the 1960s and 1970s like George McGovern were consistent in advocating the right to be innocent until proven guilty by a jury of one's peers. But liberals today, backed by situational ethics, have thrown that to the side in favor of advocating it only when it suits their agenda. So liberals in the civil rights establishment sides with O. J. Simpson during his trial, and cheered when Johnnie Cochran rapped, "If the gloves don't fit, you must acquit." They hailed the verdict as justice. Feminists, another major branch of liberals, condemned the verdict and rooted all the way for Marcia Clark and the prosecution. I was amazed to see liberal feminists siding with the prosecution. That's rare. But they did, and shed the old liberal concern with due process and instead sided with the prosecution because of the sex of the principal victim of the crime for which Simpson was tried.

Liberals have overwhelming sided with the Clintons, their lawyer Gregory Craig, Juan Miguel Gonzalez, and

Fidel Castro in wanting Elian Gonzalez sent back to Cuba. Their reasoning? Father's rights. Liberals, in domestic custody cases, almost never side with the child's father. But they do in this case because it sends Elian back to liberal (ahh... communist, rather) Cuba. But wait, this is an immigration case, not a custody battle. Liberals are usually for liberalized or even open immigration. Not in this case, liberals can't send Elian back to Cuba fast enough. Liberals used to at least be consistently liberal on the issues. Not anymore.

Liberals were big fans of another foreign communist and friend of Fidel Castro. Few liberals could hold back their support for Nicaragua communist Sandinista self-appointed President Daniel Ortega during the 1980s. Ortega took control of the Nicaraguan government through armed revolution that was backed by Soviet weapons, by way of Castro's Cuba. Liberals saw no problems with this but called the Reagan Administration terrorist for backing the Democratic Resistance in Nicaragua and a legitimate and democratically elected government in El Salvador. And that Soviet invasion of Afghanistan didn't concern liberals much either. But they demanded we stop sending aid to the freedom fighters in Angola so the Soviet-backed communist government there could go on murdering their citizens.

The Cold War was never accepted or understood by liberals, who were glad it was over once it ended. But the West WON the Cold War because liberals lost every single domestic political battle against the policies that won it. Had we been governed by liberal policies we would have not won the Cold War and Mikhail Gorbachev would still be Soviet Dictator today. Oh yeah, liberals love him too. And the liberals who fought anti-Cold War policy all that time and denied we were in a

Cold War switched their tune once it was clearly over. They then began accusing conservatives of wanting to continue the Cold War, and called for recognizing its end. But how liberals claim the Cold War was ended when they never acknowledged us ever being in one? Remember that facts never get in the way of the agenda for liberals.

Liberal feminism has collapsed in a pile of embarrassing intellectual rubble. Liberal feminists crusaded against Senator Bob Packwood, a moderate Republican but didn't utter a peep when similar sexual harassment allegations surfaced against liberal Democrat Senator Daniel Inouye of Hawaii. Liberals stood by Anita Hill while she perjured herself under the heat of Senator Arlen Specter's questioning of her dishonest and inconsistent charges against Clarence Thomas. But then liberal Democrat Bill Clinton is credibly accused by Gennifer Flowers, Paul Jones, Kathleen Willey, Juanita Broaddrick, and other women he had affairs with. Liberal feminists stood by Hillary, who stood by her man, when she so cynically and dishonestly alleged a "vast right wing conspiracy" to do in President Clinton. Clinton clearly abused women he had affairs with, and liberal feminists have been conspicuous in their silence. Not one major liberal feminist leader has stood up for any of these women.

Liberals claim to believe in privacy, unless you're a Republican activist and Craig Livingstone is looking through your FBI files in the White House while answering to Hillary. Liberals claim to believe in free speech, but if Clinton's Department of Housing and Urban Development wants a government housing project in your back yard, speaking out against it could get your prosecuted. And it is the liberals who gave us the campus speech codes at many major universities, including the U. of Wisconsin. From there, it's chancellor and speech code author Donna Shalala was appointed to the Clinton cabinet.

Liberal hypocrisy is too easy to find. Liberals are even hypocritical about being hypocritical. And they have the nerve to zing conservatives with the H-word.

Liberal Hypocrisy Again: Al Gore Alleged Slumlord

June 6, 2000

The news of the day brings yet more evidence of liberal hypocrisy, every day. It turns out that Al Gore owns rental properties and he's not upholding his responsibility as the property owner. One of his tenants has complained about problems with a toilet and sink in one of his apartments this family rents from Al Gore. Proper maintenance of the amenities in the apartments is part of what this family pays for in the month rent check and Gore is contractually obligated to such. But Gore's property manager is not responding.

Rather than pay for this with the money he collects from this family, Al Gore wants these kinds of expenses to be funded by tax dollars. That's right, more corporate welfare for liberal Democrats who own rental properties.

The family living in this apartment includes individuals with disabilities. Just days ago, Al Gore was campaigning in Maryland and called for more government programs, and the funding of more benefits, for the disabled. Yet this family pays their rent out of their fixed and limited income and Al Gore won't fix their toilet and sink.

This issue illustrates perfect how liberals, like Al Gore, live by one set of rules and seek to have others live by their rules. Al Gore and liberal Democrats enact regulations on property owner to require them to do a number of things, including proper maintenance of the buildings. Al Gore is likely to be in violation of such regulations in this instance.

Reportedly, Al Gore is blaming his apartment manager for this mishap. Even if true, Al Gore is responsible because he hired this manager. In the end, Al Gore remains responsible.

Just imagine if George W. Bush owned this apartment. Who would be the quickest to trample over a crowd, to get to the closest set of microphones and cameras, to make a statement condemning this? If you answer Al Gore, of course you're right. One only needs to look at the scurrilous attacks Gore leveled against Senator Bill Bradley in their contest for the Democratic nomination for President. Al Gore didn't hesitate to attack and bludgeon Bradley on every occasion. He engaged in blatant cynical distortion about Bradley's health care proposal. While I disagree with that proposal, I found Bradley's stance on the issue honest in comparison to Gore's cynical and dishonest politicking on the issue.

But Gore is consistent in one area on this issue. By not taking responsibility for lack of maintenance at his apartment, Gore is being consistent with the liberal philosophy he believes in. Evading responsibility and blaming someone else is typical of liberals. In this case he's blame the property manager he hired, and I suspect if called on to explain that, he would offer more excuses on how and why he hired this manager.

This story shows the true content of Al Gore's character. Voters have one easy and sure solution to this problem, at the polls in November. Simply don't vote for Al Gore.

Picnics and Outings are not Politically Correct

April 26, 2000

Political correctness never ceases to amaze me in how extreme is can be. The latest nuttiness comes from the State University of New York at Albany regarding an event to honor the 50-year anniversary of Jackie Robinson breaking the color barrier in Major League Baseball. Organizers at first called the event a picnic.

But politically correct anti-racism activities objected to the use of this term, claiming it was racist. These politically correct wackos said the terms was named such because it was used by those who lynched blacks who would "pic" which black they would "nic." This is completely made up Bravo Sierra, no such evidence of this usage exists in the history of the word's usage. These facts were pointed out to the activists, who stand demanded the university administration require the event be renamed.

Many might remember a speaker at a university last year being condemned for using the word "niggardly." Why was he condemned, because the word sounds like the infamous N-word. But it bears no relation to that word in any way. In the American Heritage Dictionary, niggardly is defined as, "Unwilling to give, spend, or share; stingy." Now I challenge anyone to tell me what is racist about that word. Perhaps any suggestion as fiscally conservative terminology is racist according to the politically correct. Remember, only a few years ago, raving liberal Congressman Charles Rangel from New York made the pronouncement, "tax cuts are racist." This comes from the same kind of liberal politically correct thinking that claims cutting welfare benefits is racist.

Political correctness has gone way overboard. You can see that when a celebration of the accomplishment of Jackie Robinson is deemed itself to be racist because of the use of a word.

In response to the protests of the politically correct activists, the event was renamed an "outing" instead of "picnic." But that term offended the gay community at the university who objected to its use. In their context, "outing" is a term used to describe an obnoxious violation of personal privacy where homosexual activists will publicly "out" the sexual preference of gays who prefer to keep that a secret.

Doesn't matter what word you use. It doesn't matter how inoffensive it might be. Someone among the many politically correct will be offended.

The Constitution's Preamble as Seen by the Politically Correct

May 17, 2000

Consider the Preamble to our Constitution as drafted and ultimately ratified in 1789:

We the People of the United States, in Order to form a more perfect Union, establish Justice, insure domestic Tranquility, provide for the common defence, promote the general Welfare, and secure the Blessings of Liberty to ourselves and our Posterity, do ordain and establish this Constitution for the United States of America.

All of the words have precise meanings in 1789 and have since been re-defined by the politically correct leftist-liberals who continually seek to move us in the direction of creeping socialism and divisive multicultural conformity that is often labeled "diversity." Realizing the importance of doublespeak, politically correct liberals have devised new definitions of these words, and it is quite common now to hear younger graduates of our public schools use these definitions without knowing any better. Below I've contrasted the accurate definitions of these words, as used in the preamble, with the politically correct ones.

We the People of the United States

Accurate definition: The Human Beings are citizens of this country and whose Rights are recognized by The Bill of   Rights.

P.C. definition: Any and all such entities, often excluding human beings, who have alleged to have been abused by human beings and therefore deserving of more rights, such as wild animals and so-called endangered species.

in Order to form a more perfect Union

Accurate definition: This simply means in order to more effective create a nation, living under this social contract we call The Constitution.

P.C. definition: This has come to mean creating a government that controls the lives of most citizens because most of us are dolts who are not equipped to make our own decisions regarding our lives and need politicians, bureaucrats, and other so-called experts to make our decisions for us.

establish Justice

Accurate definition: Equal treatment under the law, and before government agencies.

P.C. definition: Equality of outcome, economic and otherwise, enforced by government agencies via progressive taxation and intrusive government regulation. Additionally, social engineering, including so-called affirmative action, shall be necessary to insure such equality and promote multiculturalism and "diversity." Notice how anyone who disagrees with "diversity" is instantly labeled "intolerant." So much for diversity of viewpoints on "diversity."

insure domestic Tranquility

<u>Accurate definition</u>: Protect the rights of citizens and insure the peaceful nature of the community.

<u>P.C. definition</u>: Use government force to promote "tolerance" for diversity, including forcing "sensitivity training" on those politically incorrect enough to disagree with the "diversity" agenda.

provide for the common defence

<u>Accurate definition</u>: Defend our borders from attack.

<u>P.C. definition</u>: Defend and promote politically correct values throughout the world by sending our military on international meals-on-wheels missions while under-funding the legitimate defense mission of the armed forces.

promote the general Welfare

<u>Accurate definition</u>: Protect the Rights of citizens through stable Constitution government that enforces the laws against those who violate the rights of others.

<u>P.C. definition</u>: Insure equality through social engineering and social "welfare" programs, all of which are paid for by taking money from those who earn it and giving it to those who do not.

and secure the Blessings of Liberty

<u>Accurate definition</u>: Protecting and defending the Rights recognized in The Bill of Rights.

<u>P.C. definition</u>: Extending and expanding entitlements and privileges while narrowing, violating, or eliminating legitimate individual rights.

ourselves and our Posterity

<u>Accurate definition</u>: Current U. S. citizens and future citizens.

<u>P.C. definition</u>: The citizens "educated" enough to be politically correct as well as those who have yet to finish their "sensitivity training" in order to become politically correct.

Constitution for the United States of America

<u>Accurate definition</u>: A lasting and profound document that provides a social contract for us to live under in freedom, and only changes when we amend it through the process provided for in the Constitution.

<u>P.C. definition</u>: A worthless and out-dated document that we need to pay little attention to, and when we do, read it to mean whatever we want it to mean. After all, what could a group of angry white males writing a constitution in 1787 know about life in the U.S. in year 2000?

In honor the politically correct, I've re-written the preamble using the words that the politically correct really believe it means.

We the Dolts of the United States, in Order to form a socialist society, establish Diversity, insure multiculturalism, provide for the common civility and sensitivity, promote the Welfare State, and secure the Blessings of privilege to the politically correct, do ordain and establish this Constitution for the United States of America, which will be interpreted to mean whatever our justices say it means, whenever they rule that it means such.

$12,000 for Complaint on "Phallic Shaped Donuts"

June 22, 2000

"Sexual Harassment" Law is egregiously out of control.

A donut shop in Massachusetts must pay $12,000 to a female employee for "emotional distress" caused after being terminated for repeated complaining about having to make "phallic shaped donuts." This is the latest ruling on such "civil rights" cases by the Massachusetts Commission Against Discrimination. It amazes me that one could call these pastries such a name and even suggest anything sexual in relation to them based on shape only. Anyone who has visited a local Dunkin Donuts lately has seen the so-called "phallic shaped donuts." The precise name for such a donut is a cruller. It is a donut that is twisted in a straight line rather than around in a circle.

I can imagine employees made various jokes about these pastries while working at the donut shop. But joking about donuts, absent any explicitly suggestive content is simply joking and not sexual harassment. But this ruling is the latest in the move to broaden the definition sexual harassment as wide as possible. Any comments that can be construed to be sexual in any way possible, regardless of whether or not any sexual suggestion is intended by the maker of the statements, is now deemed to be outright sexual harassment. The new doctrine of sexual harassment is brought to us by the same political correct extreme feminists who advocated the speech codes on the university campuses. In this case, any comments that some believe are sexually offensive will be censored via the civil rights laws and the regulatory process of the anti-discrimination agencies.

The larger trend with all of this is what George Will calls the "new entitlement, the right to not be offended." Obviously, this one employee was offended by the task of baking crullers, calling them "phallic shaped donuts." Only in the mind of an extreme feminist is every cylindrical-shaped object both a "phallic-shaped" object and therefore automatically an object of sexual harassment. When this lunacy goes a bit further, utility poles and flagpoles will be next. Pens and flashlights are the wrong shape also. Maybe these same wackos will demand rectangular-shaped soft drink bottles. Where will this madness end? Remember that these are the same extremists as those who protested some years ago at Princeton University over the cafeteria menu listing of "manicotti." They demanded that politically incorrect dish be re-named "womanicotti." I'm not making this up. Feminist PCers on campus also demanded that "seminars" instead be called "ovulars."

The goal of all this language revisionism is the thought control that can be achieved. If the politically correct can control what we say and write, ultimately they will control how we think. Words will be banned from use and the ideas they are allegedly standing for will be shunned as well. There is only one sane response to all this nonsense. We need to expose political correctness for what it is, and do the best we can to defeat and stamp out these efforts to enforce thought control. Feel free to use terms like picnic, calling a spade a spade, etc. and refuse to live in fear that you'll be offending the politically correct.

And lastly, visit your nearest Dunkin Donuts and order a half dozen "phallic shaped donuts." While the manager, thinking liability, might prohibit employees from using that term, you can proudly use it. If they don't appreciate the humor in that, remind them of the old adage, "the customer is always right."

Artistic Guilt

April 10, 1991

The painting, done in oil paints by artist Natasha Mayers, was titled "Every Missile has a Home." The title was painted twice along the four edges of the work, once starting on the top edge and concluding on the right edge, and the second starting on the bottom edge and finishing on the left edge. In the inner rectangular area were seven painted missiles, with stars on them, sticking half or part of their length out of their silos. Next to the painting was a tag listing the title, artist, and it's price of $600.

Home -- Homeless was the name of the "art show." Several artists from Maine produced works which were displayed in this show that was touring the state and had been making its stop at the Art Gallery of the University of Maine at Farmington in February of 1991. This was courtesy of Artists for the Homeless, a project of the Union of Maine Visual Artists, for the purpose of "address(ing) the issue of homelessness."
Quoted from a brochure published by the sponsors of the project.

The introductory statement, written by Susan Drucker (President of the Union of Maine Visual Artists), states the purpose of the art show was to, "create new symbols of home and the consequence of loss of home. (sic) With these images, we hope to take a complex issue and form a visual whole, a whole which may make the statistics, and the studies, and people who are homeless themselves, harder to ignore." (italics added)

Most numerously featured at the gallery were the works of Maine Artist Natasha Mayers. The previously mentioned works included "Every Missile Has a Home," and several others by Mayers.

Another piece by Mayers was titled "Military Budget Increased."   The text painted on this one read: "Military Budget Increased 38%.   Between 1982 and 1986 Spending for Housing Decreased 82%" The work was done mostly in red, white, and blue. It indicated no years for when the military budget increased 38%. As of fiscal year 1986, the Department of Defense received $281.4 billion out of a $1.073 trillion budget, which is 26.4% of federal spending. And for fiscal year 1990, defense was funded approximately $305.6 billion from a $1.331 trillion federal budget, which is 23% of 1990 federal spending. After factoring in the annual inflation of those years, the Department of Defense has purchasing power than it did four years ago. These figures can be verified in the Congressional Quarterly Almanacs, pg. 367 of the 1986 edition, and pg. 75 of the 1989 edition.

And the artist gives no support to the claim that spending on housing has decreased by 82% between 1982 and 1986, nor did she explain what kind of spending on which individual program or programs for whatever kind of housing. Behind this text is a painted depiction of a house burning down. This piece of work fails to offer a cogent logical argument or statement to attempt to prove its claims, and it fails to show a realistic picture of homelessness or offer any footnoting for the numerical claims about spending on housing and defense. To use their words, this work does not "depict...the consequences of loss of home."

Another painting, titled "Gold Bars," by Roxanne Seitz depicted a homeless person in the fetal position with four to five story buildings surrounding this person. In the upper right corner, taking almost one quarter of the area of the work, was a diagram, somewhat round shaped, showing these four words with arrows connecting them in the following circular order: mental anguish - paralysis - joblessness - homelessness (connected back to mental anguish). So according to this work, mental anguish leads to paralysis, which leads to joblessness, which leads to homelessness, which leads to mental anguish, etc, etc, etc Logically, such a circular model would, in the absence of contrary information, suggest that mental anguish can lead to paralysis (physical or psychological paralysis?), that paralysis would lead to joblessness, etc. meaning that this is a closed cycle that only those in it would be able to be inside it (how did they enter a closed cycle?) and most of us on the outside would be unable to enter it. Obviously that's false. I, like many of you, have been temporarily jobless without experiencing "paralysis" or homelessness.   Many people experience some mental anguish (stress caused by everyday life), and some joblessness, and don't necessarily find themselves homeless. Again, this work lacks proof of its written claims; It doesn't prove that these four are necessarily connected in the manner, or the order, that they are presented on the painting.

The sponsors claim that this presenting of slogans is intended to "take a complex
issue (and)...cause a shift in some viewers' consciousness." This is also from the Introduction in the brochure.[This technique does not relay empirical facts to allow the viewer to consider the issue, it offers only slogans and assumptions. It seems to assume you are not capable of deciding based on the facts, that facts are less convincing than slogans, and that only through emotions, as opposed to intellect, will you be convinced to become concerned about homelessness.

The statement in the brochure also states, "We can

only hope that the clarity with which art can mirror society may cause a shift in some viewers' consciousness. Until the public embraces the problem of homelessness, the legislature will remain quiet. Almost any expression is better than silence."

It's difficult to believe that the sponsors of the show actually believe that "any expression is better than silence," e.g. expressions of psychopathic hatred of the homeless people, or logical refutation of the art show sponsors' claims that may in their view downplay the seriousness of homelessness would likely not be considered preferable to silence in the view of the sponsors. And about the legislature acting, if the art show sponsors were advocating a vision of a collectivist government enacting an activist social agenda, as opposed to private charity aiding the unfortunate in our society, than they should have straightforwardly stated such a vision.

Another piece, one done by Ruth Cohen, was titled, "You are Guilty," and depicted seventeen various different looking faces appearing to look right at the viewer. This piece had a price of $30 affixed to it. The message on it was and simple: everyone is to blame for the homeless problem, and is to be blamed for everyone that is homeless. Even though each and every case of a homeless person is different, and has different causes and circumstances, the message of this piece is essentially the same tactic of blaming society. One can quit his job, stop paying the rent and the bills, get evicted and become homeless, and why not blame society for his woes? It certainly can be done, if you can stand being homeless, and don't have to take personal responsibility for it; just blame society and cause uninvolved people to feel guilty for your misfortunes. Thomas Sowell, in his essay An

"Epidemic" of Irresponsibility, from Compassion Versus Guilt and Other Essays, wrote, "The decline of personal responsibility has been accompanied by a rise in social responsibility by people who had nothing to do with the individual decisions that brought on disaster. Along with this has come an increased role for people skilled at creating guilt.

They say it's "consciousness" they want to affect, but they are actually trying to create guilt, because only through causing you to feel guilty, can these artists expect you in the end to agree with their solutions to this problem. An awareness of the issue caused by reading empirical measures and definitions of homelessness and/ or personally being homeless will allow you to reasonably skeptical, and cause you to raise questions about the scope of the actual problem, and you just might suggest some logical solutions. Actually solving the problem would put all the activists, political artists, lobbyists and the whole homeless industry, the actual employment of people raising funds to advocate certain government policies in this area and those employed by such governmental policy, out of business. But through appealing to your guilt, they hope to evoke the mindless emotional response that will cause you to immediately conclude that there's a problem (before closely examining the issue yourself) and that their way is the solution, and your critical thinking faculties are lulled to sleep as you prepare to quickly satisfy your superficial conscience. The problem is magically solved; there's no longer any need to about the issue. This act of the "consciousness" promoters, as Thomas Sowell has written, "...is buying a good conscience or a good image with an I.O.U. to be paid by somebody else.

"Buy a piece of the art, or simply view it and do

nothing else, or write a letter to your legislator asking that person to advocate the Big Government/collectivist proposals or aiding the homeless, and you've done your part to solve homelessness!?

This approach only creates temporary momentary awareness of the problem, and will not, and can not, cause people take direct actions that would actually help the homeless people.   From awareness resulting from knowledge of the true problem, especially through knowing or being aware of individual people who are homeless, one can support legitimate private charities that spend the majority of their donations received on actually helping homeless people find housing, employment, education or training that would lead to employment, etc. A truly concerned person can contribute to colleges, universities, and training schools that provide people with opportunities to prepare for jobs or livelihoods that would economically and otherwise support a livable (as chosen by that individual) standard of living as earned by that individual.   Or one who has the time, money, and resources can actually provide these opportunities for some homeless people.   One can even support private organizations that help individuals in not becoming homeless and jobless.   I advocate direct help and supporting private organizations that do so because most of these charities are far more efficient than wasteful, bureaucratic government-run programs, meaning that they channel a far higher percentage of the available resources to the homeless individuals. One only needs to check the figures of the charity he proposes to donate to (and the efficient ones often keep their administrative costs less than one quarter of their annual receipts) and look into most government programs which spend most of their budgets on administrative costs.

The money made from selling this art was to contribute to efforts of advocacy on behalf of the homeless, much of which conducted by the sponsors of the show likely means lobbying efforts to secure subsidies for government programs. And the sponsors of the project clearly state that response from the government is exactly what they desire, as indicated in the statement from the introduction: "the legislature will remain quiet" unless they are pressured to spend the taxpayers' money on government programs for the homeless. After going through the act of blaming society for the problem, the art show sponsors expect taxpayers to fund such a solution to it, because the sponsors seem to believe that government programs are the only and most effective method of aiding individual homeless people. So thanks to the homeless advocates and the artists, your conscience should be relieved after you bought some of this art work, and having the pleasure of knowing that some of your tax dollars (which you could have otherwise chosen to allocate to private efforts if you hadn't been required by law to support such government mandated financial support of government programs) will be allocated to inefficient state programs that will likely treat the symptoms and not the causes of homelessness. But after two generations of government expenditures for welfare and housing programs, we have more homelessness than we did in the 1950's. Economist Walter Williams, in an essay he wrote, summarized the success of "Great Society" welfare programs. The official poverty rate was 14.7% in 1966, and 15.3% in 1983. As to why billions in welfare spending did not decrease poverty, Williams wrote, "We forgot that poor people are poor, but they're not stupid. Poor people respond to economic incentives just like the rest of us." Williams, quoting his statistics from a study by Professors Gallaway and Vedder of Ohio University, also demonstrated how state with higher benefits under the Aid to Families with Dependent Children (AFDC) program had increasing poverty rates, and those with lower AFDC benefits had falling poverty rates among children. He offered as examples: West Virginia, dropped from 24.3% in 1969 to 18.5% in 1979, and New York, whereas poverty among children rose from 12.7 to 19 in the same years. The AFDC benefits in New York are 90% higher than those of West Virginia.

In the case of this art show, the medium of art is used to promote a partisan political campaign, e. g. one that is designed to convince those who view the art to agree, without thoughtful consideration of problem and possible solution, with the philosophical and political agenda of the art show sponsors. It was displayed in the art gallery of a publicly funded University, the University of Maine at Farmington and one of the co-sponsors was the Maine Department of Mental Health and Mental Retardation, a state government agency. The tax dollars of Maine residents were used to help subsidize this campaign for increased government funding of homeless programs. Thomas Jefferson wrote, "to compel a man to furnish contributions for the propagation of opinions that he disbelieves is sinful and tyrannical." The sponsors of this program apparently saw no moral dilemma with spending public money pursue to pursue their political agenda.

The underlying support for using works of art to conduct political issue campaigns is the increasingly popular contention that "everything is inherently political." There are political explanations, and political effects, of what you ate for breakfast, if you ate anything for breakfast, according to the believers of "everything is inherently political." Not only is everything political, but politics is everything, we are supposed to believe. Politics is the ultimate aim and effect of all that we do.

That all our actions influence, and are influenced by politics, is true, but is politics the primary effect of importance of all human affairs? The light coming through the computer screen certainly generates a small amount of heat, but the important effect of the screen is to enable me to view the material that I'm producing on this computer. Likewise, politics is only one of many factors involved, and is often not the important factor (nor even a significant factor) involved in most human affairs

There is politics involved in business, economics, and international trade. There's politics involved in the local school board. In the town library. In the local art gallery. In the University. Politics is involved in all of them, but are they for the purpose of serving politics? Are all efforts for the service of politics?

Art is inherently political, the believers of "everything is inherently political" tell us, and as such, is supposed to serve politics. Art produced should depict the political issues and themes advocated by those who insist that art is inherently political in order to be judged as being quality works of art by the standards of such people, as opposed to the art being a work of unquestioned quality because it rises above the domain of debatable politics to inspire the person who views the works. Such politicized art must be every bit as political as the manifestos of political parties

And pop music singer Phil Collins recorded "Another Day in Paradise," which included slogan-type chorus lines about homelessness, which did, whether intended or not, have the effect gaining popularity due the to popularity of being perceived as being concerned with this issue. Some buyers may have believed they were satisfying their conscience by buying this album. And this is from the same man who apparently marketed his music to alleged "materialism" by naming his 1985 concert tour "The Hot Tub Club." The Irish rock band "U2" must support the politically fashionable causes, they must endorse Amnesty International, play in "Live Aid," "Farm Aid," and other events on the rock music political tour. The actors and actresses from fantasyland, USA, Hollywood that is, must also jump on the latest bandwagons. So they produce television shows such as Thirtysomething, Cheers, Wonder Years, and others that feature the trite values and issues of the new age of fashionably conceived social responsibility. After the celebrated Webster ruling on abortion by the Supreme Court that allowed states to restrict the availability of abortion, those seeking to be involved in the latest political fad had to get involved in the National Abortion Rights Action League. The Hollywood crowd also got involved in the organizing of Earth Day, the animal rights movement (including People for the Ethical Treatment of Animals, which equates meat-eating humans with serial murderer Jeffrey Dahmer), the Gay rights movement, and had to be the loudest in adding their shrill voices to the anti-war movement opposing President Bush's policy in the Persian Gulf.

Being political, and supporting the latest political fads, in the entertainment industry pays quite well. The "social critics" are (and have been since 1989) promoting the 1990's as the new era of "social consciousness" and "social responsibility," as another decade where fashionable politics will be the predominant theme, in the music, in the television programs, in all of pop culture, and the machine of American industry and American entertainment will be promoting the new values of the nineties, the values dictated by the gurus of fad politics.

And with help of the so-called critics (who seem more like advertising agents for the new political fads, and related industries), this new pop culture, through art and entertainment, will be spoon-fed to most Americans twenty-four hours per day. And this started in the late 1980's.

In concert with this new age of socially responsible fad politics, the younger generations are no longer being taught how to think for themselves, how to reason logically, how to make their own decisions, and will need to rely on the television advice shows, tips from MTV, the "Consumer" magazines, the instant public opinion and preference polls, and all of the sources of political fads in art and culture. And besides, with technology to help solve our problems and do our work for us, life will be easier if we won't have to think about it. And actual thinking will interfere with the life long party of feeling good for having let oneself get caught in latest public guilt trip of popular political activism, be it Live Aid, USA for Africa, Farm Aid, Artists for the Homeless, People for the Ethical Treatment of Animals, or whatever. Machiavelli warned that, "One who deceives will always find those who allow themselves to be deceived." Likewise, as we continue allowing ourselves to be used by pop culture to serve fad politics, the industries will continue to use us in this way.

The Clinton Era

"Several weeks ago I wrote of the "salami" effect. This is where "slice by slice" things change and no one notices until suddenly you look and realize, "My goodness, the salami is gone!" This is what has happened since the arrival of Bill Clinton on the national scene. "Slice by slice" public thinking and public acceptance of previously unacceptable behavior have eroded the nation's ethical and moral salami."

- John LeBoutillier, in a Newsmax.com commentary

I'll admit it right up front; I was against the election of Bill Clinton to the presidency from Day One. I can still remember, in the summer of 1991, while watching C-SPAN's "Road to the White House" and seeing a speech by Arkansas Governor Bill Clinton, the first I time I had both seen and heard this then possible candidate for the 1992 Democratic Nomination for president. Before I heard much about his record in Arkansas or his infamous nick-name, Slick Willie, I concluded this character was nothing more than a cheap but slick used-car salesmen-turned politician. I could just tell he was the type that would say whatever he thought would get him elected. The more I heard and read about him, the more my first impression turned out to look more and more true.

Clinton hasn't just been the most single-handedly corrupt and dishonest president in American history. He's been part of an entire generation that has seen politics and pop culture profoundly corrupted by the values and ethics of this president and the entire sewer of an administration he has surrounded himself with. Remember, this is the same president, who reacting to the minor scandals of the Reagan and Bush presidencies, said he would head up the most ethical administration in history. Once again, we see that was another one of his many dishonest promises.

Perhaps History will reflect on these years and point to the politicization and corruption of the Justice Department and legal system by this administration as its most enduring legacy. While most of the scandals of the Clinton Era will show this, I point to the disaster and cover-up of what took place in Waco early in the Clinton presidency, and Attorney General Janet Reno's Justice Department as case-in-point. I also highlight the legal mess, and ethical and moral abyss, of the whole Elian Gonzalez saga as another example.

The corruption, profound dishonestly, and complete hollowness of this era affected far more politically, and culturally, during the 1990s. Only during the Clinton Era would we see the Libertarian Party debasing itself by allowing the corrupting influence of blatant conflicts of interest surrounded by its current leadership and their favorite candidate, their 1996 and 2000 presidential nominee Harry Browne. For the party that bills itself "the Party of Principle," the Libertarian Party has quickly sold those principles down the river to satisfy the interests of the very few who've made a career for themselves in promoting the political career of Harry Browne, who has never held public office.

The politically and culturally poisonous aspects of the Clinton Era will be assessed and considered for years after the Clintons leave the White House. Clinton's Vice

*President, Al Gore, is the Democrat nominee for 2000
and Hillary Rodham Clinton has chosen New York to be
the state from which she wishes to be United States
Senator and future presidential candidate. Last time I
checked, the Constitution and its amendments says States
shall choose their senators, and not the reverse of that.
But this would be neither the first nor the last time one of
the Clintons would turn the Constitution, or the Bill of
Rights, on its head.*

China's Threats against Taiwan Warrant Swift Condemnation

March 27, 2000

The bullying of Taiwan via constant threats and provocations by China should not be tolerated in a community of nations based on respect for national sovereignty. While there is much speculation as to the real reasons (internally and otherwise) for the leaders of the Chinese regime to engage in this behavior, there is no doubt about its effects. Continued tolerance of this rogue behavior sends a signal to the outlaw states of the world they can play this game as well.

Only a few days before the recent election in Taiwan, Chinese Prime Minister Zhu Rongji warned Taiwan: "Let me advise all these people in Taiwan...Do not just act on impulse at this juncture, which will decide the future course that China and Taiwan will follow. Otherwise I'm afraid you won't get another opportunity to regret." These comments have followed months of clearly provocative acts, military training exercises by the Chinese military off the shores of Taiwan, etc.

A little history is certainly relevant here. During the revolution of the 1950s that brought the Communist Party to power in China, the previously ruling national party and many of their supporters fled to the island of Taiwan to escape the oppression of the communist system. They have since lived there as an independent sovereign nation. The United State, many other nations of the world, etc. have recognized Taiwan as such. But the Chinese communists (same ones who violently "liberated" Tibet, etc.) have always wanted to "liberate" the island and place it under communist control.

The Cold War is over in most parts of the world and most nations of the world are operating on the basis of post-Cold War assumptions. But that is not true of the few remaining outposts of imperialistic communism, places like China, Cuba, North Korea and perhaps one or two other nations. Imperial communists have no respect for the sovereignty of independent nations. They still believe all peoples of the world must be "liberated" from the capitalist system and blessed with the wonders of the "workers paradise" brought to them by Marxist-Leninist governance.

So while the Cold War is over, we also have to face the reality that there are few places in world still fighting the Cold War. That very different reality still requires a very different response. We need to make it clear that we will not condone acts of aggression against sovereign nations and that we will not tolerate these acts when committed against allies like Taiwan. We trade with China, having granted them "Most Favored Nation" trading status despite their atrocious human rights record (slave labor in their prison camps, jailing of political dissidents, etc.). Candidate Clinton criticized this policy in 1992 when he ran against President Bush, but he continued it President. Additionally, Clinton's 1996 campaign received large contributions from interests linked to Chinese industrialists who have directly benefit from that trading relationship.

At minimum, we can use relationship to insure the safety of Taiwan. While we may not be able to get China to clean up their internal human rights mess, we can at least insure they will stop their aggressive behavior toward Taiwan. The president needs to make a firm statement to the Chinese leadership: the aggressive behavior toward Taiwan ends now or "Most Favored Nation" trading status ends. It's as simple as that.

Let Elian and his Dad Stay, Send Janet STERNO Back to Cuba

March 12, 2000

Elian Gonzalez should be re-united with his father. I don't think anyone disputes that. But he should not be sent back to Cuba to live under Fidel Castro's communist regime. Both Elian and his father should be immediately granted U.S. citizenship and the issue ended right there. Fidel Castro is maximizing this whole controversy for its propaganda effect. We can quickly shut that down by granting citizenship.

The highest-ranking bureaucrat standing in the way of a sensible solution to this controversy is none other than Attorney General Janet "STERNO" Reno. Many of you will remember this is the same attorney general that in 1993 authorized the use gassing and frying of the 86 residents of Mount Carmel, the home of the Branch Davidians. Sterno order their murder via the use of cyanide producing CS gas, which our military is prohibited by international treating from using against our enemies in war. But Sterno saw no problem with using this poison on the women, men, and children, the law-abiding citizens of the Branch Davidians in Waco, Texas.

Janet Sterno also covered up the egregiously illegal fundraising practices of the 1996 Clinton-Gore reelection campaign by refusing to do the obviously needed task of appointing a special prosecutor to investigate that scandal. Janet Sterno presided over and failing to investigate and prosecute the criminals involved in the White House Travel Office crime, the illegal gathering of the FBI files on high-ranking Republicans by Hillary-hired Craig Livingstone, etc. Numerous books are being written detailing the numerous crimes of Janet Sterno in this administration.

Sterno didn't have to intervene in this case. The Immigration and Naturalization Service initially followed the applicable law and ruled in favor of Elian Gonzalez staying here. I am amazed that Sterno remains in office, but then against despite the over-whelming evidence, members of the United State Senate lacked the political will to convict and remove the most corrupt president we've had in this century.

Janet Sterno would have fit in quite well as a member of the Soviet politburo in the days Josef Stalin or Nikita Kruschev. She has exactly the right temperament and authoritarian ideology to fit in with the individuals I mentioned. Fidel Castro is nearing death or retirement, so the Communist Party of Cuba will need a replacement for him. I offer them Janet Sterno. She'll re-establish order in Cuba and subject anyone who disagrees to the gas and fry used in Waco.

Send Janet Sterno to Cuba and keep Elian and his family here. I think it would be great trade-off. We'd get two for the price of one and deport one of our most hardened criminals at the same time.

Fidel Castro: Our Psychiatrists are Ready to Get to Work on the Boy

March 15, 2000

Those are the exact words on Elian Gonzalez from the Communist Dictator of Cuba. No one has rights under the totalitarian government of Cuba. No parental rights or any other legitimate rights. Elian and his Dad will BOTH be wards of the STATE if they return to Cuba. They will have their lives controlled, and Elian's education, upbringing, and raising will be dictated by the state. One the key components of raising children under a communist government like that of Cuba is brainwashing them in the ideology of the state and reinforcing it with boot camp style child labor. Elian will be subjected to both if he's sent back to Cuba to be placed in the custody of Fidel Castro and his communist goons.

Castro's comment reveals the fact that brainwashing will be the highest priority if and when Elian returns to Cuba. Castro believes the most evil philosophy a child can be influenced by is freedom and capitalism. So they intend to counter this by indoctrinating Elian in all the glorious propaganda of the "worker's paradise" of the communist system. This is not simply the fate of Elian because his mother brought him to the U. S. by escaping Cuba, but it's the fate of all young boys in Cuba.

But Elian and his late mother are not the only ones seeking to escape the brutal Castro regime and come to the United States. Each year many others try and don't make it. Many makeshift boats filled with Cubans are sunk off the coast of Cuba by Fidel Castro's military. This policy is intended as a deterrent to others wishing to leave Cuba. Despite this, many Cubans risk their lives each year to escape a life of poverty and communism on that island ruled by the sick and demented dictator Fidel Castro.

The issue being debated here about whether Elian Gonzalez should be returned to his Dad is not the issue. If both of them go back to Cuba they will be under the custody of the state, and Fidel Castro. If one wants Elian to be under the custody of his Dad, that can only happen by his father staying here in the U. S. and raising his child here. In Cuba the state will be raising his child. That is true regardless of whether he realizes it or not. Given the nature of Cuban brainwashing, he probably doesn't realize the difference.

But those who truly do want what's best for Elian are well advised to remember what Fidel Castro has publicly said. "Our psychiatrists are ready to get to work on the boy." I'm sure they are. Give Elian and his Dad citizenship now and end this issue.

Clinton's Demagogic Gun Control Politics

May 16, 2000

Realizing he's been president for nearly eight years and lacks much of a legacy, Clinton is desperately trying to piece one together in his last year in the White House. Gun control figures prominently in these efforts. Having been a president who has always exploited tragedy for gains in his political agenda, the upcoming anniversary of the Columbine High School massacre finds Clinton shamelessly playing politics again.

Nearly a year ago the bullets were still flying inside Columbine High Schools from the terror of Harris and Klebold and politicians were already scurrying to find the nearest television camera to get before and call for enacting further restricting of the Right to keep and bear arms. Clinton and other supporters of gun control are quick to exploit bloody tragedy like this for political gain.

Gun control supporting politicians are always quick to exploit these tragedies. While it may have been badly distorted in characterization and quoted egregiously out of context, this is the issue that Wayne LaPierre of the NRA was attempting to highlight recently. He made the comment that supporters of gun control (including President Clinton) need tragedy and death to occur in order to advance their agenda. This was quickly misinterpreted to mean he was saying that Clinton and his allies WANTED such to happen.

And Clinton and other liberals were quick to put the politically correct spin on this and have their willing accomplices in the media promoted this mischaracterization. But spin doesn't change the fact that the gun control agenda does benefit when politicians and their allies use tragedy to advance their agenda.

Yesterday Clinton traveled to Denver in his latest effort to exploit the coming anniversary of the Columbine tragedy. The president and his allies are pushing to close the "loophole" in the Brady Bill to apply background checks to dealers selling firearms at gun shows. One of the students, who was injured last year at Columbine High School, spoke up against Clinton's call for additional gun control legislation, telling the president the proposal would have done nothing to prevent what happened there on April 20, 1999. Clinton backpedaled and admitted the student was right. Clinton knows this, but as usual, he's simply playing politics again.

Just a few days ago Clinton appeared with the governor of Maryland to celebrate that state enacting more restrictions against the Constitutionally recognized Right to keep and bear arms. The new legislation requires, among other restrictions, new handguns to have trigger locks on them. Once again, restrictions like this will do nothing to address the real issues of criminals using firearms to commit crimes. Does anything think a trigger lock will stop a criminal from using a gun to commit crime? It sure will prevent someone from defending himself against a criminal. Once again gun control legislation disarms the victim and makes it easier for the criminal.

Every single gun control proposal, including the banning of certain kinds of firearms, does nothing to make society safer or deter crime. But the politics of gun control aren't about addressing crime or making society safer. The gun control agenda is about disarming the public and insuring the government's ability to control people. It not ironic at all that Clinton and other liberal

Democrats who want increased government control over our day-to-day lives want to eventually reduce citizen gun ownership to zero. The best we can do, in advancing the pro freedom agenda, is to expose the demagogic politics of the gun control supporters and hope people realize why the gun control agenda needs to be defeated. The Right to keep and bear arms, as well as our freedom, depends on stopping this politics.

"What We Have Here is a Failure to Communicate"

June 21, 2000

Measuring and reporting so-called public opinion is a bizarre business. Pick up the daily papers and on any given day you're told the public agrees with this or disagrees with that or supports something and opposes something else. In an age of lazy journalism where polls alone are now "news" and detailed, well-researched reporting is rare, the daily news is filled with the result of surveys and polls. We the people are polled more often now than at any time in the past, yet most of us know very few people who've ever responded to a pollster. I'm not arguing polls are made up; I do believe most that reputable polling firms actually do call real live human beings.

What's more odd are the results of the polls and the communication involved in obtaining the results. Here's what I think is questionable about the conduct of many polls: the communication involved in asking the questions and obtaining the answers. Look at the results of polls on an issue such as the abortion controversy. Those organizations supporting the "Pro-choice" perspective, constantly release polling data showing the public agrees with their side. Pro-life organizations release poll results as well, claiming that public opinion is on their side. How can this be? Sure the public isn't both pro-choice and pro-life at the same time?

This exposes the "secret" of the polling industry. One can skew the questions in either direction to get the answer one wants. This may be done sub-consciously due to bias in the person drafting the questions. Also, it's easy to deliberately write the questions to get the desired results, if one chooses to do so. Ask people if abortion should be illegal and punishable by prison sentence for those performing abortions during the third trimester, and many would say no to that question.

Or ask if one supporting prohibiting the practice of partial birth abortion in the third trimester except to save the lift or health of the mother, and most will answer yes. Ask if all abortions should be illegal including criminal penalties for performing them and few will say yes. But if you ask should abortion be illegal except in cases of rape, incest, or to save the life or health of the mother, and most will agree. With slight differences in substance and larger differences in the communication of the substance, one can easily sway the public response to the survey toward one side or the other, and get the desired results. And then one can less-than-fully-honestly report that public opinion is in agreement with one's side of the issue.

Polling often leads rather than measures public opinion itself. I remember in 1992 the national economy was in a mild recession, according to most economists. But the media coverage of economics at the time was anything but mild. Immediately after the Gulf War ended the press heavily stressed the perception that President Bush had not done enough about the economy and needed to put more effort in that direction. As soon as reporters began asking in press conferences at the White House what President Bush planned or intended to do about the economy, the press started reporting related poll results as news.

The major networks hired polling firms to ask people if they thought, "the country is headed in the wrong direction" whatever that means. Reporters told us the question meant the President was leading the country in

the wrong direction, especially on economics. No sooner
did one of the networks get polling data showing more
than 50% agreeing the country was heading in the wrong
direction did the results make "news" in all the major
news outlets and networks. Soon after this I saw reports
of polls showing 60% or more of the public agreeing with
that statement, "the country is headed in the wrong
direction." As the media pounded this "story" in the heads
of viewers week after week more public opinion
followed, additional polling, and so on. By October of the
1992 the surveys were showing close to 80% of the same
public agreeing to that same statement.

It's no coincidence that most major newspaper and
television journalists themselves vote for Democrats for
President and mostly favor the liberal Democrat
perspective on issues. Surveys of journalists, including
those done by partisan liberal polling groups, have shown
this pattern. And so it goes, most times the major media
outlets report poll numbers on a major issue they claim
that a majority of the public supports the liberal view. The
public supports gun control, increased minimum wage,
affirmative action policies, and so-called national health
care legislation. Yet that same the public, or at least the
representative portion of it that votes, elected a
Republican majority to Congress that campaigned on the
conservative perspective on all those issues.

Why is public opinion so important anyway? If one
makes up one's own mind about the issues why does it
matter what others think about them? Maybe if we put
more focus on communicating our own views about the
issues based on our own careful study and thought we'd
be less concerned about public opinion. But many will
ask, "who has time to keep up with current events and
think about the issues?" I'll answer that by saying,

someone that doesn't want their life and their business
dictated by so-called public opinion filtered through the
media and enacted into federal law by politicians. If you
want to run your own life you can uphold that desire by
becoming informed about the issues and making sure the
press and the politicians know that your view is not going
to be dictated by so-called "public opinion."

Communicating your vision of society at the ballot box
by voting for candidates who do not allow media-created
"public opinion" to dictate their conduct helps too.

Who is Playing POLITICS with the Elian Gonzalez situation?

April 22, 2000

Spin is an amazing art and I continue to be astounded at how well it works. The Clinton Administration and their willing accomplices in the mainstream media spun this Elian Gonzalez issue so far out of recognition from the reality of the situation. The magnitude of the spinning that taken place would be like convincing the public to believe that the Tonya Harding-Nancy Kerrigan situation some years ago was the latter attacking Harding rather than what really happened. I know some won't like the analogy, but I wanted one most would clearly understand without using one from politics that would be more offensive to some.

There are numerous facts, that if one has the courage to face the truth on this issue, will show that it has been the Clinton Administration and their allies that have all along been playing blatant politics with this situation. Here are some relevant facts about this case:

** The Immigration and Naturalization Service (INS), following the Rule of Law, ruled last year that Elian must stay in the United States and award custody of him to Lazaro Gonzalez in Miami. Janet Reno over-ruled that decision and sided with Elian's Dad who is clearly controlled by the Fidel Castro regime.

** Clinton's Impeachment defense lawyer, Greg Craig, represents Elian's Dad and the Cuban side on this issue. That connection is not coincidence. These people believe in an agenda, and are clearly using the Elian Gonzalez case to further that left wing agenda.

** The Clintons paraded a so-called "expert" to claim Elian is in an abusive psychological environment as an attempt to justify the confiscation before it happened. They trotted out Dr. Irwin Redlener from New York as a "independent" expert on the matter. Well, it has been revealed that he's no expert, he's a practicing physician but he's NOT a licensed psychiatrist. Furthermore, his lack of independence, politically, is shown by the fact that he was a major supporter of Clinton's 1992 campaign, is a member of an ultra left-wing group called Physicians for Social Responsibility, has been an advisor on health care issues to the Clinton Administration, and served on Hillary Clinton's secret socialized medicine task force. One other important consideration regarding Dr. Redlener. Remember, with all of the resources at the disposal of the White House, they clearly could have found and obtained the best experts to make the case that Elian is not in the right environment with his family in Miami, if the facts supported such a conclusion. But realize that psychiatrists can lose their license to practice, and with it their careers, if they engage in malpractice and violation of the ethics of their profession. So obviously the best the Clinton administration could come up with is a single physician, who is not a licensed psychiatrists, to make this alleged "diagnosis" outside of his field of expertise and without actually seeing Elian Gonzalez. The important point here is, they could not find a legitimate and licensed psychiatrist willing to make the pronouncement that Elian should be taken from Lazaro Gonzalez without being subject to serious risk of losing his or her license to practice psychiatry. So the best they can do it trot out a old political hack who happens to be a physician who in this case it practicing psychiatry without a license.

** The 11th Circuit Federal Court ruled that Elian Gonzalez must stay on United States property until his legal rights via the court system are exhausted as they related to the political asylum petition he and Lazaro Gonzalez have filed. The administration actions, in taking Elian to return him to his Dad at the Cuban Interest Section in Washington D.C. has blatantly violated this court order. After the raid, Clinton himself said the action was consistent with the court ruling. I can't believe how much this man is so willing to brazenly tell huge lies of that magnitude. This is like claiming the sky to be green and that federal law backs up the assertion.

This administration has committed itself to the notion of sending Cubans back to slavery under Fidel Castro. They seem to think this is the way to establish better relations with Castro. The administration claims to be upholding the rule of law in this case, but they have undertaken an action that blatantly violates a federal court ruling.

We have an outlaw government in the White House in Washington D.C. This administration has done everything it could in some contexts to thwart the Rule of Law. This president has shamelessly lied under oath about his involvement and cover-up of numerous scandals, has lied while waving the finger to the American public when he said "I did not have sex with THAT woman Ms. Lewinsky" and blatantly committed perjury and told us "it depends what is, is."

This administration has gathered FBI files on high ranking Republican activists in violation of federal law and has used the FBI and IRS to frame and destroy the careers of non-partisan non-political White House Travel office employees who were fired because they didn't patronize a travel agency owned by Friends of Bill, Harry and Linda Bloodworth Thomason. This administration has just about put the Bill of Rights into a shredder and Clinton has signed numerous legislative acts that are clearly in violation of the first ten amendments of the Constitution. Clinton and Janet Sterno supervised, approved, and presided over the gas and fry of 86 innocent human being at Mount Carmel in Waco, Texas including 24 children.

The INS initially ruled in favor of keeping Elian here. No doubt his Dad could have come over here and stayed with his son, and both of them could well have applied for political asylum to escape the brutal Castro dictatorship in Cuba. All that Reno and Clinton had to do is let the original INS ruling stand. And when Juan Miguel Gonzalez sought to claim custody and return of his son to Cuba, he should been told he's also welcome to come to the United States and be re-united with his son HERE. Castro's own politicizing of this case could have been stopped right there.

But this administration joined the wrong side of this controversy and has subverted the Rule of Law to claim that law backs up his side of the issue. I guarantee you this sad spectacle would have never happened under Presidents Ronald Reagan or George Bush. But it has happened under this administration. It has happened under the presidency of the man who protested the Vietnam War while in the Soviet Union as a visiting student. It has happened under the president who inhaled far too much while in Oxford England "not violating the laws of my own country." It has happened, with blatant misuse of federal marshals by a president who has similarly improperly deployed our military, who in 1969 said he "loathes" the military. This chain of events has taken place in an administration that has appointed the most corrupt Attorney General to preside of the most blatantly partisan politicized cover-up oriented Department of Justice in the history of our Republic.

This administration is the lowest form of corrupt thugs, jackbooted goons, and cheap and debased low-rent fascists we've ever had in government. The Clinton administration is the most disgraceful in many decades and Bill Clinton's shameless and brazen playing of politics with the Elian Gonzalez case once again proves this.

Take Down the Statue of Liberty

April 22, 2000

Yes that's exactly what the title says. Take down the Statue of Liberty because obviously we no longer believe in the values that it stands for. Or at least it is clear our government lead by Janet Sterno of gas and fry at Waco fame and the first president to tell us it depends what is, is clearly doesn't believe in those values.

Whatever happened to "give us your tired, poor...yearning for freedom?" When did we a nation stop believing in the idea we'd be the beacon of hope and freedom around the world and welcome those wishing to join us in freedom by becoming productive citizens in a free society? When did we stop espousing these values and decide that we, a nation of mostly descendents of past immigrants, would pull the immigration ladder up behind us and tell people today to go back to their damned countries?

While it's the latest celebrated case, the Elian Gonzalez situation isn't the only issue from which our immigration policy has come under question. But the politicizing of Elian Gonzalez's plight is just the latest. I'm amazed at how many people think he should be sent back and would like to stop letting Cubans and other immigrants into the country.

One of the issues I hear people raising in connection to this is the claim that Cubans should not seek political asylum here in the United States but should over-throw Fidel Castro and his communist government instead. Well, I'd like to see some of these commentators and weekend warriors go to down to Cuba and try it themselves. Talk is cheap, and overthrowing the government, even a wimpy one like the Castro regime, is an entirely different issue. Let's remember we're mostly descendents of immigrants. My ancestors, some of them, came over here when people of Scotland were being taken over by the nasty British government. Should they have stayed and fought that oppression? The fact is they didn't, they came over to the "New World" seeking a new life. Cubans are doing the same thing.

Cubans and all our other generations of immigrants came here looking for freedom and a better life. That is exactly the reason why the mother of Elian Gonzalez so courageously risked her own and Elian's life to come over here and enjoy a better life. Few people realize that the "compassionate" Cuban government of dictator Fidel Castro orders its military to sink and shoot at boats and ships made by their own citizens attempting to flee the conditions in Cuba. Many Cuban citizens have lost their lives being killed at sea off the coast of Cuba by their own government.

In the Elian Gonzalez case, Clinton and his attorney general Janet Reno have sided with the Fidel Castro and against the Miami relatives of Elian Gonzalez. They have confiscated the boy and are aiding and abetting in the effort to send him back to Cuba where he will be placed in government custody in a state brainwashing facility immediately upon return to Cuba. Castro has already publicly stated, "our psychiatrists are ready to get to work on the boy."

If we as a country no longer are the beacon of hope and freedom we have no business keeping the symbol of these values standing. For those far too quick to misquote or quote out of context, of course I don't really advocate taking down the Statue of Liberty. But I do strongly believe our immigration policy should be consistent with that value that stands for. I say leave it up and take down our wall of anti-immigration policies instead. Welcome Elian Gonzalez and all like him.

We live in 1984 and not Year 2000

April 25, 2000

We, unfortunately, are living in a time where the facts and the truth don't seem to matter anymore. Too many people no longer demand to know the truth about what government is doing and seem to turn off and tune out anyone attempting to tell them. The mainstream media, for a variety of reasons, has blatantly failed in its responsibility to question those in authority. In our past history, even as recent as Watergate in the 1970s, the press viewed its role in exposing any hint of corruption, law breaking, and abuse of power by those in government. In the book 1984 George Orwell depicted how a government, excessively abusing its power to control citizens, would engage in media cover-ups and brainwashing to prevent the people from seeing what is happening. In year 2000 it's quickly becoming clearer we live in that reality.

The Waco Tragedy and the Elian Gonzalez Raid are just two of numerous incidents that prove this. In both cases the government used excessive force against peaceful law-abiding individuals. In both cases the government tried to control the media coverage and worked over-time to control the spin after the event. In both cases the government conspired to tell the people a bogus story about what happened, and did all they could to shift the blame to the victims of this abuse of government power.

Let's examine both of these cases.

The Branch Davidians were a group of peaceful law-abiding citizens living in the so-called "compound" they named Mount Carmel, which served as their home and

their church. Bogus charges of child abuse were leveled
with the help of psychiatrists obtained by Attorney
General Janet Reno. Local law enforcement officers had
previously investigated and found zero evidence of child
abuse. Bogus allegations of gun law violations were also
alleged. David Koresh was in the business of dealing
firearms and earned money doing so to help support his
family and the church community at Mount Carmel.

The rule of law was blatantly subverted. A bogus
warrant on gun law violations was obtained, but agents of
the Bureau of Alcohol Tobacco and Firearms "served"
that bogus warrant by shooting first and asking questions
later. Evidence highlighted in the documentary Waco –
Rules of Engagement conclusive prove the government
agents murdered dozens of members of the Branch
Davidians and started the fire that burned down Mount
Carmel. That film presented evidence that proved FBI
snipers fired at member hiding in the kitchen of Mount
Carmel during the fire. Many of these bodies were found
later with gun shot wounds. In this case, the government
subverted the rule of law and conspired in covering up
their lawless behavior.

The government's agents and their willing accomplices
in the media (including some journalists who were
blatantly biased as well as others simply too lazy to
conduct independent research) engaged a campaign of
smear and distortion designed to demonize David Koresh
and the Branch Davidians. Every day press conferences
were called to ridicule David Koresh, make fun of their
religion, and demonize them as a group with an
apocalyptic vision that would seek its own death in a
confrontation with the government. This was all
propaganda designed to sway public opinion in favor of
brutal government force and help the government not only

engage in murder but get away with it. Government agents, not the Branch Davidians, dragged out negotiations to give them time to demonize Koresh and get public opinion to swing they way. Blatant fear mongering was used to convince the public that Koresh's group and others like it are a threat to the public. David Koresh and his people, as the local sheriff said, were good people who threatened no one.

After the BATF and FBI agents had succeeded in murdering 86 citizens, including 24 children, they aided the government in a massive spin campaign to convince the public that what they did was justified. Evidence was destroyed. Congressional oversight committees asked for and did not receive evidence that would have proven government wrongdoing. Politicians and government officials peddled a story they knew to be a lie. They blamed the tragedy on the dead members of the Branch Davidians, claiming they started the fire and shot first when in reality the opposite has now been exposed to be true. They accused David Koresh of killing his fellow Davidians and setting Mount Carmel on fire when it was actually FBI agents who committed the murders and set the fire. The government committed murder and engaged in blatant misinformation and spin to cover it up. They reported an official version of the story, including a bogus movie parroting the official spin, all of which told the opposite of the truth.

Now let's consider the Elian Gonzalez Raid. The same thing happened all over again.

Janet Reno got former Hillary Clinton secret Health Care Task Force member, pediatrician Dr. Irwin Redlener, to engaged in practicing of psychiatry without a license and make bogus charges of child abuse against Lazaro Gonzalez. The Clinton administration refused to pursue the usual court ruling and procedures used in a child custody case and opted to carry out an armed Gestapo raid to retrieve Elian Gonzalez.

Before the Raid, government agents conducted a campaign to demonize Elian's Miami relatives and the Cuban American community. The same press who, in the same week, praised the violent protests of the World Bank in Washington D.C demonized the peaceful protestors in Little Havana. The government and their willing accomplices repeatedly carried the spin of the government and Cuban side while demonizing the Gonzalez family of Miami.

Local law enforcement agents were allowed to search the Lazaro Gonzalez residence twice the day before the raid and found no weapons there. But despite this, government agents justified the excessive use of force by knowing making false allegations of gun possession by Lazaro Gonzalez.

After the raid, the government and their willing accomplices in the press are working overtime to get the official spin put out. They are once again reporting polls and news and showing the results of the public opinion they've manufactured with this spin campaign. Based on lies and spin, polls after both events showed public opinion backing the actions of the government. In both cases the government subverted the rule of law, refused to allow due process relevant to each case, and engaged in brutal use of force. At least no one was murdered in the Elian Gonzalez Raid. In both cases the official spin covers what really happened. And in both cases, supporters of the government cite polls showing public approval of the actions. In both cases an aggressive media campaign was conducted with the obvious purpose of swinging public opinion in the direction of government spin.

The press used to take responsibility for its role as an independent outlet of information. The media used to expose government abuse of power. Apparently they don't do that much anymore. At least not when this administration, an administration of liberal Democrats, is in power. Most journalists have been shown by survey to be supporters of liberal Democrat candidates for president, and most of them are members of the "baby boom" generation. Clinton and Al Gore are the first liberal Democrats from the baby boom generation to become president and vice president. It has become more clear that members of the media have been willing to give this administration a free pass on the kind of scrutiny that Richard Nixon was subjected to by the press. Bill Clinton and his goons have engaged in actions that Nixon or Johnson would never have gotten away with.

In Bill Clinton's and Al Gore's America, we don't live in year 2000 but 1984.

Harry Browne: The Great Libertarian Con Artist

May 5, 2000

Harry Browne had a long career as an author of books and newsletters about investing and other financial topics. He also wrote a book titled "How I Found Freedom in an Unfree World," a cult favorite among Libertarians. For years, in spoken and written word, Browne urged his readers to remain uninvolved in electoral politics and politics parties, advising them such efforts would be fruitless in achieving freedom. By the end of 1994, he decided against his own advice and began his second career as a Libertarian politician. Having never run for political office, he decided his first campaign would be for the Libertarian nomination for the highest office in the Republic.

Harry Browne announced he would seek the Libertarian Party nomination for president in 1994 and believed (or stated so) he could win the nomination and create enough support for his candidacy to win the White House. All this from someone who had never even run for dog catcher while seeking the nomination of a political party that has never won an elected public office created under the Federal Constitution. The 1992 Libertarian candidate, Andre Marrou, had an idea that got him some great press attention. Knowing the tiny village of Dixville Notch, New Hampshire always casts their votes earliest on election day, Marrou spent considerable time there personally selling his candidacy to the voters in the town. During the 1992 New Hampshire primary, the same one in which Pat Buchanan shocked President Bush, Marrou gained most of the votes of the residents of Dixville

Notch, and his fifteen minutes (seconds?) of fame as well. Browne's advisers crafted a plan to have Harry Browne enlarge this concept to competing statewide in the New Hampshire primary. The idea was as follows: if Browne could poll more votes than some of the Democrat and Republican candidates, his candidacy would gain momentum, free media publicity, and enough national standing to almost assure he would be invited to participate in the debates with Dole and Clinton during the general election.

Browne played casino politics and gambled his odds in New Hampshire on a one-issue campaign. He based his entire appeal around the idea that the federal income tax be replaced with a national sales tax. While this sounded radical to many voters, it came across as a compromise to Libertarian activists who signed the party's pledge in opposition to all taxes. The Browne campaign would soon realize the idea failed to energize party activists, the much-needed backbone of any campaign for a candidate of any party. At the same time, Republican candidate Steve Forbes launched his New Hampshire campaign largely on the idea of a flat income tax. Realizing compete failure, Browne went back home to Tennessee and spent nearly the remainder of the campaign appearing on talk radio shows from his office.

On Election Day, Harry Browne polled barely one-half of one percent, or fewer than five hundred thousand votes. For a party that was founded in 1972 and showed rapid growth in presidential vote totals in 1976 and 1980, the 1996 Browne campaign was among the most well funded of Libertarian campaigns for the presidency while among the least successful of them. Simply put the Browne campaign was a complete failure for a candidate and a party that both talked about being major players on the national political scene.

By early 1997 Browne was already laying the groundwork for a 2000 presidential campaign. He sent out fundraising letters asking for donations toward a $1.5 million goal that he claimed would fund a $1 million media campaign for the 2000 election. The 1984 Libertarian nominee for President, David Bergland, ran for National Chairman of the Libertarian (with Browne's full support) claiming he would build a "Libertarian Party too large to ignore." The Bergland strategy for achieving this was a massive direct-mail campaign, to recruit new members, called Project Archimedes. Both Bergland and Browne all but promised including the party's membership, then around 25,000, to more than 100,000 by 2000. Both the party and Browne's presidential exploratory committee continually sent similar-sounding fundraising letters urging donations toward such efforts.

Direct-mail fundraising is quite expensive, but can raise large quantities of money when done professionally. North Carolina Senator Jesse Helms has raised many millions via direct mail through his National Congressional Club. But direct mail has never been successful for membership recruitment. The Libertarian Party (or at least some of its members) has learned this lesson the hard way. 2000 has arrived and Libertarian Party membership has peaked at just more than 32,000. Project Archimedes is a dismal failure. This abject failure is clearly the reason why Bergland, the party's nominee during its worst presidential campaign ever in 1984, decided not to seek a second 2-year term as LP National Chairman.

Straight through 1998 and 1999 the Browne exploratory committee continued raising money and

making grand promises about the large-scale professional
campaign that they promised to run in 2000. But many
party members questioned the 1996 campaign's excessive
use of high-paid consultants for a campaign that had a
very small budget and almost no media budget. One look
at the FEC disclosures of the 1996 Browne campaign was
enough to show the money was poorly spent at best and
the campaign badly mismanaged.

The 2000 Browne campaign has made the 1996
version look competent and effective. Browne chose the
height of the Gore-Bradley and Bush-McCain battles in
New Hampshire and South Carolina to officially
announce his bid for the Libertarian nomination for
President for 2000. The announcement was almost
completely ignored by the press. The usual campaign
books for a presidential candidate are normally released
early in the year of the election. During the open primary
in California in March, which was a chance for Browne to
show he could attract support, he was in a motel room
frantically finishing his already-way-overdue campaign
book for 2000. When the votes were counted, Browne
barely beat Lyndon LaRouche in the California balloting.
A third party candidate that can't out-poll LaRouche by at
least a 5-1 difference is one that is clearly marginal.

Browne's campaign continued raising money. Critics
within the Libertarian Party, including long time party
member Jacob Hornberger (who has twice been keynote
speaker to a national LP convention) continued
questioning the Browne campaign on how it had been
spending the hundreds of thousands it has raised since
1997. With a March 20 FEC filing deadline fast
approaching, Browne publicly announced a scheme to
forgo filing FEC disclosure, claiming he would challenge
the requirement of his campaign to file with the Federal

Election Commission. Critics instantly saw this as a way for the Browne campaign to ignore the questions about his campaign finances and trump the issue by portraying himself as challenging the government's regulations. Normally Libertarians would rally behind such a challenge, but many saw this is a cynical ploy to evade accountability for his campaign finances. Hornberger, who is also an attorney, warned that the party and the Browne campaign could face both civil penalties and criminal prosecution if it persisted willfully refusing to file with the FEC.

Jacob Hornberger has written and published damaging exposes of what he calls "interlocking conflicts of interest" in the national LP leadership and the Browne campaign. Basically the same small group of people runs both the national party offices and the Browne campaign and the same dummy companies and owners of them are constantly being paid, reimbursed, or other recipients of hundreds of thousands of dollars in money from both the Browne campaign and the Libertarian Party. Hornberger's articles can be read at www.jacobghornberger.com.

Several days ago the Browne campaign finally releases information on its campaign finances and showed just more than $1.2 million raised and spent with a debt of more than $80,000. The campaign that was supposed to raise $1.5 million to have one million for a media campaign burned through more money than that, spending most of it on overhead, consulting fees, and staff salaries. Less than a quarter of the money funded media publicity for the campaign and more than $300,000 of it went to campaign manager Perry Willis and his unregistered company Optopia Productions. At best the money was (once again) very poorly spent, at worst it appears the money was used the line the pockets of a few Browne campaign staffers, including Willis.

Browne and Bergland blatantly engaged in The Politics of Personal Destruction, launching sleazy personal attacks, via e-mail, against Jacob Hornberger. While not attempting to answer any of the issues contained in the Hornberger articles, Bergland and Browne lobbed character assassination against the messenger. Bergland's piece stooped so low as to make devious suggestions about Hornberger's use of the nickname "Bumper." Browne's response histrionically accused Hornberger of attempting to destroy the Libertarian Party as well as Browne's campaign.

Browne and Bergland have talked big ideas and delivered very little. They've shown themselves almost inept at party building as well as campaign organization and management. They've tarred the reputation of their party by engaging in sleazy, negative, character assassination politics against their critics.

After announcing the FEC scheme, the Browne campaign spent more than $25,000 printing a dishonest fundraising letter claiming to solicit $25,000 in contributions to pay attorneys for a legal opinion on the FEC challenge. Hornberger stated that far less money would hire an attorney with expertise on FEC regulations to issue advice on challenging FEC regulations. All indicators suggest this fundraising attempt was a dismal failure; it was the last solicitation from the campaign before it announced it was $80,000 in debt. Most Libertarians viewed the idea skeptically. Many Browne supporters questioned the wisdom of challenging FEC regulation when surveys showed most Americans desire more, and not less, regulation on campaign financing.

When it become clear the FEC scheme was a disaster, the Browne campaign announced it would file with the FEC and disclose its finances. Showing the campaign in debt, it sent out yet another urgent request for money, claiming the campaign would end if money did not come rolling in again. Magically, within days, the campaign claimed it had received pledges of $50,000.

Claiming this was enough to resume campaign operations, the Browne campaign said it was back on track, but still needed more money. How a campaign in debt for $80,000 can then be back in operations with $50,000 is beyond me. If most of us paid our bills this way we'd be homeless and bankrupt. But the Browne campaign rolls on, seemingly focused primarily on one goal: raising money. Despite showing poor results failing to register even one percent in any national polls, the Browne campaign continues to ask for money.

For all its money the Browne campaign can not buy a respectable campaign effort. For all their donations, Browne supporters haven't bought a respectable candidate either. They bought into continued appeals by a mediocre investment-advice-writer-turned politician who clearly realizes he's nearing the end of his second career. If the Libertarian delegates nominate Browne once again this coming summer, it will prove they are willing to bet their party's future on a candidate whose already shown himself to be a scam artist.

What is Freedom: Who Needs Enemies with Friends like These? Harry Browne's Sleazy Politics against the Arizona Libertarian Party

May 14, 2000

Harry Browne, the 1996 Libertarian Party nominee for president, wants to once again be that party's nominee for president in 2000. If he obtains that nomination, he also wants your vote in November. But Browne talks a good game, makes grandiose promises to supporters (especially the ones that send him money), and fails to deliver, and then engages in slick spin to "explain" to us how his failures are actually successes. And if you dare criticize him, Browne will show you he and his minions can practice the Politics of Personal Destruction with the best of them.

Those in the Libertarian Party know about legendary "division" in the Arizona Libertarian Party by having heard from either the right side or the wrong side of this dispute. Those of you in the LP and those who have nothing to do with the LP can now know the truth about this situation, coming from someone who is not affiliated with either faction in the dispute. This account of the situation in this article is the closest you'll get to a fair, impartial, but true and accurate telling of this story.

The story of the Arizona LP is what happens to those who cross Harry Browne, and his minions, and get in the way of their attempts to control the Libertarian Party and what little money it has. In 1995, Harry Browne began campaign for the 1996 Libertarian nomination for President. Some Libertarians considered Browne somewhat a celebrity, having been an author of several books about politics and investing. But many Libertarians distrusted Browne for a variety of reasons including claim he would moderate his politics and stray from Libertarian principles. Rick Tompkins, state chairman of the Arizona Libertarian Party, was also seeking the 1996 LP nomination for president. Supporters of the two candidates battled for control of the Arizona Libertarian Party for most of the 1990s.

Browne defeated Tompkins for the LP nomination in 1996 and his allies took control of most of the National Libertarian Party offices. Traditionally a decentralized party based largely on state and local organization, Browne and his allies in the national leadership, Steve Dasbach and Perry Willis, sought to change that focus to the national level. Efforts were made to move control of party affairs to the central office in Washington D.C. Willis and Dasbach devised a plan to use direct mail for membership recruitment called "Project Archimedes." At the same time, Browne began (in 1997) a parallel effort to build LP membership and raise money for a 2000 presidential campaign. Both of these efforts, run by the same people, focused on one main goal: raising money. Project Archimedes was supposed to raise national LP membership from 25,000 to 200,000 between 1997 and 2000. As of May 2000 national LP membership has peaked at 33,000. Project Archimedes has been a disaster, but it has made a lot of money for those employed by the LP in the direct mail business. And the "those" in this case is a firm called "Optopia Productions" which is really an unregistered business legally known as Perry Willis doing business as Optopia Productions.

How does this all relate to Arizona? Easy, those who get in the way of the Browne money machine will be destroyed. The Browne money machine supported David

Bergland for national LP Chairman in 1998, he was elected over Gene Cisewski, a critic of the Project Archimedes scam. How was Cisewski rewarded for his disloyalty to the party establishment? He was with a bogus SLAPP suit based on trumped up charges of misusing the LP mailing list in fundraising for a Libertarian PAC he was running that raised money for Libertarian candidates. The lawsuit has caused Cisewski to quit politics and has bankrupted his organization.

The other major target of the Browne money machine has been the Arizona Libertarian party, formerly headed by Browne's 1996 challenger, Rick Tompkins. After the 1996 election, the Browne faction began a long effort to try to gain control of the Arizona Libertarian Party from the Tompkins supporters who dominated and made up the majority in the ALP. Failing to win control legitimately at state conventions, the Browne supporters created a parallel organization called the Arizona Libertarian Party, Inc. Note the only difference in name is the "Inc." at the end of it.

Now that they succeeded in creating a "new" LP in Arizona, they began a battle to have this one recognized over the original Libertarian Party of Arizona, the ALP. They filed in state courts to get this done, and the Arizona Courts sided with the legitimate Arizona Libertarian Party and against the imposters. Failing at all levels in court, the Browne supporters sought a decision from the Libertarian National Committee. This one was far easier, because they were preaching to the choir. The LNC was made up of mostly Browne supporters, who would have no trouble seeing which side of this dispute their faction wanted to "win." So the LNC used membership lists made up mostly of ALP, Inc. membership lists and staged a "poll" asking which party should be the "real" Libertarian Party of

Arizona. Given the way it was jury-rigged, the results should surprise no one. They disaffiliated the legitimate Arizona Libertarian Party and then voted to grant affiliation to the Arizona Libertarian Party, Inc. The latter was the group loyal to the Browne campaign. The latter was the group that violated Libertarian principle and sought court rulings in their favor and against the legitimate Libertarian Party of Arizona. In all of those court rulings, the ALP was recognized as the Libertarian Party in Arizona, not the ALP, Inc.

So the coup was completed, and approved by Browne's minions on the Libertarian National Committee. But the Browne campaign could still pay the price for this bit of sleazy politics. The Arizona Libertarian Party, recognized by the Arizona Secretary of State's Office as "The" Libertarian Party, controls the presidential nominating process for placing the LP presidential candidate on the ballot in Arizona.

If the ALP, which is no longer affiliated with the National LP by LNC decision, chooses to nominate a different candidate as the presidential nominee of the Libertarian Party, and the convention in Anaheim this summer chooses Harry Browne, the Browne campaign might have to spend valuable time and financial resources obtaining ballot access in Arizona. And, Browne might have to run, as an independent against another Libertarian in Arizona, since his faction, the ALP, Inc. does not have ballot status in Arizona as the Libertarian Party. It will serve Browne right. His people caused this mess, and he'll be the ultimate political victim of it. He'll deserve it too. With friends like Harry Browne to divide the party, Libertarians don't need enemies.

Apply the Knight Standard of Justice to Bill Clinton

May 16, 2000

After an investigation of allegations against Indiana University basketball coach Bobby Knight, the university placed him on probation and warned the further similar violations will lead to his dismissal. Knight, who as won three national championships, has also shown excessive outbursts of temper and was accused of a few incidents of abusive treatment of players. Many among the public wanted Knight fired. But this is the same public, of which a majority if the polls are to be believed, wanted Clinton to escape any punishment of any kind for the allegations he faced in the United States Senate impeachment trial last year.

Coach Knight faced allegations of highly improper behavior, but Clinton faced a convincing criminal perjury charge that was based on his lying about allegations of behavior far worse than anything alleged against Knight. Sexual assault by Clinton, and his covering it up by perjuring himself is a far worse display of criminality then anything Knight may have done. Just about every single Republican in the House of Representatives found the four articles of impeachment convincing enough to vote for them. And the vast majority of Republicans in the Senate heard the evidence and voted to convict Clinton. If enough Democrats had been willing to vote for a conviction based on clear evidence Clinton had committed perjury, justice would have prevailed. And it would not have "overturned an election" because the elected Vice President Al Gore, not Bob Dole, would have become president.

Many of the same U.S. Senators who voted to acquit Clinton is engaging in perjury to cover up his sexual harassment also voted to block the confirmation of Supreme Court nominee Clarence Thomas in 1991 based on far less credible allegations. In 1991 staff members of Senate Democrats on the Judiciary Committee leaked out FBI documents regarding allegations against Thomas by Anita Hill. Soon after the committee held hearings which conclusively showed Hill's charges to be without credibility. Yet many of the 48 Senators that voted against his nomination in 1991 were still in the Senate in 1999 and voted against convicting Clinton on the far more convincing of perjury.

It would be reasonable to suspect that neither Clarence Thomas nor Bobby Knight would get away with a fraction of what Clinton has done. Under the probation handed down by the committee at Indiana University, Knight will be fired if he engages in the alleged behavior one more time. Democrats refused to look at the evidence acquitted Clinton. Those same Democrats intentionally and knowingly tried to push for a bogus slap-on-the-wrist censure resolution knowing it would never happen. Yet they got nothing from Clinton, neither a sincere apology for his behavior nor any statement of assurance that he would not do it again. What did Democrats reward the Criminal-in-Chief with after his display of criminal behavior? Acquittal, and Al Gore calling him the greatest president of this century.

It is beyond my ability to understand why anyone would want to vote for these people. I do not understand why more among the public, who demanded the Coach Knight be fired, didn't demand that their Senator vote to remove Clinton. That is past. There is only one way to uphold justice and end the Clinton era once and for all.

Apply the "Knight rules" to them, and send a clear
message they've abused our trust several times too many
already. Need I mention just a few of the scandals?
Whitewater, Waco, White House Travel Office, White
House FBI files, and those are only the scandals
beginning with W. Vote against Al Gore and Hillary
Clinton (if you live in New York) and end the Clinton era
once and for all. Maybe the committee that looked into
the charges against Bobby Knight should take over for
Ken Starr.

No More Clinton Bashing

June 22, 2000

No need for "Clinton bashing." Just read the words spoken by Clinton.

"African-Americans watch the same news at night that ordinary Americans do."
Bill Clinton, being interviewed on the Black Entertainment Network

Remember also, that Bill Clinton cynically engaged in divisive politics with his use of the "Sister Souljah" comments on shooting white people.

*****

"If I catch anybody using the State Department like that [searching files] when I'm president, you won't have to wait till after the election to see them gone...I just want you to know that the State Department of this country is not going to be fooling with Bill Clinton's politics, and if I catch anybody doing it I will fire them the next day; you won't have to have an inquiry or rigmarole or anything else..."
Bill Clinton, November 12, 1992.

How many FBI files did Craig Livingstone have access to in the Clinton White House?

*****

"When we got organized as a country and we wrote a fairly radical Constitution with a radical Bill of Rights, giving a radical amount of individual freedom to Americans, it was assumed that the Americans who had that freedom would use it responsibly...there's a lot of irresponsibility. And so a lot of people say there's too much freedom. When personal freedom's being abused, you have to move to limit it."

President Bill Clinton, 3-22-94, MTV's "Enough is Enough"

"We can't be so fixated on our desire to preserve the rights of ordinary Americans ..."

Bill Clinton; USA Today, March 11, 1993, p. 2A

Clinton has worked harder than any other president in our History to limit the freedom recognized by The Bill of Rights.

*****

"The Bush administration continues to coddle China, despite its continuing crackdown on democratic reform, its brutal subjugation of Tibet, its irresponsible export of nuclear and missile technology... Such forbearance on our part might have made sense during the Cold War when China was the counterweight to Soviet power. It makes no sense to play the China card now when our opponents have thrown in their hand."

Gov. Bill Clinton, Georgetown University, December 12, 1991.

Which president has coddled China the most, sold us our national interest to Chinese business interests for campaign dollars from people like Charlie Trie, and has authorized the selling of nuclear-related computer technology to the Chinese?

*****

"Yes, the president should resign. He has lied to the American people, time and time again, and betrayed their trust. Since he has admitted guilt, there is no reason to put the American people through an impeachment. He will serve absolutely no purpose in finishing out his term, the only possible solution is for the president to save some dignity and resign."

12th Congressional District hopeful, William Jefferson Clinton, during the Nixon investigations.

*****

"I will not raise taxes on the middle class to pay for these programs. If the money does not come in there to pay for these programs, we will cut other government spending or we will slow down the phase-in of these programs. I am not gonna raise taxes on the middle class to pay for these programs."

Bill Clinton, presidential debate, 10/19/92

"To middle-class Americans who have paid a great deal over the last 12 years and from whom I ask a contribution tonight..."

Bill Clinton, announcing the largest tax increase in history, State of the Union address, 2/17/93

The first budget proposed by this administration, and passed in the Senate with Al Gore's tie-breaking vote, raised taxes on the middle class to pay for their new programs.

*****

"I will have the most ethical administration in history!"
    Bill Clinton; Nov. '92

    His administration employed the most special prosecutors and independent counsels in our History.

*****

    And lastly here's a real kicker...from his Slickness...

"The road to tyranny, we must never forget, is the destruction of the truth."
    Bill Clinton, University of Connecticut, October 15,1995
    I guess really does depend what is, IS.
    What else is left to be said?

The Truth about Waco

April 9, 2000

Our government murdered 86 innocent human beings in Waco on April 19, 1993.

The facts prove this to be true beyond any plausible doubts. In February of 1993, agents from the Bureau of Alcohol Tobacco and Firearms (ATF) arrived at Mount Carmel Center (home of the Branch Davidians) to serve a fraudulent and bogus warrant for alleged violation of gun laws. Local law enforcement agencies had investigated the group for suspicion of alleged child abuse and found no evidence for the charge. The ATF brought dozens of agents to "serve the warrant" and available evidence proves the government agents fired the first shots. In response some of the Branch Davidians took up arms and lawfully defended themselves. That action unfortunately killed four ATF agents but the blame for those deaths rests with the government whose agents fired first. Additionally, a Texas court jury acquitted the 11 surviving Branch Davidians of murder. The jurors found they had lawfully defended themselves against the gunfire of ATF agents. This confrontation set up the conditions that would ultimately lead to our government murdering 86 innocent human beings in Waco on April 19, 1993.

The ATF was facing budget hearings in Congress and reduced funding because of past embarrassments of the agency, such as the criminal activity ATF agents engaged in at Ruby Ridge. They needed some great publicity to gain public approval and pressure the politicians to increase their funding. The Congressional hearings would later reveal that the agency had computers, fax machines, and phones set up on the scene to publicize the February

1993 raid but agents were unable to call an ambulance after ATF agents were shot in the crossfire. This vile government agency was so bent on publicity to shore up its public image it failed to provide ability to call 911 for its own injured agents. The ATF is just one of the groups of jackbooted thugs that murdered 86 innocent human beings in Waco on April 19, 1993.

By March of 1993 the FBI took over for the ATF in handling the situation at Waco. While the FBI negotiated with David Koresh the FBI and ATF conducted a public relations campaign designed to demonize the group. On a daily basis their religious views were ridiculed by public relations agents for the ATF and FBI, who also deliberately set the tone for the press coverage by calling the group a cult, calling their building a "compound," etc. Despite the existence of FBI and other studies showing Koresh was psychologically stable the agencies mounted a well organized media campaign to portray him as mentally unstable and a threat to the public. The FBI and ATF propaganda campaign used the "stockpiling of guns" claim to convince the public the Branch Davidians were a threat to the public. The fact is they were a threat to no one. They were "stockpiling" weapons because Koresh had been involved in the trade of weapons for nearly a decade. Making a profit as a legitimate gun dealer was one of the ways Koresh and his people earned income. But the government agents knew they had to demonize the group, and stir up public prejudice against them in order to get away with what they did later. The publicity campaign made possible for them to murder 86 innocent human beings in Waco on April 19, 1993.

When one member of the group left the building and surrendered to agents, leaving her husband behind in with the Branch Davidians. One FBI agent told her that she had probably seen her husband for the last time. At one point during the FBI negotiations with David Koresh and member Steve Schneider, they were asked how many fire extinguishers were in the "compound." They said one, to which the FBI agent suggested they get more. One another occasion one FBI agent was caught making a comment about whether the Branch Davidians had fire insurance. Clearly from these comments, the agents knew the building would be set on fire. That government set fire lead to the murder of 86 innocent human beings in Waco on April 19, 1993.

Early in the morning on April 19 the FBI agent began pumping thousands of gallons of CS gas into the Mount Carmel building. CS gas is so deadly, international treaties which the United States has signed and ratified prohibit its use against foreign enemies in war. The CS gas was injected into the building as part of a chemical combination that is deadly when ignited. That combination, after set on fire, produces the same cyanide gas used in death penalties carried out via a gas chamber. After the building was filled with gas most of the women and children of the group attempted to hide in a concrete storage room behind the kitchen of the building. FBI agents realized this, and used one of the tanks to poke a hole in this box and pumped the gas inside that area, effectively asphyxiating the members inside it. After having filled the building with gas and poke holes in many of the areas of the building the FBI agents shot detonation devices in at least two corners of the building to set it on fire. One survivor has testified to seeing a ball of flame streak through the front of the building at the same time infrared footage showed a FBI tank shooting an incendiary device into the corner of the building where the fireball originated. Our government set this fire and murdered 86 innocent human beings in Waco on April 19, 1993.

An airplane flying well above Waco covered the raid and fire using what is called Forward Looking Infrared (FLIR) camera, the same technology the U. S. military uses for nighttime operations. FLIR measure thermal energy rather than light. The FLIR footage as shown in the documentary Waco Â– Rules of Engagement clearly shows both tanks and snipers firing at the building for several hours on April 19. It is clear that those members who did try to escape the fire in the area of the kitchen were likely to have been shot by two FBI snipers shown by the FLIR shooting automatic "machine guns" in that direction. Autopsies showed that two dozen members of the group died from gunfire wounds. The FBI repeatedly claimed at the time and in congressional hearings that they never fired one shot. At the time they claimed the gunfire wounds were self-inflicted by group members. Yet the FLIR evidence clearly shows FBI snipers firing in the spot which was the only possible exit for the Branch Davidians otherwise trapped in the kitchen. This is just more evidence that our government murdered 86 innocent human beings in Waco on April 19, 1993.

It is clear to me that FBI agents were intent on one thing after the death of the four ATF agents in the February 1993 raid: revenge. They sought to make an example of the "cult" members for the deaths of the ATF agents in crossfire that occurred after ATF agents showed up at Mount Carmel shooting first. That revenge would be the murder of 86 innocent human beings in Waco on April 19, 1993.

Regardless of what crimes, if any, David Koresh might have committed, the Constitution and The Bill of Rights recognized his right of innocence and the right to a trial by a jury of his peers. But the agents of the FBI decided to act as judge, jury and executioner of not only Koresh but also the other members of his group. They murdered 86 innocent human beings in Waco on April 19, 1993.

As shown in Waco – Rules of Engagement the FLIR footage was professionally analyzed by Infraspection Institute, an organization that usually performs FLIR analysis for the Department of Defense. This evidence conclusively and without a doubt proved the FBI fired numerous shots from both tanks and snipers at the Branch Davidians before and during the fire on April 19, 1993. The television program 60 Minutes had access to this footage and the analysis. But because of fear of negative repercussions (probably involving future D.O.D. contracts) Infraspection Institute discontinued involvement in analyzing the Waco evidence and 60 Minutes did not complete nor air the story. This evidence being shown in Waco Â– Rules of Engagement shows that our government murdered 86 innocent human beings in Waco on April 19, 1993.

During the congressional hearings many pieces of evidence came up missing. FBI bureaucrats simply refused to supply the congressional committee with the evidence they requested. Immediately after the fire was put out the FBI removed the evidence. Member of the Texas Department of Public Safety testified that this is very irregular and goes against standard law enforcement procedure for handling a crime scene. There's no doubt in my mind this was a cover-up designed to keep the public from finding out that our government murdered 86 innocent human beings in Waco on April 19, 1993.

On April 14 the negotiations between the FBI and David Koresh reached a breakthrough point that made clear a peaceful settlement of the standoff was imminent.

But clearly the FBI didn't want a peaceful settlement but instead wanted to carry out the death and destruction that was in the plans for weeks. Despite knowing about this breakthrough in the negotiations, or perhaps because of it, the FBI decided it would not wait another day and conducted the raid on April 19, just 5 days later. The evidence is overwhelming. Our government murdered 86 innocent human beings in Waco on April 19, 1993.

Note: I would urge everyone to rent Waco – Rules of Engagement at a local video rental outlet and watch this documentary. Also, dial up www.waco93.com for more information on this.

Video Vertigo in the Elian Gonzalez Saga

May 2, 2000

The media spin on this case has been truly amazing. The reactions I've seen from many people on this issue are truly amazing as well. Lots of people are both sick and tired of hearing about this or simply don't want to accept the facts of what has happened. Unfortunately we live in a society that seems to care more about bread and circuses then what kind of society we live in. The government of Bill Clinton and Janet Reno has subverted the Rule of Law and has conspired to forcibly deliver a child that came to the United States to the dictator of Cuba.

The State Department and numerous human rights groups have cited the Castro regime for numerous human rights abuses. Yet despite that, our government appears to have made some kind of under-handed deal with Fidel Castro that requires we send this child, Elian Gonzalez, back to slavery in Cuba. And polling data seem to show most people either not caring or wanting to know what is really going on, or maybe they simply lack the interest and/or the courage to face the facts of what's going on. It is not easy to look at the facts, face the truth, and conclude that we have an outlaw administration in the White House that has flagrantly subverted the Rule of Law.

A whole lot of this is due to the heavily spin-laden and clearly biased media coverage. The media has bought into a lie on this case and is part of the conspiracy to tell you the lies, along with the same government that authorized the brutal Raid in Miami to steal Elian from his great uncle in Miami last Saturday. There are three casualties of

this saga. First the most obvious is the child, Elian
Gonzalez. The truth is a casualty of this, and setting the
precedent that government can get away with something
like this again and successfully lie to you about with, with
their willing accomplices in the media, means government
will be more willing to engage in further outlaw actions in
the future. And lastly, the Rule of Law has been
subverted. The more we allow the government to subvert
the Rule of Law, violate valid and established legal
precedents, procedures, and court precedents the more the
government will do as it please regardless of who's rights
are violated.

If you value freedom and your rights, you ought to be
very concerned about what's going on here. Regardless of
whether you think Elian should be with his father or his
relatives in Miami, you ought to be concerned about how
this process has been carried out. Regardless of whether
you think immigration should be legal or illegal, and
whether or not Cubans should be allowed to immigrate to
the United State, you ought to be concerned how the force
of government has been used to subvert the Rule of Law.
When these same people in government, or future ones,
use this process to violate the laws or procedures that
protect your rights or interests, you'll quickly realized
why and how you should have been concerned about it in
this case. The more we allow this kind of abusive
government action, the more it will happen.

Now are reasons for what is going on the media isn't
telling you about, otherwise it would be more difficult to
convince you of the bogus spin they're promoting. There's
a May 11th court date coming up soon where Elian's
petition for political asylum is supposed to be heard. This
is basically the process where Elian, as an immigrant, will
seek to gain eligibility for citizenship on the basis that he

would be subjected to human rights abuses if sent back to Cuba. Clinton, Reno, Fidel Castro, and their attorney, Clinton's impeachment attorney Greg Craig, realized weeks ago they could not allow this court date to come and have Elian assert his rights as an immigrant to seek political asylum. The media is not telling you this, because then perhaps you would realize THIS is the reason why these people are subverting the Rule of Law to prevent themselves from losing out to the hearing of Elian's rights in a court of Law.

Last week the 11th Circuit federal court ruled that Elian Gonzalez has legal rights that entitle him to the political asylum hearing and the insurance of those rights requires he stay here and not be moved to Cuban property or custody. This court ruling was blatantly violated by the actions of the government since last Saturday. There is one clear reason why they snatched Elian from Lazaro Gonzalez's home in Miami. They wanted to obtain control of him to begin the brainwashing of Elian and get him to (with coaching, of course) say he wanted to go back to Cuba with his father. Today's news claims that such a statement was made.

In response, one of the judges of the 11th Circuit has issued a request of Janet Reno asking why the court should not appoint an independent counsel to represent the interests of Elian Gonzalez that have been blatantly violated by her Department of Justice and subordinate government agencies. Yet this blatant transgression of the Rule of Law and the court's effort to get this outlaw administration to respect the Rule of Law get no front page attention in the major media. Instead we get bogus "feel-good" re-union stories from the father and attorney Greg Craig who have been in control of Elian since the Raid.

What's important here concerning legal rights is the court ruled that Elian Gonzalez has legal rights separate from that of his father, and his father's attorney Greg Craig. Yet Craig is seeking to nullify those rights by being named the legal representative of both the father and Elian. Craig has filed a motion to deny Elian of independent representation and claim himself as the legal counsel for Elian Gonzalez. It should be clear to anyone open minded enough to face the facts that this is an attempt to once again subvert the legitimate law and court rulings relevant to this case.

But against these facts is all the media spin. Usually such egregious use of government force and excessive violations of process spur most journalists to demand to know the truth or the government ought to be brought down in shame if they engage in this kind of subversion of the Rule of Law. The same people who would never allow the Nixon administration to get away with a "third-rate burglary" and an attempted cover up have given the Clinton Administration a free pass to operate as they see fit. It is astounding how much the press ignores from this administration that it would have scandalized beyond belief if any of this had happened under Ronald Reagan or George Bush.

And yet we are told that most people don't care. We're told that by the same media spinmeisters backed with bogus manufactured polls that the people don't care about this issue. They say ignorance is bliss. It's a shame that ignorance isn't painful, because maybe more individuals would open their minds and have the courage to be informed, look through the media spin, and face up to what is going on in this country. And maybe then, and only then, will more people get out to the polls on Election Day and make the needed changes. Either that or we can continue to be governed jackbooted thugs and media spinmeisters who make it up as they go along and tell any lies that are needed to get away with anything they want to do.

The media is supposed to scrutinize every action of the government and keep it honest. And when the government is engaging in clearly outlaw actions, the press should be the first to expose this and inform the people about what's going on. That is the responsibility of the media. But instead the press, via most major news reporting outlets, is lazily carrying the government's spin on this and many issues. We need to face up to what's happening and refuse to continue tolerating any more abusive government actions.

There's much more at stake here than Elian Gonzalez and whether he goes back to the dictatorship of Fidel Castro in Cuba. What's at stake here is what kind of society we'll live in, and whether we allow our government to operate with reckless abandon, violating legal rights and subverting the Rule of Law. If this is the kind of society you want to live in, then simply do nothing, and keep enjoying the bread and circuses. Those who remain in denial might realize, perhaps far too late, what has been going on.

Economics and Taxes

Who can oppose the notion that every individual should be assured a minimum but adequate economic standard of living? That is the question posed to us by the ideas of left-wing liberal economic ideology. We conservatives are not against this basic idea, but we disagree profoundly on how to arrive at this result. Leftists and socialist think passing a variety of laws and programs that seek to assure such a standard of living will somehow, magically, make it happen. But this is simply magical thinking, because laws and programs have not extended any standard of living to all citizens of any nation that has undertaken any extended experiment in socialist, egalitarian economics as advocated by leftist liberals. Those who wish to bring about true economic prosperity find socialist economics lacking, and seek an economic model that works.

As always, if one wants to find what works, one should simply look at what works, naturally, as opposed to that designed and put in place, by force, by human beings. The most natural and effective economic ideas known to human beings are those of capitalism. While socialism is an economic ideology, and a political one, capitalism is neither. Capitalism is simply a term used to describe the conditions that exists when human beings traded, quite naturally, products and services and forms of currency with others for yet other forms of products, services, and currency.

A free market, another term for that which exists naturally under capitalism, is every bit as natural as the weather. Heavy-handed attempts by government and its agencies to regulate the free flow of goods and service in the market have the same consequences, as would attempts to regulate the weather, if human beings had the power to do that. Disrupting the natural process exacts a large price. We pay that price in the form of higher prices, fewer products and services, inflation of the currency, and in general a lower standard of living than would otherwise be enjoyed if the free market was allowed to work.

Government and its corporate allies have concocted all kinds of ways to intervene in the otherwise natural and effective functioning of the economy. Big government and big business, through their incestual relationship, have weaved a web of relationships and economic arrangements that often makes is a challenge to figure out what institutions and corporations and agencies are controlling what and whose controlling them. The moves to deregulate industries, and bring about true free market competition, can sometimes look like attempts to undo a scrambled egg. But more of us will realize, before too long that we must move away from the statist-corporatist model of the status quo and to one of respecting the free market and getting government out of the way.

Economic Fantasy and Economic Reality

June 1999

Clinton and his willing accomplices in the media tell us every day how good the economy is. Around this time of the year they cook up the standard bogus story where they find some obscure place in the country to claim college graduates are instantly taking 60K jobs after getting their freshly minted BA degrees. Of course the media did exactly the opposite when they didn't like who occupied the White House, under Bush, Gore said it was the worst economy in 50 years and the evening news interviewed college graduates who couldn't find jobs.

But let's look at facts, that article shows that savings is at an all time low. This is a fact about economics that government can't manipulate and lie about. Personal bankruptcies, are also at an all time record high, and for the last 4 years, personal bankruptcies have set a new all time record each successive year. Again, this is a factual number that government can't manipulate and lie about, and it's a sure indicator of our economic condition. But what measures are we told prove this great economy we have? Inflation rate, the government re-defines that to suit the purposes, adding and subtracting which commodities are included in the consumer price index to produce the statistical outcomes desired. Administrations of both parties in the post Jimmy Carter era have done this to make inflation look lower than it really is.

Jimmy Carter's high inflation was in part due to honestly reporting it. Every other administration since has learned from that lesson, and realized that re-defining is the way to go. Job creation? Pure fiction. Rush Limbaugh exposed the practice of "bias-factor jobs," which is basically you're Robert Reich you believe these jobs were created, you have no empirical evidence for it, so you just add them in anyway, and say these number of jobs were created in such a period of time. Clinton goes on says "we've created 18 million new jobs." The Bush and Reagan administrations did this, but the Clinton administration raised it to an art form. Overall growth rate, that's subject to re-defining too, because the government controls the reporting of economic numbers. If we privatized that function, we'd get accurate numbers, and we would truly know what the economic conditions are.

But our true economic decline is measured in these facts:

** Two-parent families, where both work, are at an all time high. Many instances the second paycheck merely pays the taxes for that family.

** Personal bankruptcies are at an all-time high, and have set new records for the past four years.

** Savings rate among American citizens is at an all-time low.

** Our last two periods of economic growth were fueled by consumer spending, most of which was financed by credit. Our last couple recessions were caused by downturns in consumer spending, because people had to pay off the credit cards.

** The government spends a large portion of the GDP than it ever has, and that is only growing. Still growing,

Clinton said the era of Big Government is over, it has only given way to the era of even bigger government.

The colossal crash is on the way, get ready for it. You'll own what you actually own and what's in your hands, and the phony baloney paper funded completely by credit and made up money economy will crash into a black hole.

Targeted Tax Cuts Enough to Buy Twinkies

April 19, 2000

Remember 1992 when Bill Clinton, calling himself a "new Democrat" was campaigning for the votes of the "forgotten middle classes" and advocating middle class tax cuts? His rival for the nomination, former Senator Paul Tsongas saw right through this gibberish and argued Clinton was playing "Santa Claus." Tsongas calculated the impact of the Clinton middle class tax cut and announced it amounted to about a dollar per day for most affected. The late Senator from Massachusetts was right about the hollow nature of Clinton's promises.

In its actual implementation the "middle class tax cut" become the Earned Income Tax Credit (EITC) that was enacted in the 1993 Clinton budget that passed by one vote in Congress and Vice President Gore's tie-breaking vote in the U. S. Senate. An individual taxpayer, at low enough income levels, can get back a maximum of $347 from the EITC. As you can see, Tsongas was right. That's about a dollar per day.

Al Gore is proposing more such targeted tax reductions this year. The problems are both in the approach as well as the size of these kinds of tax cuts. Most revenues generated by income taxes are derived from the "middle classes." There's a simple reason for this, most taxpayers are in the middle classes because there are truly very few very wealth and those on the lowest income brackets are exempted from paying income taxes. So when the government needs more income tax revenue, there is only one way to get that revenue. The middle class will pay more taxes, either hidden taxes or the more obvious forms of taxes. And any real and substantial middle class tax cut would require the federal government to reduce spending by a substantial amount. That has not happened in the lifetimes of most living American citizens.

First, the "targeted tax cuts" reveal the basic philosophy they are based on. The main premises behind this is simple: the money involved here is THEIR money (the politicians) and they think they're being nice enough to give you back a pittance of a buck a day of money you've already paid into the system. They're quite generous aren't they? This is exactly why you hear Democrats, and some Republicans, asking advocates of larger tax increases, "how do you propose to pay for those tax cuts?" Tax cuts are not "paid for" unless one has accepted the premise that this money is owned by them and they are doing the paying when you get a tax cut. Fact is, this is the money of those who earned it and paid it in, and tax cuts are simply the individual getting a few bucks back after the government has borrowed it interest free all year due to payroll deductions.

The other major premise of this approach is the basis of the targeting. By giving you back a few bucks of what have earned and paid in, assuming you meet certain qualifications, they have decided you deserve to get your dollar per day. But the key here is politicians are deciding they know best, who should get tax cuts. This goes along nicely with the other major premise and stems from it, that the money is the property of the politicians instead of those who earned it.

In the end, the "targeted tax cuts" approach perpetuates a system that believes it controls your money, and how much of your earnings you'll keep, and ultimately would like to decide or influence how you'll spend your money.

Maybe where Bill Clinton comes from in Arkansas a dollar a day is a lot of money. But for most of us it's a joke. But in Arkansas, it's enough to buy a six pack of Old Milwaukee beer and a box of Twinkies every week.

Government Economic Statistics are Exponentially Dishonest

April 24, 2000

I've been saying for years now that official government statistics on the economy are lies. Ever since the Carter Administration was defeated at the polls due to the recession of the late 1970s the government measures of economic conditions have been changed to make report better looking economic statistics. The Clinton-Gore Administration has raised cooking the books on the economy to an art form. Throughout much of our history voters have blamed politicians for economic recessions. Like meteorologists who would take credit for having brought about good weather, politicians have always been quick to credit their policies for good economic growth. While politicians can't control weather or economics, they have figured out how to control the reporting of statistics on one of them. If reelection depended on it and it was possible, politicians would tell us we have sunny and warm weather even on days when it's cold, damp, and raining.

One economic statistic that is very much prone to manipulation by the political hacks in the labor department that makes these up is the consumer price index, or as it's informally called, the inflation rate. The old way of manipulating this was to simply take some factors out of calculating the index so the resulting number will be lower. If oil prices rise too fast, then taking that out of the index makes inflation look lower. This is one of the oldest ways the statistics were abused by politicians looking to make the economy look better than it really is and then convince voters their policies should be given credit for the "great economy."

But now they have a more underhanded and deceptive way to manipulate the official inflation measure. In a NewsMax.com article by Christopher Ruddy and Ryan Troup, government is exposed for using "geometric weighting" to adjust the consumer price index. Ruddy and Troup cite economist John Williams of the Shadow Bureau of Government Statistics as the source of this information.

Geometric weighting is a fancy term for the government statisticians ignoring real inflation. For example, as prices rise and consumers in higher number purchase less expensive generic products, government statisticians estimate this factor and essentially use this as the basic to "figure" that that product has fallen in price. Or if consumers purchase products that are better made, use more advanced technology, etc. without paying a higher price, this factor is entered in as the prices of those products in effect falling. These tricky methods of entering in lower prices in some parts of the consumer price index make it easier to conceal much of the real inflation. Ruddy and Troup estimate that real inflation is probably double what the government officially reports. I've been telling people this myself for years.

Government has made lying about economics statistics quite a business. During the first term of Bill Clinton, Rush Limbaugh exposed how the Clinton Department of Labor used an estimation technique called "bias-factor jobs" to basically claim job creation that can not be shown to have occurred. Most of the 18 or 20 million "new jobs" Clinton claims his policies have created are pure fiction, or as his Dept. of Labor calls them, "bias-factor jobs."

Lying is a bad habit, especially when it works. Because, when it works the liar will be tempted to do it more, and more and yet even more. That is the case with the government's lies on economics. They started with small adjustments, then favorable changes in the definitions, and more on to more deceptive and dishonest methods. Under this current administration they've come up with techniques like "bias-factor jobs," "geometric ratings," and other re-definitions of the statistics to exponentially lie about the current state of the economy. James Carville said, "it's the economy, stupid" in 1992. If he really knew what the Clintons were going to do with statistical reporting on economics, he might well have said "it's the lying about the economy, stupid."

"Most People Don't Pay Taxes"

April 17, 2000

In what I think was an attempt to explain the lack of political support for lower taxes, Rush Limbaugh said today on his program, "most people don't pay taxes." While I think he was referring to federal income taxes given today's day (April 17, official IRS tax day since April 15 was Saturday), this statement is not true about income taxes and less true about all other forms of taxation.

Citizens will usually object to knowingly paying excessive taxes. Of course the word is knowingly. The Boston Tea Party was in part caused by the King's attempt to collect excessive taxes. But politicians have become far better than the King was at hiding the taxes from the people. Most taxes we pay now are so well hidden few people realize how much we pay in taxes. But, WE ALL PAY TAXES, and we all pay a whole lot of taxes and don't know it.

First consider incomes taxes. I hear people talk about whether or not they are "sending money in" or getting a refund from the IRS around this time of year. A lot of people don't realize that, other than the few literally paying no federal income tax and/or getting money from the Earned Income Tax Credit, all others have actually paid a lot of money into the Federal Income Tax already. Payroll deductions have allowed the Federal government to borrow that money from you, interest-free, during all of last year despite it now being due until today. The fact that you showed a negative or positive balance at the bottom of your 1040 simply means you either get a little back from what was already taken from you and borrowed interest-free. Or it means the IRS is telling you to send in even more above and beyond what they've already had your employer send them. But for many people perception is reality, and this system has created the perception that people have been getting money from the government. By taking money from those who earn it and then refunding a little of it back, the politicians have created a scheme that hides the greater amount of money being taken. The far more obvious annual refund makes a lot of people think they actually get money from the government rather than pay taxes.

But most other taxes are far more hidden. Sales taxes are visible on the cash register receipt but I think few people worry much about the few cents-on-the-dollar in sales taxes. Then there are other taxes, such as "sin taxes" on liquor and alcohol, excise taxes on a variety of property, property taxes on real estate (which are VERY hidden for renters who indirectly pay them), taxes on investments dividends and savings account interest, etc. People often don't realize they spend money that has been taxed several times, including tax on taxes.

Corporate taxes are very hidden for most of us as well. Corporations don't grow money on trees, so the only way they pay their taxes is getting the money from the customers who purchase the products and services. WE also pay these taxes as part of the price at the cash register. Since corporations purchase products whose prices are raised by these taxes, the prices we pay at the cash register have been increased several levels by taxes.

Regulations are the other major source of hidden corporate taxes that increase the prices of the products and services we purchase. In the last 40 years Federal and State governments have imposed all kinds of needless, expensive, destructive and unconstitutional on businesses.

Regulations require all kind of policies and practices having no relation to the activity of businesses that increase costs and reduce the number of productive jobs created by businesses. The true cost of all taxes and needless regulations on the prices of products and services may account for as much as HALF the prices we pay. That is, in effect, a hidden tax and it is in addition to the sales taxes added at the cash register.

Un-funded mandates on individuals are also hidden taxes. What am I talking about, you ask? I'm referring to any law that requires you as an individual to spend money in ways you may or may not choose otherwise. State laws requiring you to purchase auto insurance, rather than self-insuring, are a classic example of this. Auto insurance is far more expensive in states where it's mandatory than in states where purchase of auto insurance is optional. Mandating its purchase, and strictly regulating its price, removes the market incentives to hold down the price. Additionally, the mandate itself attempts to force you to send your money to the insurance companies for a re-distribution scheme where those who don't have accidents finance the large bulk of the costs of those very few who do cause accidents. But this is just one example. There are numerous instances in which the individual is told by the state to purchase certain products or services. These are hidden taxes as well.

Any time you are told by the state where to send your money in these days, you are being taxed. As a means of keeping we the people from revolting against excessive taxes the politicians have gotten quite good at hiding taxes. It just means we need to do our homework and be more aware of just how much we pay in taxes and make yet more effort to keep more of our own money and property.

The New Economy is the New High Tech Sweatshop

April 19, 2000

We are in denial about the true reality of our current economic situation. There are a number of reasons for this, most of them center around the interests of the current administration in convincing us we have a booming economy and that they are the reason for this supposedly booming economy. But facts say otherwise. I've covered in a previous column how the federal government engages in fiction about economic measures, and in doing so masks any attempt to accurate measure our economic circumstances.

We are led to believe that our standard of living has increased. But actually, many citizens enjoy a standard of living that has decreased. Unless you absolutely love what you do for work and choose to work long hours to achieve future goals in that pursuit, you probably find more enjoyment and fulfillment in what you do in your leisure time. In that sense a major factor of quality of life can be measured by how much leisure time you have while still earning a living, unless you're fortunate enough to earn a living doing the same activities that you would choose to do in your leisure time. Additionally, quality of life can be measured in part by what you get paid for that activity that you receive compensation. If you receive benefits and such with it, that increases your quality of life, or if you receive additional compensation with which you can purchase the same benefits, that counts as well. These are the basic concepts I am discussing here in connection to the reality about our standard of living as it relates to the current economic situation.

Now here are some facts. Real wages and income of the "middle class" has remained stagnant over the last decade. And this fact itself somewhat masks an even more relevant fact, that many of those individuals and families are working longer hours at lower-paying, less benefits jobs than they did ten years ago. So what that means is, to match the income they made a decade ago they work more hours for what is less money (adjusted for inflation) while having few leisure hours. That is, objectively, a LOWER standard of living. And many of those people are working at jobs with fewer or no benefits at all, which means bad news if high medical expenses are incurred. If you lack medical insurance coverage and don't earn enough money to purchase it, a recommendation of surgery by a doctor is not a major medical decision but could also get you a trip to the bankruptcy court after recovery. Personal bankruptcies have been at an all time high this past decade and the number one reason for those have been medical expenses that were beyond the ability of the individuals to repay them.

Clinton claims to have created 18 million jobs during his time in office. This statistic is quite dubious, but it masks the true nature of what kinds of jobs are being created. Clinton critic and self-described progressive Democrat Jim Hightower, former politician in Texas, says he knows people who told him about these jobs. Hightower mentioned on the Larry King Show how a friend told him, "Clinton created 18 million jobs, I have three of them." This is important because it is one example. I know a number of people who work at two or three part-time jobs that pay no benefits and low wages to make ends meet. This is because most of the jobs of this so-called new economy are part-time, no benefits, temporary jobs.

Temporary you ask, what does that mean? The largest growth over the last decade has occurred in the sector of the temporary employment agencies. As a result of the actions of union bosses, government regulations, taxes, etc. corporations have hired fewer permanent, full-time employees and more part-time employees and those from temporary agencies.

The nature of the work has changed as well. I personally know many that have worked in a variety of jobs in the "new economy." The recurring themes are repeated far too often to be just isolated examples and not a picture of the real trends out there. Work is becoming increasingly repetitive and mundane, employees are often given the appearance of involvement in decision-making while actually being afforded less say over their work conditions, and employers are getting far better at paying lip service to real problems while doing absolutely nothing about solving them. So while the standard of living for the "middle class" is declining the working conditions are declining as well.

The picture here is more members of the "middle class" spending more time doing mundane work for less money and few benefits. This is the reality of an increasing percentage of the jobs of the so-called service sector, or as it is called, the new economy. To paraphrase the rock group The Who, this is the new economy, same as the old economy. Satisfying a materialistic society's desire for more bread and circuses requires the continued production of more widgets and more low-paid "factory" workers to pump out the widgets.

The new economy isn't the realization of the American Dream. If this trend continues, it's the death of the American Dream for most. The first generation in American History, so-called Generation X, to enjoy a lower standard of living than their parents might well produce yet another generation that will enjoy an even lower standard of living then their own. Social scientists tell us that economic standard of living and freedom are inter-related concepts. If you think this trend doesn't have important implications for our future, think again. The brave new world might yet be coming in our future.

More Economic Reality for Those in Denial

April 21, 2000

Today's news includes yet more fiction about economics, this time in regard to unemployment figures. My local paper included an Associated Press re-printed story on the front page with the blaring headline titled, "Jobless claims continue dip."

Government and their paid economists have been in the business of making excuses for poor economic performance for longer than most of us realize. The problem goes back to the earlier history of our republic. When we allowed the federal government to begin engaging in the business of regulating and managing the economy we also began to place expectations on the government regarding economic performance. Many of us now starting to realize this approach was a mistake. Not only does government managing of the economy not work very well, it becomes yet another subject of government lies. As I covered in another article, the same government that lied to us about Watergate, lied to us about the Vietnam War, lied to us about the Whitewater scandal, etc. also lies to us about the economy. The reason for the latter is real simple, they tell us the economy is good so we don't hold them accountable for poor economic performance at the ballot box. And many journalists both unable or unwilling to find objective data fail to do their homework and willingly report the government's economic lies as if they were facts.

Inflation and unemployment are two of the major economic indicators used by the government and the press. The statistics on both of the are also subject of rampant manipulation by government economic agencies.

The AP article claims government statistics showing jobless claims down to lowest level in 27 years. What it does not tell is how this measure is almost worthless as an indicator of reality. Again, let me explain.

The main reason one files with the local unemployment agency is to receive unemployment benefits while looking for the next job. These benefits are generally paid from an employer funded, government regulated trust fund to those that have been either laid off or unjustly terminated from full-time employment. Employees that quit know in most cases that they're not eligible so they don't apply. Workers who've been employed in temporary, free-lance, contract, or a combination of part time jobs are not eligible and do not file. Those who are not making enough money to make ends meet in their numerous (in some cases) part time jobs are not eligible to file. You see, there are millions of citizens not experiencing the "prosperity" of the current "economic boom" who are also not measured by unemployment statistics.

As I've covered in another article, most job creation that is taking place right now is part-time and temporary employment. The temporary agencies have been the sector of most rapid growth during this current economic expansion. That is why I say that temporary sweatshop work, with low pay and no benefits is truly what the New Economy is all about. The many millions of citizens stuck in low paying jobs are not counted among those who filed for unemployment benefits, and are rarely covered in reporting on current economics in the major press.

In the article, someone from a consulting firm is quoted as making the statement that perhaps the economy is creating more jobs than then there are in demand. Of course this is ludicrous. If this were true there would be NO UNEMPLOYMENT claims. But millions are still filing jobless claims every year. So obviously there are a large portion of our citizens not enjoying this "boom economy" we are so fraudulently told about.

Near the end of the article some more telling facts were revealed. That last week a total of 257,000 citizens filed for unemployment benefits, which it claimed was down 9000 from the previous week. Assuming the accuracy of those figures, that means about one million citizens file unemployment claims each month. That's at least 12 million per year. And given that probably at least as many (if not more) than those who do, do not file such claims, one can reasonably estimate there are probably at least 25 million unemployed citizens each year. This is just unemployed at one time; it could be for a week or unemployed the entire year. Does anyone want to take up the government's spin and tell me this is not a whole lot too many unemployed people?

So the facts and the claims simply don't add up. We have millions of citizens not making enough money to pay off their bills, working two or three part time jobs to make less money then they used to earn at one full time (with benefits) job. Yet we are told the economy is creating more jobs than then there are workers to take them. But how do you explain the millions filing for unemployment? We can get this answer by looking at how many people have to take on the jobs of the "New Economy."

The information is out there for those who are willing to have the courage to face reality and stop believing the government's lies about economics. And for those unwilling to face these facts, simply look at those among

your friends and family members. Most of us know
people who are among the many who've been
unemployed for long periods of time looking for work in
an economy supposedly creating more jobs than available
employees.

Do Not Underpay the IRS by One Penny

April 27, 2000

The Gestapo tactics of the Internal Revenue Service (IRS) are another sign of the times. Don't even think of underpaying your tax bill by one red cent or the IRS will really make you pay. This is especially true if you're in business. The IRS seems to really like to screw small businesses.

This latest case regards Valley Glass Co. of Roswell, New Mexico. The company paid $28,153.93 for fourth quarter taxes, but the IRS claimed the business was supposed to be paying $28,153.94. That's right, IRS agents said Valley Glass Co. owed them one more penny in taxes. I'm not making this up.

Being such a egregious violator of the tax laws and having so flagrantly evaded the paying of that one last cent, the IRS nailed Valley Glass Co. IRS agents demanded the payment of this unpaid balance and related penalties, fees, and collection costs. The company incurred an additional $500 in accounting costs to comply with the IRS request to send in an additional $286.50 in penalties and fees as well as the one cent in unpaid taxes.

Clearly the time and effort wasn't spent because it insured one more penny would be paid in taxes. Any agent in the office could have taken a penny out of one's pocket and call it paid in two seconds. But the penny under-paying allowed them to tack on a ridiculous level of late charges, penalties, and fees that no private sector collection agency would get away with in collecting a legitimate balance owed on a debt. Basically, unlike any other bill collector, the IRS can set its own collection fees, penalties, late charges, and interest. These excessive fees become a license to make up false accusations of tax evasion and simply steal more money from individuals and businesses.

A couple years ago, Congress had showcase hearings on IRS abuses and many egregious cases of blatant IRS abuse of taxpayers were exposed. But in the end, nothing was done to fix the problem. And the IRS got the last laugh when Congress voted to increases their budget. It amazes me that we put up with this nonsense. But it shouldn't.

Former Congressman George Hansen of Idaho found out what happens when an elected official challenges the authority of the IRS. Hansen, elected to Congress as a conservative Republican, actually took very seriously the numerous constituent complaints about IRS abuses. After making serious efforts to reform the IRS, he found himself being audited and investigated by the IRS. Having always paid his taxes, he did not think he had anything to worry about. They found absolutely nothing to charge him with in connection to his tax returns.

But a technical error was found on one of his filing with the Federal Election Commission, which was later trumped up into a bogus felony fraud charge, which last I heard he was cleared of the charges. But the bad publicity caused him one close call at the polls then a defeat in his following reelection bid. It sent the message clear across Capital Hill, members of Congress: "do not cross the IRS". At least not if you wish to be reelected. The message was clear: No member of Congress has mounted a serious challenge to the IRS since Hansen.

Karl Marx Praises Our Efforts at Centralized State Planning

May 15, 2000

Hillary Rodham Clinton claims to have conversed with Eleanor Roosevelt while serving as head of the secret health care task force during 1993. Likewise, I've had such a conversation with Karl Marx. I asked him what he thought of the current state of U.S. politics. This is his response:

America is very much headed in the direction of equality and social justice. Progressives know that insuring a minimum standard of living for all citizens is the most important goal of a government policy in pursuit of economic democracy. The key to effectively implementation of an egalitarian agenda is successful central planning. Where other attempts at social democracy have failed, the United States has been far more effective. The U.S. system is not perfect but if far more effective than any previous attempts.

I'm impressed with how the government has, over the years, convinced the public to accept centralized planning, and the information gathering necessary for it. I've been very impressed with the Census Bureau advertising campaign this year. It quite effectively shows why the information sought by the bureau is needed to effectively administer the numerous federal programs that distribute billions of dollars that provide all the vital government services you've come to expect in a modern democratic society.

I especially liked the radio advertisements featuring dead air space that used this as a metaphor for blank census forms. A number of government programs that improve the lives of all depend on this information. As the advertisement says, the census is your future, don't leave it blank. I'm especially pleased that subtle appeals to patriotism are effectively employed to drive home the socially responsible message of the census campaign.

Sure there are many areas of improvement I could point out as well. But the fight for social justice is a long struggle, and I congratulate the United States for having made great progress over the last seven years. There is still great inequality of income but at least the poor are less poor than they were ten years ago. Now if the problems of homelessness and regional poverty could be solved the conditions would be vastly improved. But I have confidence the progressives in the Democratic Party will continue to pursue these goals.

To continue moving toward true socialism, the best that American citizens can do this year is to fill out their census forms, vote for liberal Democrats, and elect Al Gore president this Fall.

Some Parents Sacrifice the Interests of their Children for Materialism

June 2, 2000

Many families where both parents work full time find themselves needing the extra incomes to fund an excessively materialist lifestyle. They would be better suited to be less concerned with purchasing fewer material goods and working few hours while spending more time with their children. The then president of Boston University, conservative Democrat John Silber, made this argument in 1990 during his campaign for governor of Massachusetts against liberal Republican Williams Weld. The comment was brand a "Silber Shocker" by the press, which was the name used to refer to several controversial statements made by Silber that helped propel his campaign to victory in the Democratic primary, and almost won him the governorship.

Many households where both parents work full time, the second parent must do so in order to earn money to pay their taxes while the first parent's income pays their bills. The Libertarian's candidate for Vice President, Nancy Lord, pointed this out on the campaign trail in 1992. Just last year I saw a report on Dateline NBC about such two-paycheck families that demonstrated how the "marriage penalty" in the income tax code causes most of the second paycheck to go into tax payments.

You might wonder who is right in these statements, John Silber or Nancy Lord. On the surface they sound contradictory. But they are not. Both statements are right, because both are part of the trend both candidates saw, and because the two of them were referring to different households. Campaigning in the largely upper middle class areas of Massachusetts that made up the "swing votes" in the 1990 campaign, Silber saw many cases of families where the first pay check could clearly support the family if they chose to live more frugally. So his comment was meant to convey the idea that the children would be better served to have a lower material standard of living with more personal attention from their parent. I don't think anyone, when faced with the issue in those terms, can disagree that quality time with the parents can not be replaced by any amount of material goods. You can't replace attention to your kids by buying them stuff.

Nancy Lord, on the other hand, campaigned in many lower middle class areas of rural America where clearly two paychecks was needs to pay the mortgage and finance a modest and frugal lifestyle of many parents. Talking to families she realized that elimination of income taxes would allow the second parent to work many fewer hours to make ends meet and spend much more time with their children. In short, the income taxes levied on middle class household cause the parents to work longer hours while spending less quality time with their children. Again, I don't think anyone would argue that this is not a good thing for the future health of our children and the future of our society. It is the reason why many advocate large tax reductions for the individuals and households considered "middle class."

The federal income taxes, that started at less then 4% originally, have grown to as high as 39.6% in cases because politicians can not stop recklessly spending the money. The result of that is a lower actual standard of living for millions of families and their children. But government is a reflection of society. Many among those individuals and families who are well off can not stop spending money excessively on material goods they don't need either. In many instances the excessive spending went on credit cards which are paid by both parents working full time. And those families pay way too much to income taxes as well. The combination of income taxes and paying off those high credit card bills keeps those parents from spending as much time with their children as they should.

For individuals who want to take the talk about "family values" seriously they can make the obvious choices. Living more frugally, although easier said then done, means spending more time with the children. For politicians who talk the family value talk, they can pass large middle class income tax reductions that will allow parents to work fewer hours and spend more time with their children. At a time when more people working longer hours in more part time jobs for lower hourly rate is called a "booming economy" it become obvious to myself and others that we should reconsider our assumptions on these issues. Our nation's future depends a lot more on how well we raise our children then it does on this short term so-called "economic prosperity" that is both fueled by and fuels unneeded materialist consumption. The time would be better INVESTED by spending it with the children instead of making those few extra bucks to buy just a few more things that aren't needed, or pay that extra amount of taxes to fund more programs that should be reduced or eliminated by government. Think seriously about this, I think you might just reach the same conclusion I have. Both John Silber and Nancy Lord were right. Unfortunately, despite my having voted for both of them, neither was elected.

The Watermelon Party: The Socialist Priorities of the Green Party

June 3, 2000

The Green Party portrays itself as having been founded on the environmental agenda but taking "progressive" positions on the other issues. But like with any left of center movement, when it begins to attract left-wing liberals, it becomes something else entirely. I spoke with a Green activist a few years ago that advocated making the Greens a somewhat quasi-Libertarian party with a more moderate economic agenda then the Libertarians. He referred to inner battles with the other major wing of the Green Party as the "watermelon problem." The term watermelon, to the few non-socialist members of the Green movement, means the party adopts a green image to mask "red" or socialist economic views. The watermelons have won out. The Green Party platform, as illustrated by the platform committee document of the Association of State Green Parties, is thoroughly based on socialist economics.

The Green Party claims to represent a "new politics" as an alternative to the old politics of the Democrats and Republicans. It claims also to favor decentralization of government decisions, "community based economics," and a decentralized economy as well. But the Green Party platform, at the same time, takes more specific positions on economic issues that are in stark contrast to the stated generalities. All of those specific policy pronouncements are very much in line with defending and extending centralized, statist, big government and welfare state socialism that has been enacted mostly by the Democrats over the last 70 years.

The Greens criticize the welfare reform efforts of the Republican Congress, and offer this advice to Congress: "We need to increase spending on education, job training, and child care programs." Any congressional act increasing spending on those areas is anything but decentralized and community-based. Most money already spent in those areas does nothing to fund the alleged beneficiaries, but instead funds lots of big salaries for government welfare bureaucrats who know they don't have a job if "welfare" was eliminated.

Environmental taxes, so-called value-added taxes, and progressive taxation are all concepts endorsed by the Green Party. Environmental taxes would increase the tax burden of all activities that produce the goods and services needed for living. Essentially they would hit the lower income level even harder then sales taxes. Value-added taxes should really be called value-reduced taxes. They are like sales taxes, but instead of being levied at the retail cash register only, they are levied at EVERY SINGLE level of production, all of which reflects in massively higher prices at the cash register. Both of these taxes would severely punish the lower and middle income earners.

Greens also advocate the concept of "progressive" taxation of income, which means those earning more will pay a higher tax rate on every dollar earned. For example, one making $20,000 might pay at the 10% rate while a $200,000 earner and a $2 million earner would be taxed 30% and 50% respectively. Those rates would tax 20K at $2000, 200K at $60,000, and 2 million at $1 million. I call a flat tax far fairer then this. Under a flat tax those making more would pay more, but at the same rate. But "progressive" taxes are one of the main elements of the socialist agenda as advocated by Karl Marx.

The Green Party endorses federally mandated minimum wage legislation. Not only is this inconsistent with their stated support of decentralized, local community based economics, it stands in stark contrast with the Greens claim of advocating meaningful works availability for all. When minimum wage laws are passed, many employees are priced out of the job market and into unemployment. This is simple economics; it is not even legitimately debatable. As more are unemployed, they will receive the other part of the socialist agenda advocated by the Greens, unemployment compensation. But that must be funded by taking tax money from those who do work. And the Greens would enact laws calling for even higher mandated wages under their "living wage" proposal. A healthy free market economy naturally creates enough real living wage jobs for all. It is the effects of taxes and regulations that reduce the ability of the economy to create good jobs. Enacting more regulations of the economy only makes worse the problems that socialists and Greens claim can only be solved with more regulations.

Additionally, the Green Party calls for federal affordable housing policy along with so-called single payer health care at the federal level. In plain English, that means one "payer" (the federal government) funds all health insurance for all citizens at taxpayer expense. In other words, it is socialized medicine. This is hardly locally based, decentralized, or differing at all with the socialist medicine plan advanced by the Clintons in 1993.

In short, a cursory examination of the specifics of the economic agenda of the Green Party shows it to be entirely socialist in its basic foundations. But the party promotes a "green" image while advocating a "red" economic agenda. The nickname "watermelon," chosen

by non-socialist Greens, is quite appropriate. The Green
Party member I spoke with a few years ago, is now a
former Green Party member. He is seeking the Libertarian
nomination for United States Senate.

You Should have the Right to Decide
How Your Tax Dollars are Spent

June 8, 2000

Politicians and pundits talk a lot, especially during election season, about reform. We hear about campaign finance reform, tax reform, government reform, etc. But what is the real issue all of this drives at? The issue is how the politicians spend our money, and what they spend on it, and why they do so.

The politicians think our money, that we pay in taxes, is there money to spend as they please. They spend and spend and spend more, and can not raise tax quickly enough to spend the country into even more debt. Don't believe the claim of "surplus," the national debt is as large as it has ever been.

I have a revolutionary idea for substantive reform of the process of spending our tax money. Take the decision out of the hands of the politicians and put it in the hands of we, the people, who pay these taxes. That's right, implement the concept that you have the right to decide how your tax dollars are spent. If we really do want a society where the government is literally of, by, and for the people we should adopt this proposal.

Here are some details on exactly how this will work. Every January when the income tax information booklets from the IRS are mailed to taxpayers, it will include a Taxpayer's Ballot along with the standard 1040 tax forms. Actually, there would three such ballots included, each with varying degrees of detail for voters who wish to either make broad allocations of their tax dollars or very detailed decisions on the spending of THEIR tax money. Government is basically in three levels, departments then agencies then specific programs. Each of those levels would be addressed on a ballot, with the first being the most simple while the last of the three being the most detailed. Each taxpayer would choose one of the three and use it.

Using it would be easy. For sake of explanation I'll use the simpler one, listing government by departments. It would list the major cabinet departments of the government and list a blank by each one. You the voter would fill in a number next to each, and you choose any number, which will be percentages, as long as all your numbers add up to zero at the bottom. There will also be a line titled other, where you write something in there and then list the amount of your tax dollars you wish to have spent on that line item. Then you send this in, and all these ballots from voters will be tabulated, and bingo, the federal budget for the next year will be determined. Now sending in the ballot will be voluntary, for those who don't send one in, their tax dollars will be spent as determined by the rest of the taxpayers who do send in their ballot. This is the same that happens on Election Day, those who don't vote have their decisions of candidate made by those who do vote.

Some will think this is radical. It may sound radical, but what could be more democratic then we, the people, deciding how are tax dollars are spent? Those who say our political process is corrupted because big money is buying politicians who then spend tax dollars on special interests and corporate subsidies should realize this proposal will clean up the process by putting the decisions in the hands of the people instead of politicians.

Do we want real reform of the political process? If so, we should grant the people the right to decide how their tax dollars are spent.

Schumer Comments on Gas Prices Demonstrate Economic Ignorance or Worse

June 16, 2000

Today in the news is a story that New York Senator Charles Schumer is calling on the Clinton Administration to pressure manufacturers of gasoline to lower prices. Gasoline prices have recently risen to their highest prices yet. Remember, Schumer is the same politician who, years ago as a member of Congress, declared that excessively high prices of breakfast cereals was a scandal deserving a congressional investigation. He charged the three major cereal makers of "price gouging." There are two possible explanations for this political pandering by Democrat Schumer.

He might be completely ignorant about the basic economics involved in the production, distribution, and sale of gasoline. But he has no excuse. A United States Senator surely has the resources, and staff, to gather appropriate information and do the homework to understand the economic involved. If Schumer is in fact economically ignorant it is because he chooses not to use the resources available to him.

Or maybe he's quite aware of how fallacious his pandering is here, and simply does it because he believes it to be politically expedient for him and the Clinton administration to blame the gas prices on the companies selling the product. This would not be the first time that a politician would knowingly and cynically pursue a political issue based on a premise that he knows to be a falsehood.

If Schumer would do his research he would find out how greatly the federal government regulates the production and sale of gasoline. He would also find out how ludicrous environmental initiatives add to the price of gasoline. Additionally, the regulatory process manipulates both the supply and production of gasoline. In fact, part of the problem in this instance is caused by the very regulations, that politicians like Schumer, have enacted into law in the past.

When this system of government regulation, as well as the supply manipulation by O.P.E.C., cause the increased prices we've been seeing, politicians of the liberal variety are quick to call for more regulations and blame the oil companies for the problem. But the problem is the regulatory interference with the free market. The free market works, when it is allowed to work. Regulation interferes with that working, and cause problems that economically ignorant politicians claim can be solved by yet more regulation. Those who understand free market economics can see that more regulation as a remedy is like a physician curing your infection by injecting you with more of what has caused the infection.

Regulation almost always causes the opposite of the claimed or desires effect. The Congress in 1993 heard cries from consumers that cable television service had gone up too high in price. So they stopped in regulate it, and President Clinton signed the legislation into law. Seven years later, the cost of the same service is nearly double the prices in most areas. The regulation cause cable companies to redefine what constitutes "basic service" and made prices increases more necessary than would otherwise have been the case. Once again regulation increased prices for the same service. But despite this, and numerous other examples of the complete failure of regulations to improve the providing of consumer products and services, liberal politicians are still quick to propose more regulation of the economy.

Politicians like Schumer may be ignorant, cynically manipulating the issue for political gain, or perhaps even both. But make no mistake about it; either way these politicians are motivated by one goal: the acquisition and maintenance of their political power to control the economy and run our lives. And they know that most economic activity, as well as our day to day lives, depends on the free flow of gasoline at market prices.

This is yet more proof of why the politicians' license to regulate the economy is one that needs to be revoked. And the best way voters can do that is to first understand economics in order understand why that needs to be done. Then voters can go ahead and do it by voting against liberal economically ignorant politicians who support government regulation of the free market.

Environmentalism

As if often the case there the perception and the reality. True environmentalists are concerned with clean air and water and living in a clean environment. That is what extreme environmentalists are perceived to advocate. But the reality is quite different. Extreme environmentalists advocate a radical transformation of our economic and societal structures designed to prevent non-existent plagues like global warming. The real objective of extreme environmentalists is achievement of the socialist agenda. As many commentators have observed, the extreme environmentalist movement is the new home of socialism.

The most common argument of extreme environmentalists is to circumvent logic and reason by falsely claiming crisis. Pointing out evidence that proves global warming is compete nonsense makes one the enemy, and means that one is getting in the way of THEIR crusade to save the planet from global warming. Never mind the evidence that it doesn't exist. They say it does, have junk science to prove it, and you must be ignorant, or worse, bought off by "corporate spokespersons" if you don't agree. What they will never prove, because they can't, is any real evidence of global warming. Extreme environmentalists never let facts get in the way of their agenda.

Look at every proposal advanced by extreme environmental activists. Notice that in all cases, they call for more government regulations and more taxes. Guess who else always calls for these approaches to solving problems, both real and imagined? Socialists. Governments and corporations that were agents of governments have caused the worst environmental scourges around the world. And free market capitalism, everywhere it is practiced, is the answer. Private ownership of property leads to the most effective use and preservation of natural resources since no wise individual will pollute and plunder his own property. Genuine environmentalists agree with this. But those who seek to use environmental issues to advance the socialist agenda will disagree.

Who Wants to Pay $4 a Gallon for Gasoline?

March 12, 2000

No one does, but many extreme environmentalists would love to see you paying four or five bucks for a gallon of gasoline. Look at how the price of gas has neared two dollars per gallon and how this might become an issue in the 2000 election campaign this coming summer. Just imagine how much support would be gained if the Green Party and other extreme environmentalists told you how they would love to double or triple the price of gasoline via excessive taxes. Or I should say imagine how much support they would lose from those who might otherwise vote for their candidates.

The idea, although simply wrong, is itself simple. The proposed massive gas taxes Greens and others support is designed to dramatically lower usage of gasoline. Gasoline actually burns cleaner than many other fuels commonly in use. But don't tell this to environmental extremists, they don't like having the facts get in the way of their political agenda. They believe such a huge tax would reduce use of automobiles and lead to increased use of public transit, etc. But guess what busses and other forms of public transit use for fuel? That producer of ugly black smog and filthy pollution known as diesel fuel. These people want to take cars off the road and have more buses burning that filthy diesel fuel.

Additionally, massive taxes on gasoline would increase the costs of conducting any business that relies on the use of automobiles. That in turn would sharply drive up the prices of most products and services. In short, a massive tax increase on gasoline would be highly inflationary.

And this in turn would increase unemployment and reduce the standard of living among most in the middle class. Anyone remember the late 1970s? Anyone want to return back to that? I didn't think so.

So as this election season moves forward, and the prices at the pump continue to rise, be sure to think seriously how you'll be voting. If you want to vote for those who espouse the extreme environmentalist agenda (the Green Party) or those that pay lip service to supporting that same agenda, namely Al Gore. Gas prices are sure to rise, and the political rhetoric will rise even higher. But don't vote for the candidates who will tell you that more taxes or more government regulation will solve this problem. Politicians giving that prescription are simply advocating policy that would bring back the inflation, recession, taxes, interest rates, and gas lines of the late 1970s.

The Expense and Pollution of Local Recycling

March 14, 2000

This could also be titled "how the government messes it up again and produces results very opposite of the intent." We're told recycling is supposed to help "save the planet" and cut down on pollution. But just want expense and pollution in other areas are we willing to bear for the symbolic importance of mass participation in local recycling plans?

Like many communities, this one a few years ago instituted (through its trash collection contract) a residential recycling plan. Every two weeks they send an additional truck out that collects two categories of refuse to be recycled, paper and cardboard products in large paper bags and bottles and cans in a container. These items are to be put on every other week, and put out separately from the regular trash.

This adds extra cost to the trash collection contract. The company has to hired additional staff, and purchase extra trucks (specially equipped as well) to collect this material that will be recycled. Additionally, these extra trucks are just more vehicles running on diesel fuel and pumping more of that thick, stinky, black smog in the air. All of this to make an obvious showing in favor of the CONCEPT of recycling, but obviously very defeating of the supposed environmental benefits.

This is typical of government solutions to these kinds of matters. Intentions and perceptions are really all that counts. Like Rush Limbaugh used to say, "symbolism over substance." Having the entire community participate in a program like this definitely makes people think they're doing something good. And many really think this is a good thing. But few stop to think about the true effect. Recycling a very small amount of material costs great expense and causes much pollution.

There are good alternatives to this madness. First, instead of contracting out the garbage pickup service, privatize it entirely. Let the individual choose who will pick up his trash and how they will do it. And lower taxes as well, by the amount of his and all other such "services" so the individual can contract individually for such services or voluntarily join groups that would negotiate contracts for services. Rather than a government created, one-size-fits all solution, privatizing services like this is a great way to have better services at lower prices. And it lets the customer choose rather than having the bureaucrat impose.

As for environmental concerns and recycling, these efforts are economically sustainable if profitable and efficient. Otherwise, taxing an already over-paid public for this agenda is simply not justified. If people believe recycling is so important and needed, they would contract with companies that will recycle via private contract and those companies will find a way to offer this service efficiently and profitably. If the market doesn't bear it the government, at any level, has no business forcing it.

Eco-terrorists could Finally Face Prosecution

June 2, 2000

We have recently seen an alarming number of environmental terrorism incidents. Perhaps the most notable instance was the fires that damaged several buildings and parts of ski lifts at the Vail ski resort. In a great number of these cases, the militant Earth Liberation Front (ELF) claims responsibility for these violent criminal acts. The ELF is well-organized, on-going criminal conspiracy that operates under cover and secrecy outside of its press operations. One would expect this for an organization whose primary activities involve highly illegal acts of terrorism.

A grand jury in Oregon is investigating the case of eco-terrorism against Boise Cascade, a company in the logging industry. Members of the ELF allegedly set the company's headquarters in Monmouth, Oregon on fire. The only publicly known member of the group, its spokesperson Craig Rosebraugh, has been subpoenaed twice by the grand jury to face questions about the Boise Cascade fire.

Rosebraugh was granted immunity from personally facing criminal prosecution so he could be compelled to testify. Prosecutors obviously believe he knows the who, what, where, and when that will aide in the investigation and prosecution of ELF members involved in the acts of eco-terrorism being investigated. But Rosebraugh faces contempt charges for refusing to cooperate with the grand jury. Basically he has three choices. He can refuse to cooperate and go to jail for contempt. He can be repeatedly sent to jail for contempt as long as he continues to refuse to testify. This is what happened to Susan MacDougal for refusing to testify before the Whitewater grand jury. Or, he could testify and withhold information he knows, risking criminal prosecution for perjury. Of course, he could also choose to testify and honor the oath he would take to tell "the truth, the whole truth, and nothing but the truth."

The ELF is quite conveniently hiding behind Rosebraugh, claiming that he received an "anonymous communique" from ELF members claiming credit for the Boise Cascade headquarters fire. Yet, the group claims that the government is repressing them, and Rosebraugh, by going forward with the grand jury process. In response, the group is attempting to gain sympathy as a "victim" of government repression while seeking to evade prosecution for acts of eco-terrorism for which it claims responsibility.

They can't have it both ways. The ELF can't claim it engaged in the crimes, and have their spokesperson put forth such messages via "anonymous communique" and then use this alleged anonymity as a defense when that same spokesperson, the only known member of their group, is facing possible criminal prosecution for those same incidents. But this is the nature of a purely criminal organization that attempts to gain the benefits of terrorism while hoping to evade prosecution.

We can only hope that these people are prosecuted to the full extent of the law, and via due judicial process, the guilty are convicted and given their rightful sentence of a long stay in the Grey Bar Motel. A civilized society has no place for those who deliberately engage in such behaviors. And our justice system must send a message those who engage in acts of terrorism will not go free.

I am hoping that Rosebraugh will come to his senses and realize his only choice is to cooperate and start singing. I hope this case also leads to more aggressive prosecution of other acts of terrorism by this group, its sister group the Animal Liberation Front, and other eco-terrorism groups such as Earth First. Eco-terrorism endangers human lives as well as property. We can only hope swift and effective prosecution of these criminal organizations will put them out of the eco-terrorism "business" and put their criminal members in prison where they belong.

Politics and Elections

Many of us find politics and elections just as interesting and entertaining as following sports. However, they are far more important because of the impact they have on our everyday lives. While Sammy Sosa and Shaquille O'Neil don't decide what laws and regulations we live under, our elected politicians do make decisions of that nature. It is for that reason that politics and elections do matter, and it is the reason individuals should be more on top of what's happening in politics.

Like sports, following politics requires knowing the parties and personalities involved, and understanding their role in the game. But unlike sports, politics is a game we are all involved in, whether we choose to be or not. We are involved in this game because we all have taxes levied on us by politicians. We are all affected by the decisions made by these people, so we should all be concerned with who is writing laws and regulations that shape our lives.

At the same time I've tried to make politics more interesting in entertaining, without losing sight of the fact that they are so profoundly important. If all of us were more informed and made better decisions about politics, including those made on election day, we would have better politics and public policy.

Political Reality and Political Stupidity

April 7, 2000

The Democrats have created, over the last 30 years, much of what is currently political reality. Yet, through their sheer stupidity, that political empire might come crashing down.

The Democrats have, over the years, built up huge advantages in the political system. Repeated polls have shown most journalists personally agree more with the liberal policies of the Democrats. While they may not necessarily be biased in news coverage (although many doubt that too) they can easily exercise this bias in the more crucial choices made in deciding WHAT NEWS they will cover. This was clearer to me when I visited Washington D.C. several years ago and bought a copy of both the Washington Post and the Washington Times. The Post carried a headline about a group of Democrats in Congress proposing socialist child care legislation while the Times headlined on their front page a Republican legislative proposal to reduce government spending and balance the Federal budget. Additionally, the Democrats have built up influential special interests groups among the labor unions, civil rights groups, organizations supporting public schools, etc.

But despite these advantages, the Democrats have largely squandered them. Clinton has been the only Democrat to be re-elected president since Franklin Roosevelt. Democrats lost their 40-year old House of Representatives majority to the Republicans in 1994, who seem likely to maintain their thin majority for quite some time. The U.S. Senate was won by the Republicans in 1980 and after being re-claimed by the Democrats in

1986, went back to the Republican column in the anti-Democrat election of 1994. The voters rejected the hard-left agenda of the Clinton's first term and overwhelmingly elected Republicans in 1994. While the weakest of weak Republicans incumbents were being reelected some of the most previously strongest Democrats were falling to defeat.

The voters heard the moderate message of 1992 and saw the hard left policies of 1993-94 coming from the White House. Voters returned a mandate against those policies as well as the inherent dishonesty of the candidates, who knowingly ran at moderates knowing they would govern as extreme liberals.

The rise of the supposedly moderate Democratic Leadership Council has been far more a change in image than policy. It's symbolism over substance, as Rush Limbaugh says of much that is associated with the Clinton era. Clinton and his allies at the DLC simply re-packaged liberal Democratic policies in moderate rhetoric. George McGovern warned of this in a nightly new interview at the 1992 Democratic National Convention when he called Clinton and Gore "trojan horse" candidates who would campaign as moderates and then govern as liberals. McGovern was right. The Clintons tried to nationalize one seventh of the national economy via socialized medicine.

In early 1995 Bill Clinton was in such poor shape politically that he uttered that memorable phrase "I am relevant." Until Republicans made their own mistakes, they had rendered Clinton politically impotent on most policy issues. That's when Dick Morris entered the picture with a plan to get Clinton reelected. His plan was quite simple but nonetheless brilliant strategy. He advised Clinton to re-sharpen and further intensify the process of "triangulation" that was successfully employed in the 1992 election. Essentially, this involves re-packaging your own views as sounding more moderate than they really are, and then contrasting them against an extreme straw-man version of both your opposition views as well as your own. So for a liberal like Clinton, he would claim to be a "New Democrat" more moderate than the old leftist Democrats or the newer more right wing Republicans. And Dick Morris and other adviser showed Clinton how they could get away with skirting the post-Watergate campaign finance reforms by raising tens of millions of dollars through the Democratic National Committee to be spent on "issue advertisements" to carry about the "triangulation" plan. Through the Fall of 1995 and the Winter and Spring of 1996 we saw the Democrats spend over $60 million on those ads that showed Clinton defending the various elements of the liberal Democratic establishment using the obviously conservative-sounding slogan, "President Clinton, defending our value." It worked. Clinton looked nearly unbeatable by summer of 1996.

Some Republicans blame the 1992 defeat of President Bush to the rise of the Perot candidacy. But Republicans might come to understand that third party politics could be their ticket to smashing the liberal Democratic establishment at the polls in the future.

The mid-to-late 1990s saw the rise of the newly organized Green Party in New Mexico. The Green party advocates a mixture of socially libertarian and economically collectivist views. They have been attracting a number of dis-affected Democrats who believe the Democratic Party (seen as controlled by the Democratic Leadership Council) has sold out to the right and no longer embraces "progressive" values. The rise of the New Mexico Green Party has been in direct relation to the re-habilitation of the Republican Party in New Mexico, a heavily Democratic state. The state of New Mexico has been ruled by a handful of families who've lived in New Mexico since the 1700s who have dominated state politics through the Democratic Party. They still practice patronage politics with the sheer corruption of Tammany Hall and the brutal autocratic nature of the ruling party of Mexico.

In 1994 the two-term governor of New Mexico, Bruce King, sought reelection against political novice and self-made businessman Gary Johnson, the Republican nominee. But the Greens nominated former Democratic Lieutenant Governor Roberto Mondragon as their nominee in the race. The Green candidate polled about ten percent on Election Day as Johnson defeated King by about the same margin of victory.

After Congressman Bill Richardson joined the Clinton Administration in early 1997, the Republicans saw another opportunity to win a major race with the help of the Green Party. The format of the special congressional election called on the two major parties and the Greens and Libertarians to nominate their candidate via convention. The Democrats nominated long time local politician Eric Serna, who had a reputation for being corrupt in the style of former Speaker Jim Wright. The Green Party nominated socialized medicine activist Carol Miller, who the previous year had been defeated in a Democratic primary for state senator. While Serna polled 39 percent and Miller took 17 percent carrying the Green Party banner, Republican Bill Redmond was elected to Congress with 43% of the vote. Congressman Steve Schiff, who represented the neighboring district in New Mexico, passed away in 1998, setting up another special election the following year. With the Green Party actively supporting their candidate Bob Anderson in that race, the same thing happened again. The Green candidate polled 15 percent as Republican Heather Wilson's 45 percent at the polls defeated Democrat Phil Maloof's 40 percent.

The Democrats were clueless on how to respond to this pattern of defeats. Simply put they faced a lose-lose situation in dealing with the Green Party challenge. They could try to challenge the Greens on "progressive issues" by moving to the left to regain disaffected liberal votes while giving up moderate voters to the Republicans. Or they could use the Green Party as an opportunity for triangulation and a further move to the ideological center, which would only further strengthen the Green Party and continue to divide the left-of-center vote. Clearly the Republicans were thrilled and made the most to take advantage of this situation.

A colleague of mine in the Libertarian Party of New Mexico at the time attempted to convince the Democrats they needed a similar type "spoiler" to split votes away from the Republicans. Seeing it as opportunity for his party, he talked to some personal connections he knew that were active and local Democratic Party affairs. For minimal investment politically, the Libertarian Party could gain ballot status and siphon off votes from the Republicans as the Greens had done to the Democrats. Simple common sense would say the Democrats should be very interested in this idea. But they were not, his friends connected with the Democrats laughed and ridiculed the idea. The Democrats reacted to the Libertarian Party the same way the Republican Party does: ignore them and hope they render themselves politically irrelevant. The Democrats have reacted to the Green Party that way as well. But it's the latter that has cost them some elections win and might well spell doom for the Democrats.

As it has risen locally in New Mexico, the Green Party is growing at a rapid pace nationally. In the same way the Roberto Mondragon candidacy established the Green Party as a major player in New Mexico politics, the 2000 presidential candidacy of Ralph Nader will put the Green Party in the major leagues of national politics. But Nader's campaign will not be a simple vanity campaign at the top of the ticket. His candidacy will be instrumental in helping the Green Party organize at the state level and obtain ballot access and organizational strength in most states. The Green Party will emerge from the 2000 elections as the nation's clear-cut third largest political party.

Politics can be quite predictable. We'll see the Democrats nationally acting the same way their colleagues in New Mexico did early in the last decade. The DLC type Democrats will seek to triangulate toward center in their rhetoric, re-playing the tired strategy of the Clinton years. The more "progressive" wing of the Democratic Party will urge co-option of the Green Party agenda and a move back to the left. The two factions will fight it out as the Republicans will enjoy great opportunities to win elections.

In what could be perhaps the last opportunity for the 28-year old party to gain relevancy, the Libertarian Party should want to challenge the Republicans for votes on the right. But political stupidity holds sway there as well. The Libertarians have competing factions that want to either attract more votes from disaffected Democrats with a more liberal sounding message and others who believe most of their votes will come from disaffected Republicans. But the one-half percent their candidate

Harry Browne received in the 1996 election will not worry any Republicans during the 2000 election.

The coming decade will bring opportunity to both Republicans and advocates of individual freedom as the statist coalition of the Democrats comes crashing down thanks to the rise of the Green Party. This reality could be a great opportunity for the Republican Liberty Caucus and other liberty advocates seeking to play a role in shaping the kind of victories and policies this political reality will bring. Realizing that the rise of the Green Party greatly enhances the odds of Republicans staying in the majority, the advocates of individual freedom within the Republican Party should take this as their chance to finally turn the GOP into the pro-freedom party. If that goal can be accomplished, there will be many freedom supporters who will "come home" to help make the GOP the majority party and the country more free. It's an opportunity that should not be passed up.

Which will prevail, smart strategy based on this political reality, or the political stupidity as shown by the Democrats failing to respond to the challenge of the Green Party? The future of freedom might well depend on it.

Libertarian Failure from A to Z

February 11, 2000

The Libertarians are a well-intentioned group of people who are working hard to bring issues of individual rights back to political debate. But they are so hopelessly clueless on political strategy that they are their own worse enemies. This, combined with the sheer stupidity of their two dominant factions, assures that the Libertarian Party will never win the battle for freedom.

The party's two most well known candidates for its nomination in 2000 quite neatly represent the two dominant factions of the party. On one side is Harry Browne, whom most of you haven't heard about because he spent the entire 1996 campaign as LP Presidential nominee complaining about not being invited to the presidential debates. His campaign consultants spent a bulk of the small campaign's money on themselves and their over-rated services, a fact that can be easily verified at the Federal Election Commission web-site. Browne's faction is lead by Libertarian consultant Michael Cloud, who believes Libertarians will begin winning if they water down the message and make it slick. He advocates taking the libertarian message and making it sound moderate much the way Clinton takes the liberal message and makes it sound conservative. I personally think used-car salesmen have no place in politics.

The other faction is that which is rallying behind the would-be candidacy of science fiction author L. Neil Smith. These people view themselves as the true libertarian activists and say the Browne-Cloud faction has sold out on party principle in a desire to win. Of course, this hasn't caused either faction to be in danger of winning anything in politics, besides maybe their own internal arguments.

But, without further ado, I'll chronicle the failures of the Libertarian Party, from A to Z.

A is for Anarchy. Many libertarians call themselves anarchists or anarcho-capitalists or anarcho something or other. Like it or not, the voters will never choose anarcho-anything at the polls. A is also for Archimedes, Project Archimedes, the name of the party's current membership drive. Essentially the idea was to grow from 25,000 to 200,000 members by sending direct mail (read: junk mail) to enough people until the party reaches 200,000. They ran into two problems: ran out of prospective members to mail this stuff to, and for a number of reasons, got far lower than expected response rates from this very expensive mailing. If that's not enough, A is additionally for Arizona. The LP has two parties in that state, because they divided into two parties after Rick Thompkins from that state opposed Harry Browne for the 1996 LP nomination for President. After that, Browne's allies who run the national LP dis-affiliated the Arizona Libertarian Party and then affiliated with the pro-Browne faction, who call themselves the Arizona Libertarian Party, inc.

B is for Browne. 1996 and likely 2000 Libertarian nominee for President. He's the darling of the LP's Cloud faction. Some LP members think of him as the Clinton of the LP.

C is for Cloud, as in Michael Cloud. The self-appointed leader of those who think Clinton style sales methods should be used to sell the Libertarian Party.

D is for Drug legalization. Most libertarians fail to realize how their opponents use this issue to marginalize them. The recent effort to draft New Mexico Governor Gary Johnson to run for president is an example of this. Anytime someone suggests legalizing drugs, they flock to that person like a drunk on a bottle of whiskey.

E is for elections. LP members hardly ever win them running as capital L Libertarians.

F is for Factionalism. The LP is more divided into its factions than any party I've known, including even the Democrats. The long-running dispute within the Arizona Libertarian Party proves this.

G is for Green Party. The Green Party has recently, by most measures, surpassed the Libertarian Party as the nation's third largest political party. This has happened while the Browne-Cloud faction has been running the party from their Watergate Office Complex headquarters.

H is for Howard Stern. The LP of NY nominated him for governor a few years ago, then he later dropped out of the race. It was a fiasco and the topic of jokes on Letterman and Leno. Even Dan Quayle couldn't do that to the Libertarian Party.

I is for Infighting. The Smith and Cloud factions spend so much time and effort doing this, they are hardly a threat to the status-quo.

J is for Joe Camel. Some Libertarians are the only ones left defending old smokin' Joe. L. Neil Smith urges non-smokers to become "political smokers" to protest the anti-smoking movement. That's enough to make you wonder what Smith is smoking.

K is for Karen and Gary Fincher. The Finchers have been hired by the national LP to collect signatures and register voters for the party in many states, and for the 1996 Browne campaign. Currently the two are under investigation for suspicion of Fourth Degree Felony charges in New Mexico for allegedly submitting hundreds of fraudulent voter registration cards on behalf of the LP of New Mexico.

L is for Lyndon LaRouche. He not a Libertarian, but called himself one and was quoted for saying such in a Time magazine article. The perception has stuck in part because the LP is ineffective in creating it's own image before being defined by others.

M is for Macho Flash. Cloud calls the rhetoric used by shock-jock style members of his party, "Libertarian Macho Flash." It's used as a rhetorical baseball bat to bash members of the L. Neil Smith faction.

N is for Negative. Many perceive the Libertarian message as being negative. Libertarians are always great at telling you what they're against. But voters are constantly looking for an optimistic vision to rally behind.

O is for Opportunity. The few opportunities the Libertarians have had to make themselves well known have been failures. The party long ago wasted its fifteen minutes of fame looking like extremists on unpopular issues.

P is for Preamble, the preamble to the LP platform begins with absurd language about the "cult of the omnipotent state" blah blah blah blah blah. Members try every four years to abolish this form their founding document, but the founders of the party put in a clause requiring something like 7/8 vote to amend this section. They always just barely fail to obtain the votes.

Q is for Quality of Life. Libertarian dogma fails to address quality of life issues because they don't fit into the simple concept of figuring out who's initiating force against someone else.

R is for Republican Liberty Caucus. They are the third faction of the libertarian movement, the one that gets it.

S is for Socialism. While good conservatives are never hesitant to call socialism what it is, the Cloud faction of the LP advises against using the S word. They say it offends people.

T is for Taxes. They get higher and higher every year, despite the LP's opposition to them. Perhaps it's time to reconsider their failure in political strategy.

U is for Understanding. That is, understanding the political process and how to operate within it. Smith counsels "the perfect is the enemy of the good." That's a mode of thinking that will never accomplish anything politically. As Morton Blackwell advises, which I think is far more wise advice, "never let the perfect be the enemy of the good."

V is for Values. Many LP members don't think values are important, but most voters certainly do. Or otherwise said, Dan Quayle was right.

W is for Watergate. The Watergate Office Complex is the headquarters of the national LP. These people long ago contracted inside-the-beltway disease and don't get it.

X is for X ray vision. No one in the leadership of the LP has this.

Y is for Yahoos. The LP surely has it's share. Enough said.

Z is for Zero. This is the number of Libertarian members currently in the Congress and the United States Senate.

If you acknowledge the above and still remain a member of the Libertarian Party, you will not make a difference in achieving freedom. The Libertarian Party, its competing methods of selling its ideas, and the leaders of its various factions are not now and have not and never will win any major political races. By remaining a member you're telling them failed and ineffective political strategy is the way to go.

Or you could join a team that has a chance to make a difference. Sign up with the Republican Liberty Caucus and register Republican. There's no need to dilute your philosophical principles one bit at all, just a need to accept the reality of the American political system and decide you want to make a real difference rather than remaining on the sidelines.

The Natural Law Party is a Scary Outfit, Part I

March 15, 2000

"Natural Law" was highlighted as a political issue in the summer of 1991 when Delaware Senator Joseph Biden questioned Supreme Court nominee Clarence Thomas on his alleged belief in it. Biden was referring to the definition of natural law one would find in the writings of Thomas Jefferson and John Locke.

I first heard of the Natural Law Party when I saw their booth set up in the hotel where I was attending the College Republican National Convention in June 1992. Clearly they were hoping their use of the term "natural law" in their party name would attract conservatives to take a look at their platform. I seriously doubt they signed up any new members that day, because one quick look at their platform lead one to conclude there was little or no conservative content within it.

The Natural Law Party (NLP) has a strangely new age definition of the term natural law. The term is not clearly defined by repeated throughout the NLP platform. The party says government should be run "in accordance with natural law" and that all of society's problems would be solved if all individuals lived "in accordance with natural law." Its entire platform revolves around this notion that individuals need to be living "in accordance with natural law."

One might ask of course, what I choose not to live by accordance of natural law, as defined by these people? Well, if they ever gained control of the government, it appears from reading their platform they have a solution to that as well. Your contradictory attitudes are themselves not in accordance with natural law, proving that you need to be educated in the advantages and virtues of living according to natural law. Keep in mind, they haven't clearly stipulated what this natural law is.

You see the first glimpse of what this outfit is all about. They're selling an agenda, so-called natural law, they are either unable or unwilling to define in clear language. I suspect they know exactly what natural law is, as they define it, but realize that sharing that with you will lead to most rejecting their agenda. Clearly those who don't live in accordance with natural law shall be re-educated into doing so. This is no different than Communist ideology that says it only works when everyone in society is on board with it and those who object will be re-educated. If one studies political ideologies, especially extremist ones, one finds that one common thread among them is this kind of demand for ideological compliance and some scheme of re-education to enforce it.

I seriously question any political party or movement that tells me we all have to get on the bandwagon and live our lives according to their ideas or we need to be re-educated. What they never want to tell you is the consequences of refusing to be re-educated. But we can simply examine the results of regimes based on these ideas. Those who have refused re-education in other societies have been jailed, brainwashed, tortured, etc.

Quite simply, if the ideas of "natural law" are so advantageous over others, they will be readily accepted by the masses and such re-education will not be needed. But having run their candidates for president and vice president in the last two national elections, the Natural Law Party has gained few votes. As voters become more

aware of what this outfit is all about I expect them to gain
fewer votes.

The Natural Law Party is a Scary Outfit Part II: What is Natural about their Law?

March 20, 2000

The Natural Law Party is quite slick in their image making and marketing. No doubt they understand the importance of this more than other third parties. The name Natural Law itself is very marketable to many voters. What, after all, could sound better than laws based on nature. Aren't we all in favor of doing everything we can, naturally? And on top of this, the NLP platform and candidates attempt to cloak themselves in the legitimacy of science. Technology and science has raised our standard of living, and the NLP wants to sell the notion it will improve the way we run government as well.

But behind the slick marketing hides the truth about the Natural Law Party: it's a scam. An extremely well designed, slick marketing scam that should even have the Church of Scientology jealous. This one might be even better than L. Ron Hubbard's pet project that made him a millionaire. Not only is it a scam, the NLP is a front. It's a front for the Maharishi University of Management, located in Fairfield, Iowa. Maharishi Mahesh Yogi, a guru of Eastern New Age religion originally from India, set up this institution in 1971. Maharishi has sought to invade the Christian West and spread his New Age religion. Like all fanatical religions, they ultimately realize people don't by the snake oil voluntarily, most don't anyway. And then that's when they turn to politics. By gaining control of government, a group can promote their fanatical agenda.

The university offers courses on "management" which are centered around the concepts of Transcendental

Meditation (TM), the center-piece of their New Age religion. TM is the solution to all problems, personal and societal, they seem to claim.

Both the university and the NLP sell the New Age snake oil (including TM) under the name Maharishi Vedic Science. This is not the first time a group has packaged religoius values as "science." It's striking that the web sites of both promote "natural law" as the solution to everything. The party has perpetually run John Hagelin for President and Mike Thompkins for Vice President. Both of them claims to be have obtained PhDs in the sciences from Ivy League universities. And coincidentally, both are employed as professors at the Maharishi University of Management.

A check of the internet's domain registry shows both organization are centered in Fairfield, Iowa. The Natural Law Party itself is the political arm of the movement, and the university is the propaganda arm of it.

The party's platform is a create mix of the better sounding rhetoric of the Green Party and some of that espoused by the Libertarian Party. Although it lack any consistent guiding principle other than the euphemistic use of the term "Natural Law" to promote TM, it has found some support among the Greens and Libertarians. Members of those parties see similarities in rhetoric and think the Natural Law Party supports part of their agenda. And many members of both parties consider themselves advocates of Natural Law. That is, the John Locke-Thomas Jefferson definition of the term, not the Maharishi definition of natural law.

Clearly few would support this party if they realized it's a front for promotion of New Age religion. The Natural Law Party itself will continue to market their slick message and candidates hoping you won't notice that.

The Natural Law Party is a Scary Outfit Part III: Concealment of Deceptive New Age Religion

April 20, 2000

The Natural Law Party is merely a front for the promotion of New Age religion packaged in the pseudo-science of Transcendental Meditation (TM). TM is the centerpiece of the New Age religion espoused by Maharishi Mahesh Yogi, who has founded the Maharishi University of Management and the Natural Law Party to promote TM education and politics, respectively.

The Natural Law Party (NLP), in none of the documents I've seen nor their numerous interconnected web sites, offers a clear definition of the term "natural law." Likewise, TM is not defined (except to those taking their courses and training) either. But as I read more of their materials, it become clear that TM and Natural Law are closely connected concepts. The repeated use of the phrase "in accordance with natural law" in NLP actually means in accordance with practice of TM.

In devising the marketing of this New Age religion, its creators are obviously well aware of the cultural bias toward science. They, like many contemporary New Age cults, mask their beliefs in the trappings and language of science. In this case, they claim that TM itself is science. Nothing could be further from the truth. TM is pure New Age religion without a shred of legitimate science involved.

A former student and teacher of TM, after quitting the movement, has decided to expose this fact. The open letter can be read at this web site:

http://www.trancenet.org/personal/abe/abe12097.shtml

This letter is published on www.trancenet.org, a web site dedicated to exposing New Age cults. The author describes how conducting the process of TM involves the use of mantras (that supposedly mean nothing) and other symbolism of Eastern New Age religion.

Put quite simply, TM is not only New Age religion, it is SNAKE OIL. Other than the generic benefits one may gain from relaxing or engaging in simple meditation, the rituals and New Age religion that constitute TM have no objectively verified value. Yet the whole organization that has created this industry around the "product" called TM is designed to make money for selling an essentially non-existent "product." Despite having absolutely no empirical evidence, supporters claim TM will solve all problems.

The Natural Law Party proposed sending thousands of TM counselors (at the cost of $33 million to the taxpayers) to Kosovo to solve that situation. The NLP claims all our problems in the U.S. would be solved if we all lived "in accordance with natural law" which in English is "practiced TM and learned from them how to do it."

When one reads the platform of the Natural Law Party one realizes the answer to every issue ultimately revolves around TM. Every time leaders of the NLP have lobbied before Congress on various policy issues, the answer was either directly or indirectly related to TM.

While TM is highest priority with the NLP, they conceal the definition of Natural Law they say everything must be in accordance with. It leads one to question what other values, based on their New Age religion, are being concealed. What other agendas, that would make themselves known if the NLP ever gained control of the government, are they keeping hidden from the voters?

We still don't know fully what hidden agenda lie lurking beneath the slick image of this group. Voters would be well advised to pick among the parties that are far more open about their agendas and desires. Those who wish to control government owe us a complete disclosure of their intentions and agendas. Deception and concealment should not be rewarded in the political marketplace with our votes.

Additional information on the TM cult is available at this web site:

http://www.watchman.org/tmpro.htm

They can't all be Like Barry Goldwater

March 16, 2000

"I have little interest in streamlining government or in making it more efficient, for I mean to reduce its size. I do not undertake to promote welfare, for I propose to extend freedom. My aim is not to pass laws, but to repeal them. It is not to inaugurate new programs, but to cancel old ones that do violence to the Constitution, or have failed in their purpose, or that impose on the people an unwarranted financial burden. I will not attempt to discover whether legislation is Â'needed' before I have first determined whether it is constitutionally permissible. And if I should later be attacked for neglecting my constituents' Â'interests,' I shall reply that I was informed their main interest is liberty and that in that cause I am doing the very best I can."

-    Senator Barry Goldwater

What candidate for the presidency this year is saying anything close to that? Which candidate for the presidency is advocating an approach that comes close to that? None that I see. Our political process is so dominated by special interest groups, that interest in freedom and upholding the constitution have long sense been at best secondary interests of our politicians.

I still believe there would be a massive public response, positively, in favor of a candidate who advocates both reform of the process as well as reducing the size of government. McCain had a chance to do that, but failed to offer the substantive government reform agenda. And in getting caught up in campaign bickering over negatives advertising, he got distracted from his message of reforming the political process. In the end his campaign failed altogether, and yielded to the nomination of George W. Bush.

Goldwater was a true reformer of government before it was "cool." In the 1960s he recognized that a government retirement programs run by paying benefits today from money just collected yesterday would collapse with the demographic changes and need to be bailed out several times by higher taxes. Goldwater had the courage to venture into retirement communities and tell the retired they would be living better if they had the opportunity to fund their retirement on private investment plans rather than social security. Goldwater had the courage to predict Medicare would be a financial disaster. Today those willing to admit it know he was right.

President Lyndon Johnson started the "war on poverty" in the 1960s and since we've spent billions on welfare programs to alleviate poverty. But there are as many poor as there were 35 years ago. Goldwater opposed welfare programs and predicted they would fail. Once again he was right.

Barry Goldwater had the courage to speak to farmers and tell them farm subsidies are disastrous to their industry and costly to the consumers. He didn't change his message when speaking before one special interest group or another. He didn't spin his message to sound more conservative while running in the primaries and then more moderate in the general election. He did get beat badly in the 1964 election, because his campaign allowed the Johnson campaign to define him with the sleaziest negative campaign run in this century. But the 1964 election was not a rejection of Goldwater's ideas, but a rejection of the negative image the Johnson campaign painted of the Arizona Senator.

Senator Goldwater said minimal government was necessary to establish the order that allows freedom. But he said that power is dangerous and must always be held at it minimum. Government has grown in size, scope, and authority since them. One only need to look at the news every day see how one agency or another of the government is asserting its authority to make your decisions regarding your personal life on a day-to-day basis. What decisions can you make and do without first needing an approval, a permit, or a license from some agency of the government?

None of the candidates in this year's election are saying or doing any of this.

Will Gore speak to small business owners and admit he will raise taxes and impose more regulations on them? Will he tell the auto-makers in Detroit what he wrote in his book, that the internal combustion engine is the biggest single threat to the earth? Will Al Gore tell the union bosses that union soft money has to be taken out of the political process as well as corporate soft money, as a way of backing up his claim of support campaign finance reform? I seriously doubt he'll do any of those things.

Will George W. Bush explain how he can reduce the size of government and still pay down the debt at the same time? Will he show why and how government programs must be phased out and how and why those various interests will be better off without those programs? Will he successfully cut through the media polls and spin and sell lower taxes as the only way to true prosperity for most individuals and families? I can certainly hope he will. If he did he'd not only make his campaign more viable in November. He might, instead of simply being elected as the lesser of two evils, get himself elected with a mandate to actually accomplish these things. And he might be strong enough to help his own party maintain control of both houses of Congress.

Taking Another Look at Pat Buchanan
March 14, 2000

Patrick J. Buchanan was once a favorite among conservative Republicans. Serving as Communications Director in the Reagan White House, Buchanan was as good as refuting left wing liberal horse manure as anyone. Many of us read his autobiography, Right from the Beginning, and agreed with a whole lot of what he said and a lot of why he said it. In fact, many conservatives wanted Buchanan to seek the Republican nomination for president in 1988.

Buchanan did not seek the nomination in 1988 and Vice President George Bush was nominated and then elected over Michael Dukakis. It became clear early in the Bush presidency that he was not continuing the conservative agenda of President Reagan but governing as a moderate. Bush caved into the Democrats on several issues including taxes, the Kennedy Civil Rights bill, etc. Buchanan, as co-host of the program Crossfire on CNN continued to be an eloquent critic of the Bush administration from the conservative point of view.

During the summer of 1990 I commented to friends that I both hoped, and believe he probably would, challenge Bush for the Republican nomination for president in 1992. Not only that, but I actually believed (from what I saw in his comments about Bush) Buchanan had decided in his own mind during the summer of 1990 that he would oppose Bush in 1992. During the summer and early Fall of 1991, Buchanan gradually moved closer and closer to becoming a candidate. By November of 1991, he stepped down from his post on Crossfire and soon after officially announced his campaign.

My own personal enthusiasm for Buchanan began to turn into surprise when I saw how he started his campaign. He launched his campaign using the "America First" slogan and made arguments against U.S. involvement in world politics and free trade. Having long been a strong supporter of free trade during the 80s, I wondered why Buchanan made this transition more in the isolationist and especially protectionist direction on the trade issues. I voted less than enthusiastically for Buchanan in the March 1992 primary and then in November voted for the Libertarian ticket of Andre Marrou and Nancy Lord.

In 1996 I was even more surprised by the direction of Pat Buchanan's campaign. He had not only become more protectionist on trade issues, more nationalistic, but also began using both as a way to court union support. He also used a more populist message, along with a new class warfare appeal, to garner the votes of unemployed and others. At one point, Buchanan appeared as the guest on CNN's Capital Gang, a show he used to co-host. The liberal Democrat panelist Mark Shields, long-time Buchanan adversary on the show, pronounced Buchanan's transformation to populism to be genuine. Now I seriously questioned just how far Pat Buchanan has strayed from his 1980s conservative politics when he receives that kind of praise from a dye-in-the-wool liberal like Mark Shields.

Advance forward to this year, and Buchanan started his third attempt at the Republican nomination for president. By now Republicans were tiring of his act and Buchanan received very few votes in early polls and straw votes. So he decided to bolt the GOP and seek the Reform Party nomination for president. Soon after we hear that, Buchanan is accepting the support of long-time leftist,

Marxist third party activist Lenora Fulani. Now one really has to wonder where Buchanan is taking his political act. What ideological ground is he covering in making that choice of whom to affiliate with?

I watched Crossfire the other night, and they invited as a guess, Pat Buchanan. I have to admit, he still is convincing on the issues he is still right about, and even makes a good cases (even if one disagrees) on other issues. I find him to be a more interesting candidate than George W. Bush or Al Gore even if I don't find him an acceptable choice to serve in the White House. Mark Shields said the bizarre transformation of Buchanan from a conservative Republican to a populist of some kind seems to be true.

After taking another look at Pat Buchanan, I find myself still looking for a candidate to vote for in November.

McCain Campaign Was a Lost Opportunity

April 17, 2000

A successful presidential campaign is decided on both philosophy/issues and biography/personality, and the winning candidate usually has a solid combination of some of both. While Goldwater was strong on the issues and President Bush had strong appeal as a personality, I think it's fair to say Ronald Reagan as a candidate excelled in both areas.

When I assess the McCain and George W. Bush race for the Republican nomination this year I see Bush as being marginally more right on the issues and McCain quite attractive a candidate on the personality side. But neither of them, as I see it, is strong on both counts. Bush has a limited political resume, and his limited business resume and more questionable. Clearly he lacks the biography to match the courageous background of Senator McCain. Unfortunately, I'm afraid that despite McCain great appeal due to his biography and integrity his drift toward the mushy center on far too many important issues limits his appeal to many conservative Republicans.

While taking to friends and family, who are in the military, I got a sense that support for McCain among a lot of these people is due to McCain being precisely what Bill Clinton is not. Compare and contrast the legalistically evasive "I didn't inhale" and "I didn't have sexual relations with that woman" Clinton who dodged the draft, loath the military, busted campaign finance regulations to raise oodles of money in 1996, and turned the Lincoln Bedroom of the White House into a high priced Motel 6 for the biggest contributors to the Democratic party. Against that is the "I admit I've made mistakes" and "I'll always tell the truth" McCain who spent time in Vietnam as a POW, pledges to restore the honor of the military, preaches campaign finance reform with a very populist appeal, and pledges to restore honor and credibility back to the Presidency. This makes McCain the ultimate antithesis of Bill Clinton, the perfect candidate to do just as he said in the South Carolina debate, end the Clinton era. It's not hard at all to understand the appeal of John McCain.

The tragedy I see in the McCain campaign is what I believe has been his apparent belief he needs to moderate on the issues to be more electable. Even Bush has paid lip service to this apparent direction by calling himself a "compassionate conservative." As Goldwater would say, the Conservative philosophy is inherently compassionate in its results, it needs no such moderation.

McCain staked out more moderate territory by becoming dissenting force in his own party on issues like tobacco regulation, campaign finance reform, and the spending of the so-called federal surplus. He positioned himself as a candidate of reform but his agenda lacks the kind of substantive reform proposed by the Senator he replaced: the great Barry Goldwater.

McCain has great appeal due to his impressive biography and his effective way of campaigning for his agenda as a populist candidate. He is showing appeal with independent and conservative Democrats not seen since Ronald Reagan dominated the political landscape. If McCain would have chosen to emphasize a more Goldwater type reduce the size of government, repeal unneeded laws agenda along with his other strengths as a campaigner he would have a much greater chance of winning the nomination and the election. If he had built his campaign around that kind of substance along with his appeal and populist message, he would have a chance at winning with an electoral mandate not fashioned since Reagan's 1984 landslide.

If McCain had done those things, he would prove that a candidate could be right and also be elected. He would, along with a Republican Congress, have a good chance at achieving a lot of the Barry Goldwater 1964 agenda. Instead I'm afraid the 2000 election will be the tragedy of the McCain campaign either way. Bush could win the Republican nomination and be a weakened and then losing candidate to Al Gore in November.

Or, I could see McCain winning the nomination and beating Al Gore in November in a close election. The election would be the end of the Clinton era, but it would contain no mandate for the future direction of the country. The voters will have simply ended the Clinton era in much the way they fired George Bush in 1992. The tragedy will be, once again the Republicans failed to create a mandate for smaller government and more freedom despite having a great opportunity to do so.

Why the Green Party is more Effective than the Libertarian Party

March 25, 2000

Seems like a long time ago when I used to be a Libertarian and urged my colleagues to study the success of the Green Party. After all, in a short period of time they've registered more members and gained more votes in the 1996 with a part-time presidential candidate (Ralph Nader) than the Libertarian Party has in the last three elections. I always got a knee-jerk response: the Green Party gets votes because they promise more welfare and there's nothing we can learn from their success. In other words, shut up and on to the next issue.

Libertarians often respond that way to just about anything they don't want open up their closed minds about. I could simply conclude this essay right here and that alone would explain why the Green Party is now the nation's third largest political party. But there's more to it.

First, the Greens understand how to sell their message. They've summarized their philosophy into what they called their "ten key value." They include broad themes like social justice, ecological wisdom, grassroots democracy, etc. They are, regardless of whether one agrees with this ideology, easy to understand and also easy to sell to voters. The LP has a long wordy detailed platform that means nothing to the average voter, and is rife with ammunition to be used by opponents wishing to paint them as extremists.

Secondly, the Green Party has been build by creating effective state affiliates first then a national organization. Actually they have two national organizations, the Green Party USA and the Association of State Green Parties.

But most of their activity is centered at the state level, where it should be. Some people do remember that we are a nation of 50 states. The LP was originally organized that way, but now it's a top down organization run from their office in the Watergate Office Complex in Washington DC. The Beltway mentality has caused the Libertarian Party to pretend it's a major player in national politics despite their absence from any elected federal positions.

Other Libertarians dismiss the Green Party success by using the excuse that Ralph Nader was well known before he ran for office. While that's true, the ability of the party to attract a well-known individual like Nader who agrees with their philosophy is itself a sign they are succeeding. Perhaps Libertarians want to dismiss this point because of their own party's failure to attract well known figures who agree with their philosophy to be publicly associated with their party. I saw one quite attributed to Walter Williams that he might join the LP if they would quit their habit of intellectual masturbation in public. Libertarians talk about running Clint Eastwood for president, but he won't get caught dead signing up with the LP. He's a Republican.

And there's another reason why the Green Party is more successful. They are more effective as keeping their activists involved in the party. Libertarians quit or get burned out because of the lack of success and therefore spend all their time re-inventing their party organizations, re-winning the same ballot access battles over and over, and recruiting new members to replace the ones they lose.

On the financial side, the LP raises much more money but the Greens get a lot more bang, politically, for their bucks. That's because they are a grassroots party based more on activists than money. That means they can collect the excessive number of signatures to gain ballot access, while the Libertarians have to often pay people to collect signatures or voter registrations. And in the last decade, most Libertarian Party money had gone to pay high-priced "consultants" that are cronies of the National LP leadership.

The 2000 election will prove my point quite eloquently. I expect Ralph Nader, actively campaigning as the Green Party nominee, will get as much as seven percent of the vote nationally. If he wins the Reform Party nomination, Pat Buchanan will likely win five to ten times the vote the Libertarian candidate will poll. And if the LP again nominates also-ran Harry Browne, their 1996 candidate, they will poll no more than 500,000 votes nationally.

The Libertarian Party likes to call itself the nation's third largest political party. With the rise of the Green Party and the Reform Party, the LP will soon be number five. And if the Constitution Party candidate Howard Philips is able to organize a national campaign the LP could place as low as sixth in the popular vote for president in 2000.

Ted Kennedy Already Three Cases of Beer Ahead - The Year's Most Pathetic Senate Race

May 14, 2000

Perhaps the most exciting race for United States Senator this year is the New York race between Rudolph "Rudy" Guiliani and Hillary Rodham Clinton, or as she calls herself now, simply "Hillary." But the Massachusetts U.S. Senate race is a farce that has become yet a bigger joke. It's a real three-ring circus, one in which incumbent Senator Ted Kennedy can not only claim to drink his opponents under the table, but he can clearly claim a lead of at least three cases.

Kennedy's last election campaign saw him beating back the challenge of a well funded, well organized campaign from conservative Republican Mitt Romney, the son of the former Michigan Governor. Kennedy trotted out all the usual liberal Democrat cliches, uttered them barely articulate enough to be understood, and apologized for his degenerate personal life, and convinced enough voters in the People's Republic of Taxachusetts to send this sorry character back to the Senate for another six-year term.

Six years later Kennedy looks unbeatable, and scares away any of the possible stronger challengers, including Governor Paul Celluci or former State Treasurer Joe Malone, who challenged Kennedy in 1988. A county District Attorney was the early and only candidate for the Republican nomination to oppose the nation's drunkest senator. But finding it nearly impossible to raise money, he dropped out of the raise. The Celluci and other party leaders enthusiastically invited businessman Jack. E.

Robinson to enter the raise. Robinson pledged to spend a million bucks of his own money to challenge Ted Kennedy.

Soon after his campaign began, it started to end. Accusations of driving under the influence and sexual assault came to the surface, and leading Republicans dropped Robinson like a hot potato. Never mind the fact that the charges were dropped and Robinson was not convicted on any of them, Republican Party leaders dropped their support of him and failed to find any other candidate to seek their nomination. As a result, it appears that Robinson might not obtain enough signatures to be placed on the ballot for the Republican Primary, which would end his campaign. So the Massachusetts Republican Party, perhaps the most incompetent and mismanaged GOP state affiliate in the country, may have denied themselves the chance to have a candidate running against Ted Kennedy. Nice job guys, I'm sure Senator Kennedy appreciates the free pass.

But no good three-ring circus can be complete without the third ring. This year the third ring is the candidacy of the Libertarian Party nominee Carla Howell. Normally the Libertarian Party is not the third ring, but the side show. But this candidate, Howell, has managed to attract support from a few respectable people, including Barbara Anderson of Citizens for Limited Taxation, for a campaign run by one of the Libertarian Party's slickest spinmasters, the controversial Michael Cloud.

Cloud is the perfect kind of Libertarian consultant for the Clinton era. He seems to think if one SPINS the Libertarian message just right, that voters will magically start voting for Libertarian candidates, even those who take extreme Libertarian positions on the issues but use his "kinder and gentler" rhetoric. So the Carla Howell campaign is being marketed like a cheap brand of diet cola, using the slogan "small government is beautiful." While many think government is far too large and expensive, reducing the size of government does not make most of us think first of the word "beautiful." Effective, more efficient, more in line with the Constitution and The Bill of Rights are accurate descriptions of a smaller government, but not "beautiful."

What's really beautiful for Cloud and his brand of Libertarians is the money. Cloud, who by profession is in the direct-mail business, convinces his clients to spend large amounts of money on direct mail fundraising of very questionable effectiveness. The Howell campaign's disclosures with the Federal Election Commission show its expenses for fundraising are not much below the money those efforts brought in. So after Cloud receives his 15 percent fundraising commission, and his preferred mailing house gets their cut, there's not much money left for the actual campaign. Given this track record, including his work in the Howell campaign, Senator Kennedy won't have to worry about seeing too many 30 second spots promoting "small government is beautiful" on the television screens this Fall. Most of the money will be pay for Cloud's expensive direct mail strategies, and campaign-overhead for a campaign that will do very little campaigning.

Ted Kennedy has little to worry about politically. If he can manage to keep from getting behind the wheel of an automobile, he'll be almost assured of re-election. But I thought the purpose of an election is to give the people a choice over whom to elect as their representatives? That is the purpose of an election, but it requires the other parties to nominate good candidates and run competent campaigns. But in this three-ring circus, it is tough to tell which one is the biggest joke; the most disgraced incumbent senator in the country or his two pathetic would-be challengers. Too Massachusetts didn't put "None of the Above" on the ballot. NOTA would have a chance in this race.

Smackdown Hotel California: Presidential Nominating Conventions of the Reform and Libertarian Parties

June 5, 2000

We know two political parties that will hold conventions to choose their candidates for president this summer. Two other parties will hold convention shows for the coronation of the presidential candidates they've already chosen. Though Jesse Ventura won't likely appear at the Reform Party or Libertarian Party convention this summer, there will be more body-slamming, bashing, arguing, and drama then seen at any night at the World Wrestling Federation.

Jesse, The Governor, Ventura slammed his former party out of the cage and former Republican Patrick Buchanan jumped in. Launching a hostile takeover attempt, which could only find analogy in the Ted Turner owned and owned WCW sending his best wrestler to compete for the WWF title, is John Hagelin of the so-called Natural Law Party. Hagelin's party is a slick front for the Transcendental Meditation (TM) scam of the Maharishi Mahesh Yogi, a new age religious guru originally from India. TM is all about "you feel good spend your money, Yogi get very rich from it thank you." If Hagelin, continuing to front for this scam, can take over the Reform Party they will have federal matching funds, earned by Perot's 1996 campaign, to push their scam to even greater heights. This kind of greed knows no bounds, and according to Natural Law Party press releases, the Hagelin juggernaut claims it can steam-roll the Buchanan forces at the Reform Party's Long Beach, Cal. convention.

The Perot supporters, without apparently signal from their man, don't like Buchanan or Hagelin. It would appear they're pushing for Ross the Boss to slam his way back into this contest, but we must remember that both of Perot's campaign was orchestrated by his paid "volunteers" who created the illusion of spontaneous citizen demands to draft Perot. But old Ross cynically knows that, in politics, perception can often be reality. A lot of people bought into the Perot campaigns of 1992 and 1996, even after he dropped out and re-entered the race in 1992. A lot of people call 1-900 numbers too.

The Libertarian Party will start the month of July convening in Anaheim. This is Anaheim, the home of Disneyland, oh yes also the Tragic Kingdom form where the rock band No Doubt hails. Thinking of the fly-riddled oranges on the cover of No Doubt's Tragic Kingdom album seems quite fitting. There will be no shortage of fear and loathing at this convention. I hope the great Gonzo Journalist, Dr. Hunter Thompson, will be there to chronicle this. If Harry Browne and David Bergland are not evidence of the Death of the American Dream, I don't know what is.

The Libertarians have two interesting smackdown contests going on, one for their presidential nomination and one for their party's national chairman. Bergland, who was the LP's candidate for president in 1984 while the party ran its worst national campaign, is not seeking for reelection as national chairman. He's a one-termer, a Jimmy Carter as Dana Carvey would say in Bush imitation, in that position. The current party leadership has anointed James Lark to succeed Bergland, who apparently would continue the status quo. George Phillies, who has written an entire book on how he would change the party's direction and strategy, opposes him.

The presidential nominating contest is between the current leadership's darling and 1996 LP candidate, Harry Browne, and a candidate who's actually been elected to office, New Hampshire State Representative Don Gorman. Other parties believe in running people for president who've already proven themselves in public office. The Libertarians have always run candidates that lost elections. The Gorman supporters promote the idea of choosing someone who's been elected to office. They are also advocating the strategy of focusing on electing more of their party members at the local level. But Harry Browne, who's made a career of giving speeches and writing books, wants another four-month glorious national campaign because he thinks he can do better than his failed showing in 1996.

Lately, the fit has really hit the shan as disclosures from the Browne campaign show he's raised well more than $1.2 million in the last 3 years and has nothing left to show for it except well paid consultants with full pockets and a half hour campaign infomercial that will only be shown on free cable-access (think Wayne's World) channels because the campaign has not money to buy television time for it. Despite all this, Browne could still defeat Gorman in Anaheim. If they do, LP might just stand for Lemming Party instead of Libertarian Party.

As always, C-SPAN will televise these events. Be sure to watch them, or set your VCR to tape them. They'll both be entertainment of the highest value. Political Smackdown is perhaps the best of all. Republicans and Democrats govern us, and third parties have obviously committed to entertaining us. Why not enjoy it? After all, this is free. It's the Republicans and Democrats that are expensive, we pay for them on April 15 every year.

Massachusetts Libertarians Bask in their Own Hypocrisy

June 16, 2000

The Libertarian candidate for U.S. Senator in Massachusetts thinks the best way to beat the Republicans is to knock their candidate off the ballot. Ted Kennedy agrees. He has also filed a challenge to the ballot-access signatures of African-American Republican Jack E. Robinson. While Democrats dominate the state, it has elected Republicans to the governorship the last three times that office was up for election. But the Libertarian Party claims to be different than all the other parties; they call themselves "the party of principle." But we see how quickly principle gives way to political expediency when opportunity knocks.

Politicians that like to assert principles will often quickly forget they have to live by them as well. A candidate who preaches family values should be sure to live up to those standards himself. If one is going to crusade against corruption of politics by special interest group money, then one shouldn't take money from those same groups. Likewise, if a party and its candidates are going to advocate opening the political process to parties and candidates, it has no business seeking to shut a party or candidate out of the process.

As the self-proclaimed "third largest" political party in the United States, Libertarians have crusaded for years to lower ballot access requirements. Libertarians claim high signature and voter registration requirements were set by Democrats and Republicans to keep other parties out of the electoral process. In some cases, the third parties are able to meet these requirements and obtain ballot status.

Carla Howell, the Libertarian candidate for Ted Kennedy's Senate seat, has joined the incumbent in challenging the signatures of Republican Robinson. The politics of this are obvious. Howell would like to be Kennedy's most prominent challenger, regardless of how this condition is to be achieved. The usually consistent advocacy of open ballot access falls by the wayside on the first chance Libertarians have their ballot access and wish to not compete with the Republican candidate.

Robinson's candidacy, for reasons that are beyond simple explanation, has attracted controversy from the beginning. When their previously anointed candidate dropped out of the race, Republican leaders were desperate to find an opponent to run against Ted Kennedy. Governor Paul Celluci, and other party leaders, quickly endorsed Jack E. Robinson, who pledged to spend $1 million of his own money to finance the campaign. Immediately after, the press was filled with stories of unproven and unsubstantiated charges from Robinson's past. Robinson denied the allegations, but Celluci and other Republican leaders withdrew their endorsement of Robinson.

The Massachusetts Republican Party has, in the past, been a case study in sheer incompetence. The party had an even worse disaster in 1986 attempting to find a candidate to run against, then governor, Michael Dukakis. The party anointed, at its convention, a little-known state legislator who then dropped out weeks later when he was exposed for lying about his military record. Soon after that, another candidate dropped out of the after being accused of bizarre practices, including nudity, in his office. But this candidate remained on the ballot and actually won the primary against a few unknown names that were on the ballot. Two days later he declined the nomination, allowing the party to choose another candidate.

More recently the party has been embarrassed by the Republican administration of Governor Paul Celluci and Lt. Governor Jane Swift. They've been rocked by numerous scandals, from funding homo sex student groups in public high schools to the disastrous mismanagement and financial corruption of the "big dig" highway construction project in Boston. Swift, whose name has proven quite ironic, has embroiled their administration in her own scandals, including using state employees to baby-sit her child and an especially favorable law school teaching assignment for which she was massively over-paid.

Against this backdrop of incompetence, scandal, mismanagement, corruption, and failure the Libertarians had an opportunity to stand by principle and still gain political advantage. They could have let Ted Kennedy do the dirty work of challenging Robinson. They could have stood by their support of open ballot access and criticized Ted Kennedy for attempting to eliminate one of his opponents in the race. Instead, they've bellied up to the bar with Kennedy; they've ordered a double hypocrisy cocktail as well as one for Ted Kennedy.

Celluci has opposed Robinson's campaign since the unproven charges against him were published. Kennedy and Howell have joined in on The Deal by challenging his nomination signatures. If they think Robinson's campaign has so little chance of winning, they aren't showing it by challenging his right to seek the office that he earned by collecting 10,000 signatures to get on the ballot. In joining Kennedy on this deal, the Libertarians are showing themselves to be the biggest of hypocrites.

The Problem with Campaign Finance Deform: Congress Shall Make No Law
June 13, 2000

The target of all attempts to enact so-called campaign finance reform is limiting or restricting political speech. Every proposal of this sort will limit how much money you can spend to support or promote the candidates and political causes you support. And every one of them is unconstitutional, because they violate the First Amendment prohibition against legislation that limits free speech. But these continued attempts prove that we have far too many politicians who take an oath to uphold the Constitution and The Bill of Rights and quickly violate that by advocating campaign finance deform. They need to tell us what part of "Congress Shall Make No Law" they don't understand.

Most campaign finance deform proposals are supported by liberal Democrats and opportunistic moderate Republicans. Liberals constantly whine about how much more money conservative Republicans raise to spend on campaigning. Liberal Democrats have no problem taking money from union dues and spending it on promoting their liberal agenda. In fact, most campaign finance deform proposals, including the McCain-Feingold version, exempt the spending of union-dues money for political activities.

The reason conservatives raise and spend so much money on political advertising is to get their message out over the chorus of liberal politicians and their willing accomplices in the mainstream media. Every night the news broadcasts of the three networks, the Clinton News Network, and PBS (Public Broadcasting of Socialism) routinely report on the liberal issue agenda as set by the left. And that "reporting" is strictly from the spin of the leftwing liberals. The competing sources of information to this deluge of liberal spin are primarily the paid media of conservative organization and candidates, and the various sources of "new media," including talk radio and the Internet. Liberals constantly try to regulate all three, because they would like the public to get their news from Dan Rather, Tom Brokaw, and Peter Jennings rather than from these other sources.

Liberals have sought to regulate talk radio by re-introducing the "fairness" doctrine that would require conservative talk show hosts to give "equal time" to liberal viewpoints. Liberals have sought to regulate the internet, through the cynical ploy of the "communications decency act," a proposal that hoodwinked many conservatives to support something that would quickly get the government into the business of regulating content on the internet. They failed to realize that regulating "porn" on the internet today quickly leads to regulating political speech on the internet soon after. And finally, political speech is the target of liberal regulation attempts through campaign finance deform.

The latest attempt is the proposal of John McCain and Wisconsin liberal Democrat Senator Russell Feingold. This proposal would have limited the money that could be spend on campaigning by corporate and other supporters of political candidates, while exempting the spending of union money on political activities. That is because the union bosses spend nearly all of that money supporting liberal Democrats while most corporate political money goes to conservatives and Republicans. McCain-Feingold was an attempt to disarm, financially, the political opposition. It's that simple.

Senator McCain was simply using the issue in a cynical attempt to build an image of himself as a reformer and use that image to be nominated and elected president. It worked to some extent, he was taken seriously as a reformer by Bill Bradley and gained some support among independents and Reform Party members. But it failed to get him nominated by the Republican Party. Liberal Democrats, like Feingold, really do support the campaign finance deform agenda. These are the same socialists who think the government should have unlimited license to spend your tax dollars on propaganda while you should not have the right to spend your own money to buy a microphone for your political speech.

But there remains one problem with these proposals: they violate the First Amendment, which states "Congress Shall Make No Law" restricting political speech. Politicians who fail to understand this, and vote for legislation that violates it, need to be immediately retired out of office by the voters on Election Day.

Some Libertarians Show Contempt for the Voters

June 16, 2000

It amazes me that some members of a third party, one that has a history of poor performance at the polls thinks political success comes by showing absolute contempt for the voters. Some Libertarians show they don't trust the voters to make the right decisions on Election Day, and think voters prefer to have those choices made for them by limiting the choices that are available on Election Day.

The Libertarian Party is supposed to be different from other parties. They accuse the others of selling out principles for political expediency, and call themselves "the party of principle." But the party is bitterly divided between those who want to stand on principle and another faction that sell that out in the interest of expediency. One of the leaders of the expediency faction is the popular Libertarian political consultant Michael Cloud.

Cloud has made a career out of trying to be essentially the James Carville of the Libertarian Party. If the Libertarian Party would operate like the Democrats and Republicans, and play the same kind of game, Cloud seems to think his party could also win elections. Cloud is the consultant managing the campaign of Carla Howell, who is running for Senator against Ted Kennedy in Massachusetts this year.

Howell and Cloud have betrayed Libertarian principles on equal ballot access, and shown their contempt for the voters, by seeking to have Republican candidate Jack E. Robinson disqualified from the ballot. Cloud claims that Robinson recently moved to Massachusetts, from Connecticut, and therefore has no business being in the race. In other words, he thinks the voters aren't smart enough to look at the allegations against Robinson and decide for themselves, so they should have that decision made for them by not having Robinson on the ballot. I doubt the voters appreciate having Michael Cloud decide what's in their best interest. This behavior directly contradicts the stated Libertarian claims to respect the rights and choices of individual voters.

Many Libertarians are more honest about why they want Robinson off the ballot. They say that most Republican voters will support their candidate over Ted Kennedy if they don't have a Republican nominee to vote for. I fail to see the logic of this. How is that Republican voters, denied the ability to select their candidate on election day, will be ready to cast their votes for the candidate of the party that helped deprive them of their own candidate? Clearly some Libertarians live in a different world than most of us do.

Yet other Libertarians claims that Robinson, by being on the ballot, will get thousands of votes from those voters who choose to cast straight Republican ballots on election day. This built-in advantage isn't fair, say some Libertarians. So the answer is once again to show contempt for the rights of voters, and deprive straight-ticker Republican voters of their candidate for Senator. Once again, these Libertarians are showing their contempt for the rights of voters to make their own choices.

This is not the first time that Libertarians from the Cloud camp have shown their complete contempt for the voters, and their right to register their political choices through the electoral process. In New Mexico the Libertarian Party lost "major party" ballot access status after the State Election Bureau investigated more than 2000 questionable voter registrations. The state chairman of the Libertarian Party of New Mexico, Joseph Knight, considers himself a support of the strategies and ideas taught by Michael Cloud. I've personally attended one training session, taught by Knight, in which the Cloud methods of persuading voters to register Libertarian were demonstrated.

Those methods lead to hundreds of voter registration cards being submitted where it was clear the voter selected Democrat, Republican, or Independent and the Libertarian party staff member processing the voter registrations crossed out the voter's chosen party and wrote in Libertarian. Still other voters' registration cards appeared to be entirely fraudulent, including forged signatures and incorrect social security numbers. Clearly they had no respect for the rights of individual voters or the sanctity of the political process. Under New Mexico law, a voter's party affiliation choice limits which party primary they are allowed to vote in. In other words, voters who had their party registration changed, against their wish, by the Libertarians might find out the consequences on the day of the primary election. They might attempt to vote Democrat or Republican, only to be told they're registered Libertarian and be given a Libertarian Party primary ballot. The state election officials did the only thing they could do to protect the rights of voters; they changed those voters back to their former party registration unless they confirmed the switch to Libertarian.

It is beyond my ability to understand how Libertarian activists, who show this contempt for voters, expect to win the support of those voters at the polls. It is a shame because most Libertarian Party members are good people who believe in the principles of their party. But they have such strong desire to improve their showing at the polls they find themselves supporting questionable tactics and strategies concocted by less-than-honest members of their party. Those who show this kind of contempt for voters, and their right to make their choices in the political system, have no business being political operatives in any party. And clearly they have no business tarring the name and image of the group that call themselves "the party of principle."

Disastrous Decision Made in the Tragic Kingdom

July 2, 2000

Second Browne Nomination at Anaheim Convention Spells Doom for the Libertarian Party

"Once was a magical place, over time it was lost.
The king has been overthrown by jesterly fools.
And the power of the people shall
come to believe they do rule.
They pay homage to a king,
Whose dreams are buried in their minds.
His tears are frozen stiff; icicles drip from his eyes.
Welcome to the Tragic Kingdom.
Cornfields of popcorn have yet to spring open."

Tragic Kingdom, by No Doubt

Convening in Anaheim this past weekend, the Libertarian Party faced the choice of either continuing its rendezvous with irrelevance and inevitable future non-existence or changing course. Anyone open minded enough to look at the evidence and acknowledge the obvious could see trend. The Libertarian Party has been ineffective at making any significant difference in national politics and has recently shown no signs of changing any time too soon.

Critics of the current ruling faction in the Libertarian Party presented a mountain of evidence. Long time Libertarian activist and Future of Freedom Foundation President Jacob G. Hornberger, and others, documented a systematic pattern of interlocking relationships and blatant conflicts of interest within both the Libertarian Party at the national level and the on-going Harry Browne for President campaigns of 1996 and 2000. Essentially, party rules and common sense requires that a political party and the various competing candidates for its nomination for public office remain separate affairs. But in this case the evidence proved that the Browne organization and the party were so closely related and overlapped that it compromises the integrity of the party. This put serious doubt to the idea that any of Browne's rivals for the LP nomination for president stood any chance of winning the nomination.

Esteemed libertarian publication, Liberty, looked into the charges and found merit to most of them. Still many other critics within the party found reason to not only conclude the behavior was wrong for the party, but also engage in an organized effort to change the direction of the Libertarian Party. Massachusetts Libertarian activist George Phillies and others organized a plan for change called the Clean Slate Action Plan. Phillies ultimately lost his bid for party chairman to the handpicked candidate of the party's incumbent leadership, Libertarian National Committee member James Lark. Incumbent national chairman David Bergland, the party's failed presidential candidate of 1984 and architect of the party's failed Project Archimedes membership recruitment plan, declined to seek reelection to his post.

The party had a chance to make change by electing the Clean Slate candidates to leadership posts and nominating Don Gorman for president. Just weeks before the convention, long time Arizona Libertarian Party activist Ernest Hancock predicted the national leadership would insure enough loyal delegates to nominate Browne and elect their chosen candidates to party leadership positions.

For the Libertarian Party's full-time staff located in the Watergate Office Complex in Washington DC the most important things were at stake. Their jobs working for the party hung in the balance. The Clean Slate candidates made it clear they would change the direction of the party, and most viewed this, as meaning change in personnel would follow. So despite the overwhelming evidence that the party is failing to make any substantial improvement in it political fortunes, the leadership easily obtained what they wanted at the convention. They obtained ratification to stay the course and continue to be politically irrelevant.

This has been the history of the Libertarian Party for most of its existence. The faction that currently runs it gained control of the party on the very idea it would run the party more professionally and obtain big league results at the polls. And nothing close to this has yet to happen. The party was founded in 1971 and grew rapidly during its first nine years of existence. It peaked in 1980 when Libertarian Presidential candidate Ed Clark polled more than 900,000 votes in the national election, which also featured Ronald Reagan, President Jimmy Carter, and John Anderson.

The "new breed" of libertarians who sought to "professionalize" the party gained control of the Libertarian Party during and after the Clark campaign. The history of this group's control of the party has shown their methods don't work. The party has received fewer than 500,000 votes in every single presidential election since 1980 and has shown no signs of improving. Furthermore, all the past predictions of electing members of Congress and Senators have failed miserably. No Libertarian has even come close to being elected to Federal office in any state. And in the few cases where the

Libertarians elected state legislators, they were defeated soon after in their reelection bids.

The purpose of a political party is to elect and reelect candidates and move national politics in the direction of the public policy priorities of that party. In the case of the Libertarians, the stated desire is to reduce the government to that which is minimally necessary to insure freedom and eliminate government activity that violates individual freedom. But the only way to move in that direction is to elect candidates to public office that will move policy in that direction by repealing laws and regulations as well as promoting the defense of individual liberty. And in that goal the Libertarian Party has proven itself to be a spectacular failure.

The premise of most Libertarian candidates is about building momentum, or something else, in hopes of winning future elections. Still other Libertarian candidates say the goal of their candidacy is to recruit more party members. Yet party membership growth has been anemic and that future major partisan race the Libertarian Party is supposedly going to win never comes. The Libertarian Party is an eternal act of organized political procrastination. One need only be involved in the party for a few election cycles to realize that next election the LP will have a shot at winning just simply never comes around. A political party that constantly says it will win at some point in the future will never win. A political party that waits around for some catalytic, earth-moving crisis that will cause people to "wake up" and vote Libertarian will never win at the polls.

We don't have time to wait for the Libertarian Party to finally get a clue and take itself in the right direction. We don't have time enough left, in the fight for freedom, to wait for the Libertarian Party to finally get its act together and begin acting like a political party that takes itself seriously enough to take seriously enough an effort to win public office and change the course of history before it is too late. Statist politicians are well served by those who decide to stick with this cultish, irrelevant, little party that the Libertarians have become.

By staying the course the Libertarian Party has proven it is not yet prepared to make a difference and has little hope of ever making any real difference. Electing Bergland's handpicked successor as national chairman and nominating failed candidate Harry Browne again proves this. The cult of the omnipotent Watergate Libertarians refuses to give up their control of the party. In doing so, they've chosen to maintain their control over a rapidly shrinking party pie rather than build a dynamically growing and vibrant political party where all Libertarians and libertarians could share pieces of a growing party pie. The decisions made in Anaheim, in my view, doom the Libertarian Party to failure and their inevitable place in the dustbin of history. Those of us who are serious about advancing freedom in our lifetimes will move and advance the individual freedom agenda elsewhere.

Bill Janklow controversy – liberal hypocrisy on parade

August 28, 2003

Ralph Nader and Joan Claybrook, dubbed "safety advocates" by the dominant liberal media, are calling for Cong. Bill Janklow (R-SD) to resign from office and give up his drivers license. For those not following the news, Mr. Janklow is reported to have sped through a stop sign colliding with a motorcycle and killing the rider. In most states this would warrant a prosecution for vehicular homicide or some similar charge.

The hypocrisy from liberals like Nader and Claybrook is so loud that the Moose can not remain silent. Liberals like Nader and Claybrook NEVER call for other liberals to held accountable when THEY cause auto accidents and the deaths of others on the roads. Of course the most notable case is Ted Kennedy and Chappaquiddick. Ted Kennedy should have prosectued for vehicular homicide and abandoning the scene of the crime. That's usually good enough for a decade sentence in the joint. It would have saved us from having Ted Kennedy in office.

Obviously Janklow should be held accountable for his irresponsible driving and the deadly consequences of his actions. The Moose would like to congratulate these liberals for once getting it and calling for personal responsibility. The hypocrisy, however, speaks so much louder. Liberals always want the rest of us to live by the rules while they break them.

Jacquis Ch-Iraq and Tony Blair

July 28, 2003

Foreign Affairs: Jacques Ch-Iraq and Tony Blair

President Bush came to Washington promising a "new tone" after the eight years of Bill Clinton. Many, quite correctly, perceive the "new tone" to be same as Bush senior's "kinder and gentler" tone. The Democrats didn't hesitate to attack the first President Bush for breaking from the "kinder and gentler" tone at any time when Bush would criticize the Democrats for their policy decisions. It will be no different with George W. and the "new tone."

Like the first Bush presidency, the current president is strong on foreign policy issues while being weak on domestic policy because of compromising to the liberal agenda of the Democrats. Like 1992, we are also in a recession and when Democrats are out of power they will exploit that for all its political value. Bush has little or no ability to distance himself from the Democrats on domestic policy, and because of the new tone, has little or no ability to use his advantage on foreign policy. The Democrats are taking an extreme position on Iraq, but the "new tone" renders Bush politically impotent in taking the Democrats to task for their political extremism.

George Bush has a decision to make. He can either go after the Democrats on their foreign policy extremism or he can stay with the "new tone" and sit by while becoming yet another one term president. The Moose is unsure which option the president will take. The decision would seem to be an easy one.

Three Cheeers for Freedom in Baghdad
April 9, 2003

Iraq is finally nearing liberation as our tanks are rolling in the streets of Baghdad amid the welcomes of the Iraqi people who are more than overjoyed to see us there. Many Iraqi citizens cheered as some of their own helped topple a statue of Saddam Hussein in Baghdad. This contrasts nicely with the absurd agitprop coming from both the Anti-American leftists here in the U.S. as well as our misguided libertarian friends. Those who said the Iraqi people didn't want us there and that our presence would lead to more 9/11 type attacks have been rendered politically impotent, as Rush Limbaugh said after the Gulf War in 1991, and they should go see their urologists.

Never again should we listen to the discredited word of the leftist and the other members of the Anti-American coalition that opposed the just involvement of the Coalition of the Willing that lead Operation Iraqi Freedom. But you should remember these aren't just the few crackpots and charlatans of the extreme fringe, they are the mainstream of the American left and "progressive" side of American politics. The Hard Left, as seen in the flat earth society like anti-Nuclear movement of the 1970s and 1980s, has hijacked and taken full control of the foreign policy direction of the Democratic Party. With few exceptions (the candidates that have no chance of being nominated in 2004 such as Sen. Joe Lieberman or Sen. John Edwards) the leading presidential candidates of the Democratic Party march in lockstep with this view. You see this in the crass comments of Sen. John Kerry of Massachusetts who called for a "regime change" in our own country. The Moose thinks the next two senate elections in Massachusetts should be time for regime change in the two seats held by Mr. Kerry and Ted Kennedy.

The Moose says, never again grant any credibility to the crackpots and charlatans of the far left. And while they are rendered intellectually and politically impotent, join with the people of Iraq to begin celebrating their freedom.

Conservative Reform

As my views evolved to a more reformist conservative direction, I began writing some commentaries and essays under the name "Bull Moose" and my own at the web site www.conservativereform.us. The selections in this section come from those writings.

Take an Axe to the Federal Budget, Mr. President

March 9, 2003

The Washington Budget battle heats up with the latest report from the Congressional Budget Office. Showing that they still don't get it, the Democratic Leadership is quick to blame tax cuts for the coming budget deficits and call for President Bush to roll back or cancel planned tax cuts. The Democratic leadership is acting quite predictably, and the Republican leadership, with the president, can act predictably themselves. Or they stake out a bold position on the deficit, and rather than repeating the mistakes of 1990-91, win both the policy battle and the political battle.

The Moose remembers all too well how Bush senior was rolled by the Democrats into accepting the budget deal of October of 1990. Bush lost both the political battle, when an all-but-likely congressional win for the GOP was turned into a loss of seats, and the policy battle was lost because taxes were increased and the capital gains tax cut promised by Democrats was killed in the Senate under the leadership of Senator George Mitchell, the Majority Leader.

Washington DC always needs new ideas, and I have a simple but revolutionary idea on how the Congress and President Bush might solve this latest deficit crisis. It's really simple, but it's so out-of-the-ordinary, I may have to repeat myself. Here it is…

Cut Spending.

That's right, don't reduce the rate of increase in federal spending, but actually cut spending. Cause the federal government to spend less this year than it did last year. If

the deficit is going to be $287 thousand million, as says
the Congressional Budget Office, simply reduce federal
spending to balance the budget. The Moose knows this
idea is so revolutionary to the politicians inside the
Beltway, and the K Street crowd that lives off of federal
pork, so a repeat is in order.

Cut Spending.

It's that simple. The Democratic leadership, the special
interest groups, and those addicted to government largesse
will protest. Mr. President you can establish moral clarity
on this issue; make it clear that tax cuts are needed for
economic growth and the ONLY route to a balanced
budget this year is spending cuts. If the Democratic
leadership, the K Street Crowd, and the government
addicts want to stand in the way of this, they can take
responsibility for thwarting a balanced budget. The
Moose says, by taking a firm stance on this issue, the
president will likely win both the political debate and the
policy battle. The worst the president can do is show the
people where the real impediments to government reform
lie and the people can make the appropriate changes on
Election Day.

Let Us Now Praise Joe Camel

March 5, 2003

Few recent political crusades have captivated both the politically correct left and the Hollywood community (if you forgive the Moose for redundancy here) like that of the anti-smoking crusade. A notable feature of this crusade was the death of the cartoon character Joe Camel. The cartoon character, commonly seen in magazines read by adults, was claimed to be the cause for younger children taking up cigarette smoking.

If this age of celebrity voyeurism can apply to even non-celebrities like The Moose, The Moose will disclose here. I do not smoke myself but regard the decision of adults to smoke one that should be their own. One who knows the health risks associated with smoking and still decides to take on that risk has every right to do it. But The Moose is very much concerned with the very real and legitimate issues of how pop culture and infotainment media impact and influence those young people who unfortunately make the unwise decision to take up cigarette smoking.

It is both fashionable and politically correct to be against smoking and seek to ban smoking in bars and restaurants and other public accommodations. Marching in lockstep with the politically correct agenda, the Hollywood elite toes the party line on this issue. While completing some online research on another issue The Moose found a most provocative website - the "celebrity smoking list" at the website www.smokingsides.com. The site claims to be one offering views on both sides of the whole smokers right v. anti-smoking debate.

Keeping in mind Hollywood's official endorsement of the anti-smoking agenda The Moose was quite interested (can't say surprised) to find just how many in the entertainment communities themselves partake in the same evil weed they condemn officially. You too might be surprised how many of your favorite celebrity entertainers or actresses or the like have their publicists issuing official denials while they sneak off to chain-smoke a few Marlboro Reds out of public view. The Moose remembers all too well the obvious example of Hillary Rodham Clinton's anti-smoking stance while Chelsea was witnessed smoking on many occasions.

The celebrity smoking list includes virtually every well-known female celebrity among entertainers and athletes and even includes links to pictures to document their claims of who has been puffing away. Links for motion pictures that depict smoking are also included. This all got The Moose thinking. More than 70 percent of public identifies as non-smokers or ex-smokers. American society becomes more predominantly non-smoking every year. But not in Hollywood. It's clear that the in the unreal world of movies almost everyone smokes. It's as if Big Tobacco has the motion picture industry entirely bought and paid for because almost every most depicts smoking. Movies glorify smoking and The Moose sees that reaching many more teenagers, showing them a positive image of smoking, than Joe Camel every did. And to ponder the sheer hypocrisy of it. The very people who made it a priority to ban harmless old Joe Camel are doing more to glorify and promote smoking to teenagers in the movie theaters than Joe Camel could ever dream of doing.

The Moose says it's time for a change. How about BRINGING BACK Joe Camel and having Hollywood

voluntarily agreeing to completely stop the glorification
of smoking in movies, and even BAN smoking in motion
pictures. The anti-smoking crusade has ended the Virginia
Slims sponsorship of professional tennis tournaments and
may stop the NASCAR championship from being called
the Winston Cup.

The Hollywood crowd marches in lockstep with this
movement while most among that crowd smoke like
chimneys. You can view that list yourself if you don't
believe The Moose. Perhaps The Moose shouldn't
overreact to the obvious hypocrisy of this community.
Madonna once wrote a letter to a then young Gwyneth
Paltrow to urge her to stop smoking but has been seen
publicly puffing away herself. Fans of many sitcom stars
have seen their idols smoking off-camera and think it's the
coolest thing that they smoke. It's bad enough that
marijuana smoking is now thought to be more "cool" than
ever before among teenagers. Hollywood can cast Tonya
Harding and Anna Kournikova in movies playing
characters that smoke like chimneys on screen, which is
no different than what most in this entertainment
community do off-screen. That is, if the smoking list site
is to viewed as credible. And the Moose thinks it is. Why
don't the two previously aforementioned celebrities model
for advertisement for Virginia Slims? Why not also bring
back the Marlboro Man? And Joe Camel. That would be
more honest, and certainly less inconsistent. The Moose
can no longer take this hypocrisy. The Moose is feeling
very much like former Congressman Jim Traficant at the
moment. Beam me up mister speaker.

(for some reason The Moose is reminded of the song
"Shredding the Document" by John Hiatt.)

Term Limits Redux – the Old Religion Lives

February 26, 2003

The Moose has little patience for reforms that truly do not reform government. One such example is term limits. The ides is that limiting the term of politicians keeps them from accumulating two much power. That makes sense on the surface, but the idea falls apart with a little examination.

In the past, Republicans were the most prominent supports of terms limits, especially when the GOP remained the minority in the Congress. It was believed that terms limits would give the GOP more open seats to contest and aid the Republican effort to regain control of Congress. Reality, however, didn't bear that out. The real reason the Democrats maintained their control of the Congress during the Republican 1980s is because they won 57% of all open Congressional races during that decade.

Without term limits, the GOP won control of the Congress by smashing the Democratic majority behind the leadership of Newt Gingrich and the Contract with America. The old term limits religion had clearly been refuted and shown to be practically obsolete for those who supported it only as a means to a GOP majority. The Republican congressional majority has been maintained by winning open seats more often than the Democrats and also the help of some good old-fashioned gerrymandering.

But the old term limits religion never dies. The Moose read with great interest and fascination the latest term limits screed in Rational Review by Stacie Rumenap, executive director of US Term Limits. Ms. Rumenap sums up the thesis of the term limits religion according, "Most establishmentarian-type politicians bitterly oppose term limits. That's because term limits curb the power of career politicians and open the door to a less power-hungry breed of representative."

While that may be convincing for some, it fails to hold up under any scrutiny. The Moose laments the trend in local government, the "professionalization" of local government that has transferred much real power OUT of the hands of elected officials and INTO the hands of appointed, unelected, and unaccountable "professional" managerial staff. Term limits are yet one more idea proposed by the "let's run government like a business" pseudo-reformers. Government is government and business is business and they are very different for good reasons. Terms limits in reality does decrease the power of politicians but transfers that power to the Congressional staff. When the average congressional staffer is on Capitol Hill longer than the elected member of Congress, Real Power transfers to the unelected fraternity of Career Congressional Staffers, who stay on to work for the next term-limited member of Congress.

This is not reform at all. When power is taken away from the elected and given to the unelected, the people lose their power to control their own government. Does the Moose have to remind anyone how popular the term limits religion remains with the K Street crowd? Think about that.

The New Democrats Get It

February 23, 2003

Bruce Reed of the Democratic Leadership Council has sketched a road-map by which the Democratic Party might reclaim the White House in 2004. But that question is, will the Democrats follow it?

Writing in the Democratic Leadership Council's Blueprint magazine, Al From and Bruce Reed offer an agenda a Democratic candidate for president can advocate for effectively recapturing the White House in 2004. The Moose can't help but notice how strikingly similar most of the ten-item agenda is to that supported by Reform Conservatives.

Reed and From include in that agenda making America safe through more support for law enforcement, restoring economic growth through fiscal responsibility in the federal government, corporate responsibility, asking Americans to serve their country, family-friendly tax reform, education reform that demands competence from educators for better pay, strict enforcement of child responsibility (including child support from absentee parents) from parents, and energy reform. The Moose can't help but see the New Democrats gearing up to attempt to win another election by shamelessly pilfering Conservative Reform ideas.

The Moose can already hear some conventional conservatives shouting that the Clinton Democrats didn't really steal those ideas; they paid lip service to them while backing little of the substance of the ideas in policy. The Moose also knows that in politics, perception is reality, and when the other side has conceded the debate over ideas, our ideas have won the day. Conservative Reform ideas have vanquished the old debate between old style liberal ideas and the backward negative incremental compromise agenda of the country-club Republicans. The Third Way is the Conservative Reform agenda. The Democrats now realize this political reality. The Moose asks you to enjoy this victory for our ideas, and press forward. The Moose, truly is, loose.

Social Security Reform and Transcending the Industrial Age Retirement Paradigm

March 2003

The current federal social security system compares to currently available retirement options as an old obsolete ENIAC computer made of 18000 electron tubes would to a new personal computer running an AMD Athlon XP 3000 processor. Unlike the computer, our government retirement system has changed little since its inception as a depression-era safety-net program. Demographic changes and evolving assumptions about retirement have entirely changed the very nature of the social security program.

The Congress legislated the retirement age of 65 in the 1930s at a time when the average life-expectancy was not much more than 65 and the percentage of the American population over the age of 65 remained quite small. The other major drawback of the current system is that it has been a pay-as-you-go system from day one. The money going into the system in part went right back out to those who were eligible for benefits. This was financially strong when social security had a very high ratio of payers to payees. But the demographics trends that have increased the number of retired individuals to those still working have rapidly made that ratio less financially beneficial to the social security system. The program, history, has received several bailouts, all of which involved increases in the payroll taxes funding social security. Barring real reform, future bailouts that will be forced by the continued demographic trends will always involve more increases in the social security payroll taxes. The bleak future will become reality when we reach a point where social security payroll taxes meet or exceed the rate possible at the Laffer curve peak and sufficient revenues to fund social security are truly not available. That disastrous economic reality would force true reform of the system at time when it will be far too late.

The time for reform is now and yesterday would have been better. Every day we don't reform social security is just one more day closer to the financial explosion that will make reform both necessary and far less advantageous. A solid reform will first transcend the old collectivist system that puts all employees in the same system and moves everyone below a certain age out of the current system and gives them the option of having an individualized retirement account through the social security administration. The reform should also recognize the right of individuals below a "beyond the point of no return age" to simply opt out of the system entirely and never pay social security taxes again. The plan can offer a disincentive for middle-aged individuals by offering than an alternative of the individualized retirement account administered through the social security administration. The second component should be individualized control of those accounts. The owner of that account should have full discretion over where the money is invested, be it the stock market or corporate bonds or even government bonds. And lastly, unlike the social security "account" fund that disappears into nothing when the individual dies, this individualized account must be a financial asset that can be passed along to heirs who themselves can either cash out or reinvest that money. The current social security system forces the individual to pay into a fund for their entire working lives that will be worth zero upon death. That is fundamentally wrong.

A reform plan that revolves around individual choice, individual control, and ownership of the "nest egg" is one that will help us transcend industrial age assumptions about retirement and begin to consider paradigms about how we live our lives in the post-Industrial age. The old paradigm involved one spending most of the productive years making widgets or some comparable industrial type work until reaching a designated age of retirement, at which time one gets off the industrial treadmill to have some time to do other things in life. Many individuals are realizing the better route to a fulfilling and meaningful life involves finding ways to make a living doing what they truly enjoy and finding time to do the "other things" in life during the more productive and healthy years of their lives rather than procrastinating to the magical "retirement" years. Our post-Industrial society values the judgment, expertise, experience, and wisdom of older individuals who want to make those attributes available in ways not possible by retiring.

Individuals are beginning to want an increased control over their lives and will demand alternatives to the industrial-age paradigm of 40 years of work followed by retirement. Our reform proposal must offer the opt-out arrangements that will accommodate this growing demand for new self-chosen and self-designed retirement options. A truly dynamic social security reform plan capable of meeting the challenges of the future must be one able to meet the needs of individuals in the future.